THE BIG BOOK OF TAROT SYMBOLS

This book is dedicated to you, wherever you find yourself. May you be guided and enlightened as you walk your tarot path.

Quarto.com

First Published in 2025 by Fair Winds Press, an imprint of The Quarto Group,
100 Cummings Center, Suite 265-D, Beverly, MA 01915, USA.
T (978) 282-9590 F (978) 283-2742

Fair Winds Press titles are also available at discount for retail, wholesale, promotional, and bulk purchase. For details, contact the Special Sales Manager by email at specialsales@quarto.com or by mail at The Quarto Group, Attn: Special Sales Manager, 100 Cummings Center, Suite 265-D, Beverly, MA 01915, USA.

29 28 27 26 25 1 2 3 4 5

ISBN: 978-0-7603-9707-7

Digital edition published in 2025
eISBN: 978-0-7603-9708-4

Library of Congress Cataloging-in-Publication Data available.

Design and Page Layout: Cindy Samargia Laun

Printed in China

The Beginner's Guide to Decoding the Cards

THE BIG BOOK OF TAROT SYMBOLS

LIZ DEAN

Author of *The Ultimate Guide to Tarot*

CONTENTS

INTRODUCTION

The Big Book of Tarot Symbols invites you to connect with the spirit of each card through its symbols. From sunflowers to sphinxes, crowns to towers, every card element holds an energy you can sense intuitively. When you allow your intuition to interact with a symbol, a doorway opens; the symbol becomes a portal to new insights and understanding.

The symbols you find in this book are for you; in fact, you can let the symbols find you rather than consciously seek them. Move through this book with openness and curiosity, and let your intuition guide you to the cards and pages you need at this time.

This book is for everyone. If you are a beginner, finding a symbol on a card that calls to you is a beautiful way into its meaning. If you're a more seasoned reader, the symbols highlighted here invite you to deepen your knowledge and discover new ways of seeing. If you're an experienced reader, working with card symbols can refresh your practice. Sometimes when we know our cards well, we can unthinkingly revert to traditional card meanings rather than respond to a card in the moment and glean something new.

In the following pages, join me to explore all 78 cards of the tarot through more than 200 individual symbols—and find those that will speak to you in every reading.

How to Use This Book

You may wish to start right at the beginning, or dive into a card or a spread straight away. One way to begin is to use the old technique of bibliomancy—close your eyes and flip through the pages, stopping when you feel it is right. Wherever you land can be your starting point whenever you choose to work with this book.

Chapter 1 explains how to tune in to the language of symbols by learning to identify them and sense their meaning.

Chapters 2 and 3 present the major and minor arcana. Arcana means "secret"—so the 22 major arcana cards reveal big secrets, or life issues, while the 56 minor arcana reveal the lesser, or day-to-day, events in our lives. The card profiles include the following associations:

CARD NAMES: ALTERNATIVE AND ESOTERIC

A card's alternative name gives us insight into the way our ancestors may have interpreted it, as well as revealing something of its long history. V The Hierophant or Pope, for example, was briefly known as the Roman god Jupiter during the wars between Catholics and Protestants in Europe (see V The Hierophant, page 38).

The cards' esoteric titles originate from the Hermetic Order of the Golden Dawn (founded 1888), the British occult society from which the Rider Waite Smith Tarot evolved. Arthur Edward Waite, a leading light of the Golden Dawn, co-created the Rider Waite Smith cards with artist Pamela Colman Smith, also a member of the Order.

Some of these esoteric titles appear to describe the cards' imagery—such as "Dweller Between the Waters" for the Star, as we see the star maiden kneeling between a large and small pool. Others draw upon the card's element, planet, or astrological sign. For example, Justice is "Ruler of the Balance," a reference to the scales of Libra, the card's zodiac sign. Some esoteric titles are majestically obscure—such as Child of the Forces of Time for XV The Devil—as they refer to the card's magical associations that were part of the Golden Dawn's philosophy.

NUMBER AND NUMEROLOGY LINK

A card's number is more than a quantity or reference to its place in the deck. Like other imagery, number is a symbol. Numbers resonate with us, offering imaginative and intuitive ways to approach a card. For this reason, you will find a number interpretation for each card, plus a card's numerology link. The numerology link refers to a number relationship with another major arcana card. For example, VII The Chariot's relation is XVI The Tower (as 16 is 1 + 6 = 7, the number of The Chariot). These two cards often represent a story of light and shadow, which gives context to the card in hand. The determined charioteer riding out in sunlight contrasts with the dark night of the Tower's storm; the charioteer must control his ego to stay on track but if not, disaster looms—illustrated by the tower's collapse. Likewise, The Chariot can also signify the recovery after lightning strikes, so the two cards become a circular story, just like the major arcana itself (see chapter 1).

In the minor arcana, you will see a heading: Major Arcana Link. These show you the connection between some minor and major arcana cards to give you insight into their meaning. All the Aces link to I The Magician, card of beginnings. All the Knights relate to VII The Chariot, cards of journeys; also, the sphinx on VII The Chariot symbolizes the fixed signs of the zodiac, which are aligned with the four Knights (see The Chariot, entry on the sphinx, page 48). Queens relate to III The Empress, the mother archetype, while the Kings relate to the IV The Emperor, the father.

THE ELEMENTS, PLANETS, AND ZODIAC SIGNS

Next in the listing is the card's element. The element of Earth, Air, Fire, or Water gives us insight into the nature of the card—if it expresses material concerns (Earth), or thoughts and decisions (Air), or passion (Fire), or emotions (Water). Likewise, the card's ruling planet or astrological sign tells us more about its character, based on the qualities associated with the planet or sign.

In the minor arcana, you will see that the court cards have two elements. One is the element of the card, and the second element is for the suit. Pages are Earth, Knights are Fire, Queens are Water, and Kings, Air. So, the Page of Cups, for example, is Earth of the suit of Water. This alignment differs from the traditional associations of Fire for Kings and Air for Knights. To me, the Kings, as holders of wisdom and authority, align with the mind-oriented suit of Swords. In medieval social hierarchy, Swords also signified the noble warrior, which taps into the archetype of the King as warrior; we see the King of Pentacles in armor, just like IV The Emperor. (The Kings can be understood as four aspects of the Emperor, as the Queens are four aspects of III The Empress.) Fire suits the Knights, as these are action cards, bringing change.

HEBREW LETTERS AND THE TREE OF LIFE

The major arcana cards have a Hebrew letter and a Tree of Life pathway. The 22 cards of the major arcana, numbered 0 to XXI, correspond with the 22 letters of the Hebrew alphabet. Each letter has its own symbol and meaning, which offers a deeper understanding of the card. The Tree of Life is the central motif of the Judaic mystical system of Kabbala. It has 10 spheres, or sephira, and 22 pathways between the spheres that correspond to the 22 major arcana cards. The minor arcana cards each have a Tree of Life sphere, rather than pathway (see the Tree of Life in the Appendix, page 222).

SEASON OR DAY OF THE WEEK

The minor arcana cards have their own season: Wands for spring, Cups for summer, Pentacles for autumn, and Swords for winter. Wands suit spring as they bear the buds of new life; circular Cups signify the fullness of summer sun. Pentacles represent harvest—the material gifts of the earth—while the cold metal of Swords symbolizes the harshness of winter. Some people prefer Wands for summer, given its element of Fire for hot summer days, with Cups for spring—as winter's snow melts and new life flows. Go with what resonates with you.

You will also see each major card has its own day of the week, should you like to practice that card's spread on its favored day. For example, you might lay the Magician spread on a Wednesday, ruled by Mercury, the card's planet. See the chart in the Appendix on page 228 for further details.

CHAKRAS AND CRYSTALS

Chakra and crystal associations are included for all major arcana cards to help you work with their energy in meditation (see chapter 4, page 222). Note that these are my associations, and of course you may have your own; it is always wise to go with what most resonates with you.

COMPOSITIONAL AFFINITY

Compositional affinity means resemblance to another card. This might be VI The Lovers and XV, as the two lovers with the presiding angel mirror the two demons with the devil. Attuning to these visual connections can help you with your interpretations because you get to contrast the two cards. In this case, we see the devil as the shadow side of love.

ANIMAL SYMBOLS

Living and mythological animals, birds, reptiles, and insects are also listed in the card profiles so you can see at a glance what is depicted on the card. Animals speak to us, whether represented as statues, as symbols in the sky, or as living creatures.

ARCHANGEL ASSOCIATIONS

The four major arcana cards featuring or associated with archangels are VI The Lovers (Raphael), XV The Devil (Uriel), XIV Temperance (Michael), and XX Judgement (Gabriel).

UPRIGHT AND REVERSED CARD MEANINGS

Keywords plus upright and reversed card meanings are given for all cards. See chapter 1 for further information on reading reversals.

Chapter 4 gives you the techniques you need to read a card with "instant intuitive focus"—to see beyond the traditional card meaning to attune to what your card's symbols are saying in the present moment. You'll also discover ways to work with a card's associated crystals and chakras in meditation and use tarot journaling as a powerful way to record and explore your insights and reflections. Finally, try the spreads in this chapter, too, which are based on several key symbols in your cards.

ABOUT THE RIDER WAITE SMITH TAROT

The deck shown throughout this book is the Universal Waite, a recolored version of the original Rider Waite Smith tarot first published as the Rider Waite tarot in 1909. (Rider is the name of the publisher; Waite as A. E. Waite, the co-creator; and artist Pamela Colman Smith.) Working with the Rider Waite Smith symbols and the techniques in this book will equip you to interpret the symbols on other tarot decks, too; it's all about developing a symbolic mindset.

XVII
IV
VII
O

CHAPTER 1

HOW TO READ THE SYMBOLS IN YOUR CARDS

Symbols give expression to our thoughts. We seek out symbols, often unconsciously, to give form to our thoughts so that we can examine them and discover more about ourselves and others. The Latin word for symbol, *symbolum*, translates as "index" or "collection." When we work with our tarot cards, we can see a card symbol as an index that unpacks itself whenever we look upon it. Working intuitively with symbols helps you naturally find your way to a card's meaning. It's a journey of curiosity and connection that will bring you deeply rewarding and intuitive readings.

When we contemplate a symbol—whether an object, color, or number—we open up to our own wisdom and to the wisdom of the cards, too. In the Rider Waite Smith tarot, shown in these pages, there are hundreds of card symbols; some of them may be familiar—a sword, a crown, a child. Others, less so—a crayfish, a man upside down, or golden droplets emanating from a tower. And then, we have color, number, and esoteric symbols, all of which are powerful signifiers of meaning. Together on a card, they present a rich landscape of possibility. Every tarot card is rather like an advent calendar—each symbol is a door waiting to be opened. We see the outline but don't know what is behind each little portal until we venture through it.

When you focus on a symbol, your sensory awareness heightens. You feel its form and color more intensely as it comes alive under your gaze. This happens because symbols stimulate memory and our higher consciousness; they're a bridge via which we communicate, self to self (as in the images in our dreams), or from the self toward other realms of knowing. In this way, symbols are portals to a world of interpretation.

What's a Symbol?

Symbols refer to imagery. In your tarot cards, this may be

- Numbers
- Figures and their pose
- Hand gestures
- Hair and clothing
- Landscape features, such as mountains, valleys, rivers, and sea
- Weather features, such as rain, clouds, rainbows, and lightning
- Heavenly bodies, sun, moon, and stars
- Buildings, towers, churches, walls, bridges, and pillars
- Colors
- Geometric forms, such as squares, triangles, and crosses
- Objects, particularly those held by a figure
- Animals, such as dog, cat, lion, and horse

When contemplating symbols that call to you, consider that a symbol does not need to be contained, or even something you can immediately name. For instance, if you're drawn to a color that appears in several areas of a card, that color is still your symbol. You may be drawn to a series of lines on a card that doesn't resemble a familiar object—if so, this is again your symbol. You can connect with it using the latter part of the Instant Intuitive Focus exercise in chapter 4 (page 228).

NUMBER AS SYMBOL

A brief guide to number meanings:
One (Ace): Beginnings
Two: Duality. Partnership; alternatively, the tension of opposites
Three: Acknowledgment
Four: Stability
Five: Disruption and challenges
Six: Harmony; a stage of completion
Seven: Potential and mystery
Eight: Reward, change, and progress
Nine: Intensity
Ten: Completion, release, endings, beginnings

SUIT SYMBOL MEANINGS

Cups: Element of Water. The heart: Emotions, relationships, imagination, flow
Pentacles: Element of Earth. The material world: Money, home, work, property, the body, environment, nature
Swords: Element of Air. The mind: Decisions, conflict, strategy, anxiety, thought, intelligence
Wands: Element of Fire. The soul: Energy, creative force, drive, desire, travel, communication

Finding Your Way into This Book

This technique is known as bibliomancy—or divination by book. To find the card you need today, close your eyes, flip through the pages, and stop when it feels right. The card illustrated or described on that page is your card for the day. Another way to use bibliomancy is to repeat the above, but this time looking at the page numbers. If the page you stop at is numbered higher than 21, add that number together until you arrive at a number lower than 21. This number is the major arcana card you need today. When you have your major arcana card, see the exercises below on finding a symbol on the card.

FINDING YOUR WAY INTO A CARD

To approach a card through its symbols, begin with an attitude of curiosity: take a step into the card by describing it internally or aloud. For example, take 0 The Fool. Here is a young person with a strange motif on his tunic, holding a rose; there's a white dog, mountains, sun, a knapsack. Ask a question: Where might he be going? Why is the dog jumping up? Sit with these questions. Slow down and allow yourself to be drawn in rather than feel you must crack a code, and your senses, rather than your logical left brain, will start to do the interpreting. Say you notice how the white rose looks out of place on the rocky cliff top; maybe the Fool is somewhere new, or risky too. There you have your first meaning—that the card is about risk, about trying something new.

EXERCISE 1: ONE-CARD READING THROUGH A SYMBOL

In this first exercise, we spend just a few minutes interpreting one card. The focus is on working quickly and intuitively rather than taking time to (over)think.

Center yourself (see Your Basic Techniques, page 14) then shuffle the deck, asking, "Which card can teach me about symbols today?" Stop shuffling when you feel a subtle shift in your solar plexus. Then dip into the deck with your left hand (traditionally known as the hand of fate), and pull one card. Place it before you, face up.

Hold the card and turn it around—sideways, upside down, and diagonally, too. Release what you think you should know about the card: today, it has something more to show you.

Begin by looking at the card's border and its corners. Be curious: Does anything there call out to you? Maybe the artist's signature, or the edge of another symbol? Look at the number, too, from different angles. For example, the Roman numeral III on its side looks like a ladder. That might mean ambition, a step up. Then, see what else calls to you.

Practice finding detail and potential meaning. Remember, this is practice for yourself, so there is no pressure to be right.

When you feel comfortable with this exercise, try the Instant Intuitive Focus exercise on page 222.

EXERCISE 2: CHOOSING A SYMBOL WITH A PENDULUM

You can work with a pendulum to find the symbol or symbols that hold a message for you today. All you need do is flip through the book and stop at a card (see Finding Your Way into this Book, page 13). Then take the pendulum chain in your dominant hand, supporting your elbow on your desk or table so you are comfortable.

Hold the pendulum above the card. Ask "which symbol do I need today?" Close your eyes and sense the flow of energy from your fingers, down the chain and to the pendulum.

Take a breath and feel how the pendulum is beginning to move a little. When the movement has begun, open your eyes and see where the pendulum goes on the card.

Tip: *You can use a pendulum to select a pile of cards to read from (see The Three Piles, opposite). Hold the pendulum over each pile and sense its energy through the pendulum. A pile of cards might feel flat, heavy, fizzy, or light, for example. The pendulum magnifies the vibe so you can choose the pile of cards you most align with for reading.*

Your Basic Techniques

If you're an experienced reader, skip ahead. Otherwise, here's how to prepare for a reading and lay out your cards.

CENTER YOURSELF BEFORE YOU READ

This helps you relax and connect with yourself before you connect with your cards.

- Get comfortable and close your eyes. Pay attention to your breathing, feeling that you are breathing into the present and breathing out what is past.
- Place your right hand on your solar plexus, under the rib cage, sensing the movement of your breath.
- When you feel settled, open your eyes and pick up your cards.

SHUFFLING IS KEY

Shuffling is more than simply randomizing the cards. When you shuffle, you give your hands and logical left brain a task, which means you stop judging your thoughts. This is why we can have the best ideas when our hands are busy washing up or tidying, for example. With the left brain distracted the right brain, seat of intuition and creativity, can be heard. You naturally begin to tune in to your intuition.

- Shuffle and speak your question or request aloud or in your mind; shuffle it into your cards. Ask three times.
- Stop shuffling when you sense a subtle shift. You might feel this a little flip in your solar plexus or heart, or feel it as a knowing.

Tip: *Keep your questions open. For example, ask "what do I need to see today?" rather than a yes-or-no closed question such as "should I go to this event?" When you ask what you need to see, you open yourself up to possibilities beyond the specifics—your cards can pinpoint how you might be feeling and reasons for your current situation, as well as the likely outcome.*

CHOOSE YOUR LAYOUT, THEN CHOOSE YOUR CARDS FOR A READING

There are various methods, below. Use your left hand to choose cards, as traditionally this is the hand of fate. Also, the left hand connects with the right brain and your intuitive knowing. You'll always place your cards face down, then turn them over sideways so they are face up (see Reading Reversals, below); then, you're ready to interpret your cards.

The dip: To choose one card, hold your deck with your right hand, and splay it out a little. Close your eyes, and dip in with your left hand. Pull out that card, and place it face down.

The fan: Spread all the cards face down in a fan shape. With your left hand, choose the cards you need. If you are reading for another person, ask them to point out the cards, then you take them from the fan. Place your chosen cards in a spread, face down.

The three piles: With your left hand, cut the deck twice so you have three piles of cards in a row—to your left, center, and right. Choose the pile that feels right to read from. If you are reading for another person, ask them to point to a pile; if you are reading online, ask them to visualize three piles—one to their right, the center, and one to their left, and ask them to choose a pile for you to read from. (Remember that their left-hand pile will be your right-hand pile, and vice versa.)

Reading Reversals

A reversed card comes out of the deck upside down. You might begin with a deck of upright cards, but somehow, during shuffling, one or more cards invert themselves. For most cards, the reversed meaning is negative; for cards that are already challenging, however, the reversed meaning can say that the worst is over. Many readers today prefer not to read reversed cards because they prefer to interpret the card as they feel it—and understand that the shadow side of a card is always present in its upright meaning. (The exception to this is XIX The Sun, which chases all the shadows away.) It is your choice whether to read reversals or not, but it is always worth reading the reversed card interpretations to broaden your understanding of a card. If you get reversed cards and prefer not to read them, simply turn them the right way up and continue your interpretation.

Jumping Cards as Symbols

When you shuffle, you'll often find that one or more cards jump out of the deck. They convey a message that needs to be shared with the querent (the person being read for) when the full reading begins.

The jumping card can also be a message for me, the reader, about the querent: it tells me something about them in advance. For example, Ten of Wands as a jumping card says the person may be feeling overwhelmed or overloaded and it may take a little time for them to relax into the reading.

When you get a jumping card, you can do one of three things:

- Place the card face up to the left, keeping it in sight but away from the cards you'll lay down. This way, you can bring its interpretation into the reading when it feels right to do so.
- Look at it, take a mental note, and place it back in the deck then continue with your shuffle.
- Lay it down as the first card of your spread.

There is no right or wrong way to work with jumping cards. Do what feels best to you, but always pay attention to their message.

B
J
TORA

VII

VIII

IX

X

XII

XIII

XIV

XVII

XVIII

XIX

XX

CHAPTER 2

MAJOR ARCANA SYMBOLS

0 THE FOOL

Other Names: The Jester, The Idiot, The Joker, The Foolish Man

Esoteric Title: The Spirit of Ether

Number: Zero

Alternative Number: XXII or no number

Numerology Link: None and all of the major arcana cards

Astrological Sign or Planet: Uranus

Day of the Week: Wednesday

Element: Air

Hebrew Letter: Aleph

Symbol: The ox

Meaning: Instinct

Tree of Life Pathway: First, between Kether and Chockmah

Chakra: Crown, for spiritual connection, and base, for survival

Crystals: Clear quartz (crown chakra), red carnelian and red jasper (base chakra)

Animal Symbols: Dog, eagle

DESCRIPTION

In a mountain range, a young traveler holding a white rose is about to step off a precipice. His dog barks a warning, but the youth gazes up at the sky.

KEY MEANINGS

Beginnings, journeys, innocence, risks, ideals, leap of faith, optimism, naivety, exploration

UPRIGHT MEANING

The Fool is the card of beginnings—of new adventures and goals. This is a time for discovery and to follow ideals, providing you consider the potential risks. There may be danger in rushing ahead too quickly, so you may need to plan—or look—before you take your leap of faith. The card also shows starting an educational course, relationship, or other new venture to inspire your courageous, romantic spirit. More broadly, the Fool ushers in a new phase of life, as something within you is born. A further meaning is a young person leaving home to embark on their own adventure.

REVERSED MEANING

The reversed Fool can indicate the dangers of an idiotic decision; it is best to hold back and consider the options.

THE FOOL'S SYMBOLS

1	Number 0	Links with all and none of the other major arcana cards
2	The Fool	Innocence
3	The white sun	Pure consciousness
4	The sleeve lining	The womb
5	Tunic design	Cycles

6	Leaf crown	Growth
7	The red feather	Life force
8	White rose	Idealism
9	Dog	Instinct
10	Knapsack	Resources

What the Symbols Mean for You

When you are drawn to a particular symbol or feature of a card, it's because it holds a special meaning for you. Here is a guide to interpreting your symbols.

1 THE NUMBER 0

The Fool's number 0 is the zero, the no-thing before he evolves through the cards in the major arcana cycle. The zero is the shape of an egg and the Fool is the embryo within, symbol of potential. As the first card in the major arcana, the Fool takes the first letter of the Hebrew alphabet, Aleph, for the breath—the beginning of life. The Fool's Tree of Life pathway is first, between the spheres of creation and wisdom: our Fool gains knowledge as he travels.

See the zero/egg symbols on XXI The World.

2 THE FOOL

The Fool's pose is one of openness—with his arms wide to the air, his natural element, he is ready to embrace the world. The Fool is the archetypal young hero or heroine who sets out on a quest to follow his dream. Free-spirited—a quality of his planet, Uranus—he represents the birth of an idea.

3 THE WHITE SUN

The early morning sun is the Fool in his early stage of life. Its whiteness links with the crown chakra for this card, for the Fool's connection to spirit, and is also the color of innocence: he steps into a sunshine world, not cognizant of the pitfalls ahead.

4 THE SLEEVE LINING

The red lining suggests the lining of the womb, a reminder that the Fool is newborn, a novice in life.

See this symbol on the Nine of Pentacles.

5 TUNIC DESIGN

The Fool's tunic of yellow, black, and red symbolizes the colors of alchemy. There are twelve motifs—for the twelve zodiac signs and months of the year. Nine of these look like the spokes of a wheel, to symbolize life's cycles. The other three motifs might be pomegranates, symbols of fertility. Collectively, the motifs represent life and life's cycles.

See the wheel motif within X The Wheel of Fortune. See the pomegranates on II The High Priestess.

6 LEAF CROWN

The Fool's laurel wreath is a symbol of victory. The esoteric author Paul Foster Case says that the wreath represents the vegetable kingdom while the red feather (see below) symbolizes the animal kingdom. As the vegetable kingdom is about growth, this gives us a meaning more fitted to the inexperienced Fool who is yet to experience victory.

7 THE RED FEATHER

The red feather is a symbol of the life force. Here it resembles an umbilical cord linking with the meaning of the sleeve lining as womb (see above).

See the red feather on XIII Death and XIX The Sun; also the box overleaf.

8 WHITE ROSE

The white rose is a symbol of purity and innocence. The Fool is a romantic, full of airy ideas, holding the rose as a magical object to guide him forward—regardless of the perilous ground ahead.

9 DOG

The Fool's dog symbolizes instinct; he jumps up to warn his master that he is about to walk off the edge of the cliff, but the innocent Fool is oblivious to his dog and the danger.

10 KNAPSACK

The Fool's knapsack bears the emblem of the eagle, for vision and freedom. It contains the four suit symbols we see on I The Magician's table, but the Fool does not yet know their power; in this way, the knapsack is the Fool's undeveloped personality. He needs to meet the Magician to realize he has the resources to survive on his journey: light (the Wand), water (the Cup), air (the Sword) and food (the Pentacle).

See the symbols of the four suits on I The Magician.

The Fool's Red Feather

The red feather, symbol of the life force, appears at significant points in the major arcana sequence: with the embryonic Fool, on Death's helmet on card XIII, and in the child's hair on XIX The Sun. These represent key turning points on the journey—from birth (Fool) to transformation in the death of the ego (Death) then the beginning of the second transformation with XIX The Sun. After the Sun comes Judgement as the soul ascends, XXI The World as reintegration with the One, or Universe, followed by rebirth with the Fool—as so the wheel turns.

THE BIRTHDAY READING

As the Fool is the newborn beginner of the major arcana cycle, this birthday reading helps you look at the year ahead.

To begin, take out 0 The Fool and place it face up as shown to oversee the reading. Then shuffle the cards, asking, "show me what I need to see now" and choose three (see page 14). Place them face down below the Fool as shown. Turn the cards face up and begin your interpretation.

What you have learned from the past twelve months
Example: Three of Wands. The benefits of travel and exploration; new concepts and ways of seeing the world.

What is seeking you now
Example: IX The Hermit. Quietude; time for reflection and healing.

Spiritual guidance for the year ahead
Example: The Ten of Cups. Tending to family and chosen family; finding a supportive group.

I THE MAGICIAN

Other Names: The Magus, The Juggler, The Minstrel, The Mountebank

Esoteric Title: The Magus of Power

Number: One

Numerology Links: X The Wheel of Fortune and XIX The Sun

Astrological Sign or Planet: Mercury

Day of the Week: Wednesday

Elements: Air, also Ether, the quintessence or fifth element

Hebrew Letter: Beth (Biet)

- **Symbol:** House
- **Meaning:** Creativity

Tree of Life Pathway: Second, between Kether and Binah

Chakra: The palm chakras, for manifesting

Crystals: Aquamarine, fire agate

Animal Symbol: Serpent, dove

DESCRIPTION

Standing by a table displaying the four suit symbols, a man dressed for sacred ritual holds up his wand to the sky. His left hand points earthwards, where roses and lilies grow.

KEY MEANINGS

Action, manifestation, self-expression, creativity, communication, enterprise, energy, willpower

UPRIGHT MEANING

The Magician signifies action, so now is the time to begin a new project. At work you take the lead or benefit from strong leadership, and in your personal projects you discover a new creative path. If you are looking for a relationship, this is the time to meet someone new; in a fledgling romance, love develops as you make plans. Under the influence of the Magician, you communicate with clarity and have the energy to act upon your inspired ideas; travel is favored, too. The Magician also represents manifesting, so be ready to receive what you desire.

REVERSED MEANING

The reversed Magician suggests manipulation and dishonesty—so what you hear may not be accurate or true.

THE MAGICIAN'S SYMBOLS

1	Number I	Links with X The Wheel of Fortune and XIX The Sun
2	The Magician	Magic
3	The wand	Directed energy
4	The four suit symbols	Elemental power

5	Robes	Action and purity
6	Roses and lilies	Authenticity
7	Serpent-girdle	Infinity
8	Dove	Peace
9	The lemniscate	Cycles and renewal

What the Symbols Mean for You

When you are drawn to a particular symbol or feature of a card, it's because it holds a special meaning for you. Here is a guide to interpreting your symbols.

1 NUMBER I

Through his number I, The Magician is related to X the Wheel of Fortune (X = 10; 1 + 0 = 1) and XIX The Sun (XIX = 19; 1 + 9 = 10; 1+ 0 = 1). Number I means beginnings and new cycles: we see this in X The Wheel of Fortune and in XIX The Sun, which carries the seed, the "I" of the beginning to come after the end of the cycle at card XXI—before we return to 0 The Fool.

In Pythagorean numerology, number one means divine intelligence and the sun, which fills this card with light. Further, "I" symbolizes the self or individual, and the Magician is certainly self-directed, taking action to manifest his own desires.

As the second card in the major arcana, the Magician takes the second letter of the Hebrew alphabet, Beth, for creativity. He is associated with the second Tree of Life pathway, between the spheres of Kether, divine light and Binah, for understanding: for the Magician, this means spirit in action.

2 THE MAGICIAN

The Magician performs magic: as a conduit of universal energy, he makes the link between heaven and earth to manifest thought into reality. Historically he is associated with the winged traveler Hermes, god of communication—the Roman Mercury, whose namesake planet rules the card. Determined and focused, he is mindful of his task, which is signified by his headband.

See the headband on the Three of Wands.

3 THE WAND

Signifying power and purpose, the wand directs energy from heaven to earth. It is double-ended to illustrate the Hermetic axiom "As above, so below"—what happens in the higher realms also manifests on earth.

See the double-ended wand on XXI The World.

4 THE FOUR SUIT SYMBOLS

The suit symbols represent the suits' associated elements of Earth (Pentacles), Fire (Wands), Water (Cups), and Air (Swords). The Magician harnesses the power of these four elements to create the fifth element of Ether or Spirit—the Magician's elements are Air and Ether.

5 ROBES

The Magician wears a white tunic and red cloak. The red stands for action in the material world and the white, purity of intention. These meanings are echoed in the red roses and lilies below.

See the red cloak on IV The Emperor, V The Hierophant, and XI Justice.

6 ROSES AND LILIES

Red roses represent love and passion while lilies symbolize purity; the Magician wears their colors as a statement of his authenticity. The flowers appear beneath his downward hand, as if he had just made them appear: the blooms are an example of his magic.

See roses on III The Empress, VIII Strength, and the Nine of Swords; the roses and lilies on the gowns of the supplicants in V The Hierophant

7 SERPENT-GIRDLE

The serpent eating his tail is the ouroboros, alchemical symbol of infinity and eternal energy. The serpent design is a symbol of Mercury, the card's ruling planet.

8 DOVE

The dove means peace; its form echoes the dove on the Ace of Cups, which is also a symbol of spirit.

9 THE LEMNISCATE

The lemniscate or infinity symbol illustrates the eternal flow of energy. Above the Magician's crown, the symbol shows that he works with this universal flow, harnessing it to manifest his desires.

The Magician and the Aces

There are many correlations between the major and minor arcana—from III The Empress overseeing the four Queens to the Kings as facets of IV The Emperor. The four Aces of the minor arcana are aspects of I The Magician: the Aces, representing their suit elements, illustrate how a beginning may actualize in our day-to-day lives:

Ace of Cups (Water): The beginning of love, of devotion. An outpouring.
Ace of Pentacles (Earth): A new opportunity in the material world. A gateway.
Ace of Wands (Fire): A new spark; feeling inspired to move, to create. A passion.
Ace of Swords (Air): A resolution; success and clarity. A breakthrough.

MAKING MAGIC

With this spread, discover your potential to create what you desire.

To begin, take out I The Magician and place it face up as shown to oversee the reading. Then shuffle the cards, asking, "what can I create?" and choose three (see page 14). Place them face down below the Magician as shown. Turn the cards face up and begin your interpretation.

1 **What you can create**

2 **What kind of resources you need**

3 **The magic ingredient: What turns your idea into gold**

II THE HIGH PRIESTESS

Other Names: The Papess, The Priestess, Juno

Esoteric Title: The Priestess of the Silver Star

Number: Two

Numerology Links: XI Justice and XX Judgement

Astrological Sign or Planet: The Moon

Day of the Week: Monday

Element: Water

Hebrew Letter: Gimel

  Symbol: Camel

  Meaning: Wisdom

Tree of Life Pathway: Third, between Kether and Tiphareth

Chakra: Fifth eye (angelic or soma) chakra for psychic activation

Crystals: Lavender quartz, selenite, moonstone

Compositional Affinity: V The Hierophant, XI Justice

DESCRIPTION

A woman sits between two pillars with a veil decorated with pomegranates behind her. She wears a horned headdress and cross; a scroll with the letters TORA rests on her lap.

KEY MEANINGS

Intuition, clairvoyance, secrets, wisdom, teaching, spirituality, divine feminine

UPRIGHT MEANING

The High Priestess is a card of spiritual advice, so a mentor, new teacher or other guide finds you. You intuitively sense a stronger connection with the Universe or the divine, and your dreams hold messages: new spiritual pathways beckon. In your personal life you tap into your inner wisdom and may need privacy to process your insights; the theme of confidentiality also applies to work, as you may be asked to keep certain information confidential. In established relationships, the card means secrecy or a secret relationship, but otherwise, the High Priestess can symbolize celibacy or being single.

REVERSED MEANING

When reversed, trust issues arise as you feel you have been influenced to follow a path that is not right for you. Listen to your intuition.

THE HIGH PRIESTESS'S SYMBOLS

1	**Number II**	Links with XI Justice and XX Judgement
2	**The High Priestess**	Divine feminine
3	**Moon crown**	Stages and cycles
4	**Scroll**	Wisdom
5	**Blue cloak and white robe**	Truth and purity
6	**Pillars**	Severity and mercy
7	**Pomegranate and date palm**	Fertility
8	**Crescent moon**	The unconscious

What the Symbols Mean for You

When you are drawn to a particular symbol or feature of a card, it's because it holds a special meaning for you. Here is a guide to interpreting your symbols.

1 NUMBER II

Number II links with Justice, card XI (XI = 11; 1 + 1 = 2) and Judgement, card XX. Both the High Priestess and Justice with their two pillars guard a portal. The High Priestess's portal leads to the world of spirit; its existence validates our intuition, while Justice's portal leads to freedom, a validation of innocence. Both cards have a veil behind them to symbolize the dualities of heaven and earth, innocence and guilt. The High Priestess is also related to XX Judgement (2 + 0 = 2), which illustrates the impact of the past on the present.

As the third card in the major arcana sequence, the High Priestess takes the third letter of the Hebrew alphabet, Gimel, for wisdom. She is placed on the third Tree of Life pathway, between the spheres of divine light (Kether) and beauty and rebirth (Tiphareth); her work is the care of the soul, mediating between the earth plane and those in spirit.

2 THE HIGH PRIESTESS

The High Priestess represents the divine and lunar feminine, counterpart of V, The Hierophant or High Priest. Her world is internal; she is the psychic, the clairvoyant and intuitive, whereas The Hierophant occupies the external world of the church and public teaching. As the nun—she is dressed like a nun in her robes—she relates, too, to IX The Hermit or monk, who also seeks arcane wisdom. The High Priestess's cross symbolizes her spiritual devotion.

3 MOON CROWN

The moon headdress references the Egyptian deity Hathor/Isis, goddess of fertility, life, and magic. Within it we see the moon in three phases to symbolize the moon's cycles and the life stages of youth, maturity, and older age.

4 SCROLL

The scroll is the Sefer Torah, a hand-written scroll that is one of the sacred texts of Kabbala. *Torah* means law and teaching.

See the letters TORA on X The Wheel of Fortune.

5 BLUE CLOAK AND WHITE ROBE

The High Priestess's flowing robes are symbols of her element of Water. Her white robe symbolizes purity, which aligns with her identity as a nun while the blue cloak signifies truth.

6 PILLARS

Two temple pillars symbolize duality and boundaries—they are gateways to the mysteries, to what is unknown. The shape of the pillars resembles upright lilies, with the pillar as stem and the fluted tops as the flower. Lilies symbolize the High Priestess's purity.

See the pillars on V The Hierophant and XI Justice.

7 POMEGRANATE AND DATE PALM

The pomegranate is a symbol of fertility, death, and rebirth. In Greek myth, Persephone ate pomegranate seeds in the underworld and was cursed to spend six months of the year there and the other six months with her mother in the upper world. The story is an allegory of nature's cycles and the duality of life and death (see also V The Hierophant). With the pomegranate is the date palm for masculinity; together they symbolize fruitfulness.

See the palm frond on the Ace of Swords.

8 CRESCENT MOON

The crescent moon illustrates the card's ruling planet, echoed on the moon crown (see above). Placed by her feet almost like an anchor, the moon is a reminder that the lunar, unconscious mind is always present.

Pillars of Severity and Mercy

The two pillars on II The High Priestess are the pillars of the Temple of Solomon, named in the Bible's Old Testament as Boaz and Joachim (the B and J on the card). In Kabbala, the pillars are part of the Tree of Life, its central mystical symbol. The left-hand (black) pillar is called "Severity," while the right (white) pillar is "Mercy." The Severity pillar is named after the sephirot or sphere of Geburah for violence and destruction, while the Mercy pillar is named after the sphere of Chesed, for love, kindness, and evolution. There is also a central pillar on the Tree that represents balance. The High Priestess sits between the pillars, maintaining this balance, or harmony.

THE OTHER SIDE OF THE PORTAL

As the High Priestess sits between two temple pillars, she is the guardian of the gateway to wisdom. By the placing her card in the center, we travel from card 1 through the portal to card 2 and the future.

Take out II The High Priestess and lay the card face up in the center, as shown. Then shuffle the remainder of the deck and lay two cards face down, one below the High Priestess and one card above. When you are ready, turn cards 1 and 2 face up and begin your interpretation.

The present:
What I am learning now
Example: The Hierophant. Learning to be the teacher; listening to guidance and learning more about yourself.

Future:
How this wisdom will affect my life
Example: I The Magician. Being empowered to take action, to create what you desire in physical form.

III THE EMPRESS

Other Names: The Mother, The Grandmother	
Esoteric Title: Daughter of the Mighty Ones	
Number: Three	
Numerology Links: XII The Hanged Man, XXI The World	
Astrological Sign or Planet: Venus	
Day of the Week: Friday	
Element: Earth	
Hebrew Letter: Daleth	
	Symbol: Door
	Meaning: Attainment
Tree of Life Pathway: Fourth, between Binah and Chockmah	
Chakras: Heart, for love, and sacral chakra, for fertility	
Crystals: Rose quartz, emerald, orange carnelian, orange calcite	

DESCRIPTION

A pregnant woman wearing a crown of stars sits comfortably on her throne. A fertile landscape surrounds her—ripe corn, trees, a waterfall.

KEY MEANINGS

Abundance, love, generosity, comfort, sensuality, security, productivity, pregnancy, creativity, resourcefulness

UPRIGHT MEANING

The Empress symbolizes the female partner in traditional tarot meanings, but the card has many further attributes—beginning with enrichment, security, and abundance. Money grows, you feel content within and, if you are looking for love, now could be the right time for a new relationship. As this is the card of mothering, you feel nurtured and support others, too, so all your relationships benefit. In work, you get creative and resourceful; at home, you enjoy a deeper sense of comfort and may invest in redecorating or other improvements. Physically, the Empress also symbolizes pregnancy or incubating an idea.

REVERSED MEANING

The reversed Empress shows discord—so there may be financial problems and miscommunication in relationships.

THE EMPRESS'S SYMBOLS

1	**Number III**	Links with XII The Hanged Man and XXI The World
2	**The Empress**	Abundance
3	**Pearl necklace**	Cosmic wisdom
4	**Rose motif**	Love
5	**The starry crown**	Authority
6	**Venus glyph**	Love
7	**Corn**	Well-being
8	**Lush landscape**	Creative flow

What the Symbols Mean for You

When you are drawn to a particular symbol or feature of a card, it's because it holds a special meaning for you. Here is a guide to interpreting your symbols.

1 NUMBER XII

The Empress's first relation in the major arcana is XII The Hanged Man, whose number reduces to III The Empress (XII = 12; 1 + 2 = 3). The pregnant Empress waits for her unborn child to grow, as the Hanged Man, as initiate, waits as he undergoes spiritual rebirth. The second relationship is with XXI The World (21 as 2 + 1 = 3). The World is the card of expansion, completion, and success—the goals of the Empress and the Hanged Man. Both III The Empress and XXI The World also feature the laurel wreath, symbol of victory.

Number three is also the child of I The Magician and II The High Priestess. I The Magician is the masculine principle, and solar consciousness, and II The High Priestess, the lunar unconscious, represents the divine feminine—hence III The Empress's meaning of fertility and motherhood.

As the fourth card in the major arcana sequence, the Empress takes the fourth letter of the Hebrew alphabet, Daleth, a door; this links with the Empress as mother, as birth as the gateway to new life. On the fourth Tree of Life pathway, III The Empress is placed between the spheres of Binah and Chockmah, or compassion and wisdom. As Binah is the feminine principle and Chockmah the male, this symbolizes creativity and wholeness.

2 THE EMPRESS

The Empress is the female archetype. She is Gaia, Mother Earth (Earth is the card's element), symbol of abundance, fecundity, and nurturing. Surrounded by nature, her throne, or place of power, is adorned with luxurious cushions from indoors. In this way, the Empress embodies both the inner domestic world and outer world of wildlife. She nurtures and is sustained by both.

3 PEARL NECKLACE

The Empress wears a necklace of seven pearls, a symbol of wisdom. The number seven relates to the seven principal chakras and seven classical planets—which connects with the starry crown (see below).

4 ROSE MOTIF

The red rose is a symbol of love and passion. On the Empress's gown, it is illustrated with leaves and stem to resemble the glyph for her planet, Venus, also seen on the shield (see Venus Glyph, below).

See roses on VIII Strength and the Nine of Swords; the roses and lilies on I The Magician and on the gowns of the supplicants in V The Hierophant.

5 THE STARRY CROWN

The Empress's crown is a half-crown, or diadem, of twelve stars, seen in depictions of the Virgin Mary. On the card, the twelve stars can signify the twelve tribes of Israel or the twelve signs of the zodiac. Beneath the crown is a wreath of laurel leaves, symbol of victory.

6 VENUS GLYPH

The circle and cross on the stone heart is the astrological glyph, or symbol of love goddess Venus, the card's associated planet. The motif is repeated on the cushion to the left of the throne.

7 CORN

The ripe corn represents harvest, symbol of wealth and well-being. Corn is also a symbol of Demeter, the grain goddess and mother of Persephone. (See the story of Demeter and Persephone in V The Hierophant, page 40.)

8 LUSH LANDSCAPE

A waterfall at the edge of a forest, a cornfield under a sunshine sky: the Empress's landscape symbolizes growth and creative flow. All life is supported.

Empress Day: Friday Meditation

As III The Empress is associated with the planet Venus, her day of the week is Friday, also ruled by Venus. Meditating with the Empress or doing her reading, below, on a Friday helps strength your connection with the card and with her nurturing, creative energy (especially helpful if you feel depleted at the end of a long week). Here's how to begin:

- Take the card, close your eyes and center yourself for a minute or two.
- Hold The Empress to your heart. Take three deep breaths in and out, breathing in light and breathing out any negative experiences or thoughts from the past few days. Then, return to normal breathing.
- Ask the Empress to bring you energy and abundance (phrase this request in a way that's right for you).
- Tune in. Listen with your heart.
- When you are ready, give thanks and open your eyes.

MONEY AND ABUNDANCE

This spread uses three cards, including The Empress, to tune in to the energy of creative number III. Use it to check for any blocks in abundance—so if you are focusing on money just now, you can see what may be in the way and discover what to do next.

First, take out III The Empress and place her face up as shown to oversee the reading. Then shuffle the remainder of the deck and lay two cards face down, in positions 1 and 2. When you are ready, turn over the cards and begin your interpretation.

1
What's in the way of abundance

What to do or focus on to grow in abundance

IV THE EMPEROR

Other Names: The Father, The Grandfather

Esoteric Titles: Son of the Morning, Chief Among the Mighty

Number: Four

Numerology Link: XIII Death

Astrological Sign or Planet: Aries the Ram

Day of the Week: Tuesday

Element: Fire

Hebrew Letter: Hei (Heh)

  Symbol: Window

  Meaning: Progress

Tree of Life Pathway: Fifth, between Tiphareth and Chockmah

Chakra: Base, for security and belonging

Crystals: Red jasper, red calcite, garnet

Animal Symbol: Ram

DESCRIPTION

A mature bearded man in armor and red robes sits on a stone throne in an arid landscape. He holds a golden scepter in his right hand and an orb in his left.

KEY MEANINGS

Stability, order, authority, boundaries, control, ambition, territory, leadership, protection

UPRIGHT MEANING

The Emperor, while symbolizing the father and traditionally the romantic partner, has broader meanings. The card represents calmness and stability after a time of disruption, so order returns. At work, The Emperor shows strong leadership and new structures that will please or challenge you, depending on how well you respond to authority. As a card of advice, The Emperor encourages you to manage your time and energy. You may also need to protect your boundaries, whether with neighboring properties or in maintaining personal boundaries for good self-care. In relationships, you find love and loyalty.

REVERSED MEANING

When reversed, The Emperor is domineering—so you may need to say no to unreasonable demands.

THE EMPEROR'S SYMBOLS

1	**Number IV**	Links with XIII Death
2	**The Emperor**	Maturity and power
3	**The golden apple and ankh**	Male and female archetypes

4	**Ram's heads**	Sign of Aries
5	**Robes and armor**	Action and defense
6	**Crown**	Authority
7	**Desert terrain**	Fire and flow

What the Symbols Mean for You

When you are drawn to a particular symbol or feature of a card, it's because it holds a special meaning for you. Here is a guide to interpreting your symbols.

1 NUMBER IV

The Emperor as card IV relates to XIII Death (XIII = 13; 1 + 3 = 4); The Emperor brings peace and protection after Death's disruption. The number four is the number of the element of Earth, which combines with the card's element of Fire. These two elements are comfortable together—they do not empower each other directly, as do Fire and Air (Air feeds Fire to make flames), but nor they do not weaken each other. (Air and Earth, for example, are seen as contrary.) In this way, Earth and Fire are stable together, and stability is the prime meaning of the card.

As the fifth card in the major arcana sequence, The Emperor takes the fifth letter of the Hebrew alphabet, Hei, which means "progress." On the fifth Tree of Life pathway, The Emperor is placed between the spheres of Tiphareth and Chockmah. Tiphareth is associated with beauty and rebirth and Chockmah, wisdom: the Emperor passes on his wisdom to future generations, so he lives on.

2 THE EMPEROR

The Emperor symbolizes traditional male authority, and more broadly, being the authority in your own life. The four kings of the minor arcana are aspects of IV The Emperor: the pragmatic King of Pentacles with his wealth, the fiery King of Wands with his eloquence and culture, the King of Swords with his honor in battle, and the King of Cups, for empathy and intuition. The Emperor's beard is a sign of maturity and wisdom. Note his eyes—he looks to the side, wary of those who approach or oppose him.

See the beard on IX The Hermit.

3 THE GOLDEN APPLE AND ANKH

The Emperor holds the ankh and an apple-like orb. The ankh represents male virility and the apple, female fertility. The ankh symbolizes life and the apple, love, and sexuality; the apple is the symbol of Venus, goddess of love. In this sense, these objects can represent the Emperor as head of generations of a family—hence his alternative name, The Grandfather.

See the Venus symbol on III The Empress.

4 RAM'S HEADS

The four ram's heads on the front and top of the throne are the zodiac symbol of Aries the Ram, associated with Fire, the card's element.

5 ROBES AND ARMOR

The Emperor's red robes signify action and passion. Underneath he wears armor, showing he has the power to fight to protect his territory.

See the armor on XIII Death.

6 CROWN

The crown is a symbol of authority. The Emperor's crown is closed, a symbol of self-containment; he guards his power.

7 DESERT TERRAIN

The desert-like landscape of fiery orange echoes the card's element of Fire. The river at the foot of the rocks symbolizes boundaries and the flow of life; the river may be thin as a ribbon, but it ensures the land is not barren.

The Emperor's Clothes

The Emperor and V The Hierophant share the same red and blue in their attire—they both wear a red robe with a blue garment underneath. Blue symbolizes truth and red, action—so the Emperor and the Hierophant are associated with truth in action, or integrity. They also connect to Chockmah, the sphere of wisdom on the Tree of Life (see page 222). In elemental terms, the colors are used in proportion to create balance. Too little blue (for Water) means a fire gets out of control; too much Water and the fire dies—so the red-blue ratio is just right, creating the meaning of stability.

BEING THE EMPEROR

This spread takes the Emperor's excellent organizing skills as inspiration and reveals what you most need to manage at present.

First, take out IV The Emperor and place the card face up as shown to oversee the reading. Then shuffle the remainder of the deck and lay three cards face down, in positions 1, 2, and 3. When you are ready, turn over the cards and begin your interpretation.

1

Past success
Example: I The Magician. Resourcefulness; creating desired results.

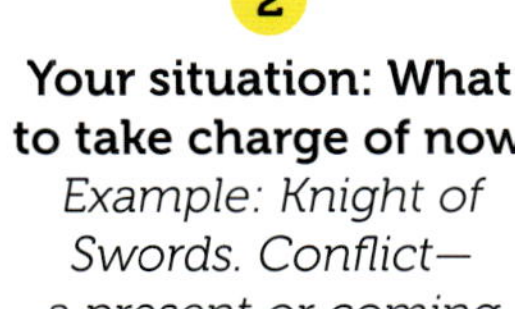

2

Your situation: What to take charge of now
Example: Knight of Swords. Conflict—a present or coming battle that needs a strategy from you.

3

Guidance: Moving on from card 2
Example: XVII The Star. Healing after the battle in card 2; tuning into spiritual messages through intuition. All will be well.

V THE HIEROPHANT

Other Names: The High Priest, The Priest, the Pope, Jupiter

Esoteric Title: Magus of the Eternal Gods

Number: Five

Numerology Link: XIV Temperance

Astrological Sign or Planet: Taurus the Bull

Day of the Week: Friday

Element: Earth

Hebrew Letter: Vau (Vav, Wav)

- **Symbol:** Nail or connector
- **Meaning:** Kindness

Tree of Life Pathway: Sixth, between Chesed and Chockmah

Chakra: Causal, or fourth eye, for spiritual connection

Crystals: Apophyllite, celestite, sapphire

Compositional Affinity: XI Justice, II The High Priestess, The Six of Pentacles

DESCRIPTION

A priest in red and white sits between two pillars. At his feet are crossed keys and two supplicants. He holds the papal cross and makes the gesture of blessing with his right hand.

KEY MEANINGS

Education, advice, spiritual authority, tradition, unity, higher awareness, improvement, commitment

UPRIGHT MEANING

The Hierophant's meanings may appear diverse—from learning and education to conformity, religion, and commitment—yet the common denominator is unity and development. When the Hierophant appears, work and finances improve. You take on a leadership role or find an inspiring teacher; you discover higher wisdom, find the right advice and benefit from years of experience. The card also relates to communities, so you may find a project or group that brings learning and personal growth. In relationships you make a commitment, which may mean marriage. Symbolically, this marriage can be within as you feel aligned and at one.

REVERSED MEANING

The reversed Hierophant can show a wrong spiritual direction or mentorship and generally, poor guidance.

THE HIEROPHANT'S SYMBOLS

1	**Number V**	Links with XIV Temperance
2	**The Hierophant**	The revealer
3	**Supplicants**	Guidance, love, and purity
4	**Crossed keys**	Power and unity
5	**Benediction gesture**	Heaven and earth

6	**Pillars**	Order
7	**Papal crown**	Spiritual authority
8	**Zodiac symbol**	Taurus
9	**W symbol**	The letter Vav
10	**Small crosses**	The Trinity
11	**Red and blue attire**	Authenticity and action

What the Symbols Mean for You

When you are drawn to a particular symbol or feature of a card, it's because it holds a special meaning for you. Here is a guide to interpreting your symbols.

1 NUMBER V

The Hierophant's number V links with card XIV, Temperance (XIV = 14; 1 + 4 = 5). As the High Priest and angel, both cards represent divinity and higher consciousness. In Pythagorean thinking, number five represented human experience. Comprising three and two—three was believed to be a male number, and two a female number, a further meaning of five is marriage, linking to the Hierophant's role as officiating priest. The process of integration is also part of XIV Temperance, in which an angel measures the flow of water between two chalices.

As the sixth card in the major arcana sequence, the Hierophant takes the sixth letter of the Hebrew alphabet, Vau (see W Symbol, opposite). On the sixth Tree of Life pathway the Hierophant is placed between the spheres of Chesed for divine love and mercy, and Chockmah, for wisdom: the values he must communicate as an emissary of God.

2 THE HIEROPHANT

The Hierophant represents religion and belief systems. As the Pope, he is called pontifex, or "bridge-maker" between our outer and inner worlds. The word *hierophant* means "revealer of sacred things"—he officiated the annual Eleusinian Mysteries, an ancient Greek ritual that honored death and rebirth through the story of the goddess Demeter and her daughter Persephone (Persephone's pomegranate appears on card II The High Priestess). Persephone was kidnapped by Hades and taken to the Underworld. While later released, she was forever bound to return for part of every year because during her captivity she had eaten pomegranate seed. In this way, the Hierophant is also the natural counterpart of II The High Priestess (see Number V, above).

3 SUPPLICANTS

The two supplicants have monk's tonsures, a symbol of religious devotion. One supplicant has a rose motif on his robe, a symbol of love; the other wears the white lily design, which signifies purity.

See the roses on III The Empress, VIII Strength and the Nine of Swords; the roses and lilies on I The Magician.

4 CROSSED KEYS

The crossed keys signify unity of heaven and earth and access to the kingdom of heaven. The keys were once an emblem of the Roman god Janus (for January), deity of beginnings, transitions, and endings who unlocked the gates of the solstices—so they also symbolize exclusion or inclusion; the keyholder holds the power.

5 BENEDICTION GESTURE

The hierophant makes the gesture of a blessing, with two fingers bent and two extended to represent the seen and unseen, or earth and heaven. A further meaning is that the three raised digits—thumb, index, and middle fingers—signify the Holy Trinity of the Father, the Son, and the Holy Spirit.

6 PILLARS

Two pillars symbolize duality and boundaries. The boundaries are religious doctrine and rules that the Hierophant lives by—and expects others to conform to. The pillar's gray color also signifies wisdom, as gray integrates the opposites black and white.

See the pillars on II The High Priestess and XI Justice.

7 PAPAL CROWN

The crown is an authority symbol worn by the Pope as God's representative on earth (Earth is also the card's element). Its three tiers symbolize the holy trinity of God the Father, the Son, and the Holy Spirit.

The Hierophant: Other Interpretations

Although the Rider Waite Smith card shows the Pope, you can interpret it in a way that resonates with you. As spiritual adviser, the card can mean a shaman, lecturer, inspirational speaker, magus, esoteric teacher, or author whom you follow; this may be a preferable interpretation if you feel uncomfortable with orthodox religious imagery. In the nineteenth century the Hierophant, then named The Pope, was replaced due to wars between Catholics and Protestants. In the Tarot de Besancon of 1818 he became the Roman god Jupiter, and the High Priestess, Juno.

8 ZODIAC SYMBOL

The zodiac glyph for Taurus, the card's zodiac sign, is just visible above the corner motifs on the Hierophant's throne. Taurus is associated with stability, loyalty, the body, and the senses. The Hierophant is linked to the sense of hearing and listening, as the Hierophant of the Eleusinian Mysteries (see The Hierophant, opposite), was renowned for his enchanting voice.

9 W SYMBOL

The W symbol above the Hierophant's crown is attributed to Vav, the card's Hebrew letter, which means "nail" or "connector," a reference to the Hierophant as the bridge between earth and heaven (see The Hierophant, opposite).

10 SMALL CROSSES

The trinity of Father, Son, and Holy Spirit is symbolized by the three crosses on the Hierophant's gown. Further crosses appear on the Hierophant's gown and shoes, by his feet, and within the crossed keys.

11 RED AND BLUE ATTIRE

The Hierophant's robe is red for action, a color associated with his sign of Taurus. His undergarment is blue for the truth; truth underlies every action.

LESSONS AND BLESSINGS

This spread helps you acknowledge and appreciate what you are learning. When you bring gratitude into learning, you open up to further spiritual lessons and guidance.

First, take out V The Hierophant to oversee the reading and place the card face up as shown. Then shuffle the remainder of the deck and lay three cards face down, in positions 1, 2, and 3. When you are ready, turn over the cards and begin your interpretation.

The situation now

Your current lesson. What you are learning about yourself through your immediate situation.

Blessings: what you can be grateful for; what skills and challenges will help you with your current life lesson.

VI THE LOVERS

Other Names: The Lover, Love

Esoteric Titles: Children of the Voice Divine, The Oracles of the Mighty Gods

Number: Six

Numerology Link: XV The Devil

Astrological Sign or Planet: Gemini the Twins

Day of the Week: Wednesday

Element: Air

Hebrew Letter: Zain

- **Symbol:** Sword
- **Meaning:** Soulfulness

Tree of Life Pathway: Seventh, between Tiphareth and Binah

Chakra: Heart chakra, for love and healing

Crystals: Aventurine, agate, rose quartz

Animal Symbols: Snake

Archangel: Archangel Raphael

DESCRIPTION

Two lovers in paradise stand before a huge angel in the rays of the sun. The woman looks up at the angel, while the male figure looks at her. A snake curls its way around an apple tree.

KEY MEANINGS

Love, decisions, doubt, relationships, maturity, commitment, opportunity, growth, harmony, healing

UPRIGHT MEANING

Given the card's title, it seems clear that the theme can only be love—so you may meet a new potential partner now. However, there is much more to the card's meaning: this is a time for a decision, and this applies to every life area, not purely relationships. At work, there may be an opportunity to take a new path and on the home front, a key decision on whether to stay, improve, or move. This decision will have lasting impact, so you need to choose wisely, to see beyond the immediate situation and consider your long-term future. The card can also show a point in an existing relationship when you commit or walk away; do what feels right and is for your highest good, long term.

REVERSED MEANING

The reversed Lovers reveals poor choices often driven by materialism. In relationships, the card can show imbalance.

THE LOVERS' SYMBOLS

1	**Number VI**	Links with XV The Devil
2	**The angel**	The power of love
3	**The couple**	Innocence
4	**Tree of Knowledge of Good and Evil**	Temptation and sexual experience

5	**Snake**	Risk and wisdom
6	**Clouds**	Doubt
7	**Tree of Life**	Healing and eternal life
8	**Mountain**	Distance and aspiration

What the Symbols Mean for You

When you are drawn to a particular symbol or feature of a card, it's because it holds a special meaning for you. Here is a guide to interpreting your symbols.

1 NUMBER VI

Number VI links with card XV The Devil (XV = 15; 1 + 5 = 6), the shadow side of the Lovers. The composition of the card is similar, with one dominant figure and two subservient figures, a male and female, below. Number VI symbolizes a stage of completion or point of recognition—we must decide if this love, endeavor, or place is best for us in the long term.

As the seventh card in the major arcana sequence, the Lovers takes the seventh letter of the Hebrew alphabet, Zain, a sword, suggesting division: being in two minds. One of zain's interpretations is analysis, which also describes the decision aspect of the card. Placed upon the seventh Tree of Life pathway, the Lovers bridges the spheres of Tiphareth for beauty and rebirth and Binah for compassion and understanding. All these qualities ideally characterize a positive relationship or opportunity.

2 THE ANGEL

The angel is Archangel Raphael, angel of love healing. He symbolizes higher consciousness and the healing power of love.

See the angels on XIV Temperance and XX Judgement.

3 THE COUPLE

The female and male figures are Adam and Eve in the Garden of Eden before the Fall. Eve was Adam's twin as she was created from him, hence the card's astrological sign of Gemini the Twins. The Lovers' paradise symbolizes the heady first phase of a new relationship before life's realities hit. We see what is to come through the couple's gaze—Eve looks up at Archangel Raphael while Adam looks across at Eve, a sign of potential differences and the coming decision that the card represents.

4 TREE OF KNOWLEDGE OF GOOD AND EVIL

The tree to the left of the female figure is the Tree of Knowledge of Good and Evil, which represents the female principle. The tree's apples are the forbidden fruit that Eve ate in the Garden of Eden; they symbolize temptation and sexual experience. The four fruits also suggest the four elements, which represent life.

See the fruit on the tail of the female demon in XV The Devil.

5 SNAKE

In Christianity the snake is temptation and evil. Satan in the form of a snake tricked Eve into eating the fruit of the Tree of Knowledge of Good and Evil, after which she and Adam were banished from Eden. In other belief systems, the snake represents wisdom and can also be a symbol of healing. On the card, we can interpret it as a symbol of wisdom and the risk we take when we break a rule.

6 CLOUDS

The clouds between the Lovers symbolize the card's element of Air. They communicate the idea of haziness and doubt—the relationship is not yet clear.

7 TREE OF LIFE

To the right of the male figure is the Tree of Life, which signifies the male principle. Its twelve fruits signify the twelve signs of the zodiac; the three flames of each suit are believed to symbolize the three decans within each sign. The Tree of Life has also been referred to as the Tree of Mercy because Adam believed its oil could soothe his ailments—so this meaning of healing also accords with Archangel Raphael, the holy healer (see above).

8 MOUNTAIN

The mountain between the Lovers creates visual separation—she to the left, he to the right. This couple may occupy the same ground, but they are emotionally distant. Equally, the mountain offers the meaning of aspiration—or relationship goals.

Is it Love?

The meaning of love for the Lovers card is in a reading when certain cards appear next to it in a reading: these include the Two of Cups (the soul mate card) and the Hierophant, which can predict marriage. The Lovers with the Three of Cups reveals that a flirtation leads to a relationship, while the Eight of Cups (the card of departure) indicates that nothing may develop.

The card's other meaning of decisions is highlighted, again according to the cards around it: look for the Two of Pentacles, Seven of Cups, and Two of Swords. Further, The Lovers' shadow card, XV The Devil, urges a choice between love and lust, materialism, and empathy, and freedom rather than entrapment.

YOU AND THEM

Here's a fast way to look at what you each bring to a relationship—whether your connection is new or established.

First, take out VI The Lovers and place the card face up as shown to oversee the reading. Then shuffle the remainder of the deck, choose three cards (see page 15) and lay them face down. When you are ready, turn over cards 1 through 3 and begin your interpretation.

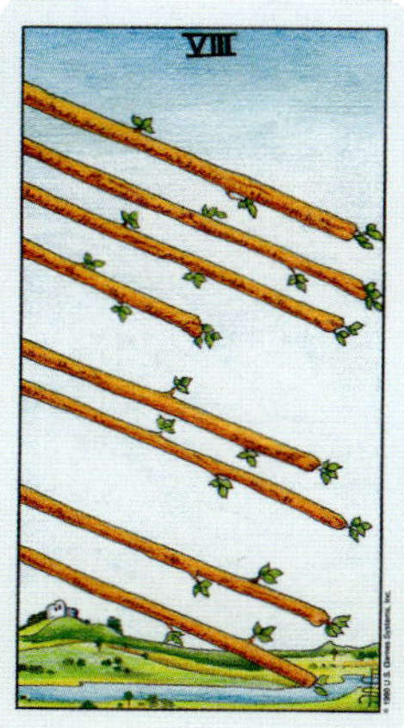

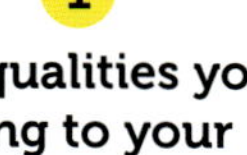

The qualities you bring to your relationship
Example: Eight of Wands. Extroversion; being talkative and adventurous, and valuing self-expression.

The qualities the other person brings to the relationship
Example: The Six of Cups. The other person is kind and forgiving and may seek a quiet life. They value harmony.

The outcome
Example: Seven of Pentacles. Ideally, they will find practical ways to give each other space. Appreciating one another is the key—if this happens, the relationship can deepen.

VII THE CHARIOT

Other Names: Victory, The Triumphal Chariot

Esoteric Titles: Child of the Power of the Waters, Lord of the Triumph of Light

Number: Seven

Numerology Link: XVI The Tower

Astrological Sign or Planet: Cancer the Crab

Day of the Week: Monday

Element: Water

Hebrew Letter: Heth (Chet, Cheth)

Symbol: Fence or Enclosure

Meaning: Guidance

Tree of Life Pathway: Eighth, between Geburah and Binah

Chakra: Throat, for truth

Crystal: Blue lace agate

Animal Symbol: Sphinx

DESCRIPTION

A male figure in armor is upright in a stone chariot. With the city behind him and two unharnessed sphinxes before him, he is about to embark on a journey.

KEY MEANINGS

Journeys, departure, new directions, success, determination, progress, spiritual connection, vehicles

UPRIGHT MEANING

The Chariot means success and progress, so travel and discovery are favored now. In your relationships you find a new and meaningful path together or decide to venture out alone (the surrounding cards will reveal which). In projects and work, you find success and abundance. In readings, the card often appears as the result of a major decision, as the energy locked up in the process of choosing is released—so you feel revitalized and ready to move on. This is a time for assertiveness, excitement, and spiritual connection, too. On a practical level, the card can show a new vehicle or simply a journey.

REVERSED MEANING

The reversed card can reveal delays to plans or arrogance rather than assertiveness; try to regain your balance.

THE CHARIOT'S SYMBOLS

1	Number VII	Links with XVI The Tower
2	The Chariot	Self-containment
3	The charioteer	Determination
4	Armor	Protection
5	Belt and tunic	Spirituality

6	Star crown	Authority and guidance
7	Canopy of stars	Divine navigation
8	Sphinxes	Negotiation
9	The shield	Unifying forces
10	Staff	Purpose

What the Symbols Mean for You

When you are drawn to a particular symbol or feature of a card, it's because it holds a special meaning for you. Here is a guide to interpreting your symbols.

1 NUMBER XVI

The Chariot's number VII links with XVI, The Tower (XVI = 16; 1 + 6 = 7). While the Tower reveals the power of higher forces beyond the self, or ego, the charioteer's success depends on managing his own drives to keep his vehicle on track. Number seven means potential, a number also associated with mystery, luck, divinity, and magic. Seven combined with the card's element of sensitive Water means the charioteer must stay in tune with himself—and not let his ego rule—while staying connected with divine guidance. As card VII, The Chariot marks the end of the first stage of the major arcana sequence (see Temperance as a Gateway, page 77).

As the eighth card in the major arcana sequence, The Chariot takes the eighth letter of the Hebrew alphabet, Heth (see The Chariot, below). Placed upon the eighth Tree of Life pathway, The Chariot rides between the spheres of Geburah for power and destruction and Binah for understanding. The charioteer must balance the extremities of these influences to keep his vehicle moving forward.

2 THE CHARIOT

We can see The Chariot as the vehicle of the personality; a physical representation of self-containment referred to by the card's Hebrew letter, Heth, meaning fence or enclosure. The chariot is made of stone and has four pillars, symbol of stability and the four elements of nature.

3 THE CHARIOTEER

The charioteer sets out alone on an adventure. He brings with him everything he needs to support him as he travels, but he must create the momentum to go forward. In this sense, he symbolizes willpower and determination.

4 ARMOR

The moon faces and crescents on the charioteer's shoulders link to his zodiac sign of Cancer the crab. Like the crab, he must protect himself as he travels. They also represent the divination stones urmin and thummin, which in the Old Testament were cast to divine the will of God. His armored cuffs are frilled like shells, again a reference to Cancer and his element of Water. The breastplate has the alchemical symbol for earth, for the four elements of nature and the four corners of the earth; the charioteer's ambition is limitless.

5 BELT AND TUNIC

The belt is decorated with zodiac glyphs and the tunic with protective talismans, a reminder of the charioteer's connection to spirit.

6 STAR CROWN

The crown is an authority symbol; the eight-pointed star is a symbol of guidance and cosmic order, as the star is just beneath the canopy of stars (see below). The laurel wreath beneath represents victory, one of the card's alternative titles.

See the star crown on III The Empress.

7 CANOPY OF STARS

The golden stars on blue cloth evoke the night sky and the signs of the zodiac; the charioteer uses the positions of the stars to guide him physically and spiritually.

8 SPHINXES

The sphinxes are a symbol of negotiation. The sphinx has long been associated with riddles, mysteries, and wisdom. Here, the black and white sphinxes represent duality—the dark and light side of nature and the self. The charioteer controls the sphinxes through his willpower, rather than a harness—so they signify the need to balance opposing forces

Echo and Symbol in The Chariot: The Fool to The Lovers

The Chariot is the last of the first set of major arcana cards (see Temperance as a Gateway, page 77); look within, and you will see a little of every card that has come before him. As the traveler, the charioteer is 0 The Fool, beginning a quest. His intuition is symbolized by the moons on his shoulder plates, a link with the crescent moon of II The High Priestess, while the star crown evokes the diadem of III The Empress. The chariot, made of stone, suggests IV The Emperor's throne; and V The Hierophant's pillars appear as part of the chariot, holding the canopy of stars. Finally, the lush landscape calls up VI The Lovers' Garden of Eden. Carrying the echoes and experiences of the preceding cards, the charioteer is ready for his onward journey.

within. In Freemasonry (the card's co-creator A. E. Waite was a Freemason) the black and white sphinxes represent the Egyptian deities Isis, goddess of healing and magic, and Osiris, god of fertility, life, and death.

See the sphinx on X The Wheel of Fortune and the black and white pillars as duality symbols on II The High Priestess.

9 THE SHIELD

The winged disk represents the conscious mind (it is an ancient symbol of the Egyptian sun god, Ra) while the red yoni-lingam symbol represents the union of male and female. The charioteer must pay attention to every element of his chariot to ensure balance.

10 STAFF

The staff symbolizes support, travel, and self-determination. As a wand, it represents magic and purpose—this is charioteer's potential, provided he manages his energy and his thoughts.

See the magic wand on I The Magician; see the staff on 0 The Fool and IX The Hermit.

WHERE AM I GOING?

VII The Chariot is the card of progress, so in this small spread we look at what can progress next in your life.

First, take out VII The Chariot and lay it face up as shown. Then shuffle the remainder of the deck, laying down three more cards in positions 1, 2, and 3.

1 Where you are now

2 Where you are going

3 What to do next

VIII STRENGTH

Other Names: Fortitude, Force
Esoteric Titles: Daughter of the Flaming Sword, Leader of the Lion
Number: Eight
Numerology Link: XVII The Star
Astrological Sign or Planet: Leo the Lion
Day of the Week: Sunday
Element: Fire
Hebrew Letter: Teth
  Symbol: The serpent
  Meaning: Courage
Tree of Life Pathway: Ninth, between Geburah and Chesed
Chakra: Solar plexus, for self-empowerment
Crystals: Citrine, tiger's-eye
Animal Symbol: Lion

DESCRIPTION

A young woman in white holds open a lion's jaws; he licks her hand like a cat. She wears a rose garland and a flower crown, and above her is the lemniscate, symbol of infinity.

KEY MEANINGS

Strength, courage, patience, resilience, healing, solutions, self-guidance, boundaries, grace, compassion

UPRIGHT MEANING

Strength's meaning is just as the image portrays—having the courage to hold your ground when facing potentially fierce opposition. Rather than play by others' rules to avoid conflict, you negotiate a solution. In love the card brings hope, but also shows a relationship test and the need to work through issues; in health matters, Strength shows recuperation and resilience. A further interpretation is having compassion for others and compassion for yourself. You may need to wrestle with your wild side and your conscience—and go with what is morally right rather than let instinct drive you.

REVERSED MEANING

Reversed Strength means weakness, which may be expressed as avoidance of necessary challenges and experiences.

STRENGTH'S SYMBOLS

1	**Number VIII**	Links with XVII The Star
2	**The lion**	Courage
3	**The maiden**	Moral victory
4	**Rose crown**	Taming the wild

5	**Lemniscate**	Cycles
6	**Yellow sky**	Clarity
7	**Mountains and pasture**	Growth and challenges

What the Symbols Mean for You

When you are drawn to a particular symbol or feature of a card, it's because it holds a special meaning for you. Here is a guide to interpreting your symbols.

1 NUMBER VIII

Eight is the number of fulfillment, change and renewal, also symbolized by the sideways number eight or lemniscate (see Lemniscate, at right). As number VIII, Strength is numerologically linked with XVII The Star (XVII = 17; 1 + 7 = 8). The Star also features a maiden, and both cards share the meaning of healing.

As the ninth card in the major arcana sequence, Strength takes the ninth letter of the Hebrew alphabet, Teth, meaning courage. Placed upon the ninth Tree of Life pathway, Strength is positioned between the spheres of Geburah for power and destruction and Chesed, for love and peacefulness. The lion aligns with Geburah, while Chesed is the maiden, who treats the animal with love and kindness.

2 THE LION

The lion symbolizes power and wildness; the creature illustrates the card's element of Fire and Leo, the card's zodiac sign. The allegory of Strength as a woman subduing a lion or holding a broken pillar is seen in the oldest tarot cards dating from the fifteenth century and was a common motif before then. The eleventh-century tomb of Pope Clement II depicts a maiden holding open a lion's jaws, just as we see Strength today.

3 THE MAIDEN

The maiden signifies a moral victory. The composition of the card is similar to that of a 1909 painting by the American artist Frederick Stuart Church (1842–1924) entitled Lady Placing a Wreath of Flowers on a Lion. The painting's theme is the same as our Strength card—in a pastoral setting, a lion is subdued by a maiden wearing a flowing white dress, symbol of purity. This is the allegory of Strength—the wildness within bowing to the civility of the maiden. There is something divine in this command of nature, which leads us to I The Magician, the manifestor who creates heaven on earth: the maiden's white dress and garland worn as a belt echo the white robe and belt of the magus.

4 ROSE CROWN

The maiden wears stems of rambling roses as a crown, and she has fashioned more stems into a loose belt—a symbol of taming wild things.

See the roses on the Empress and the Nine of Swords; see the roses and lilies on I The Magician and on the gowns of the supplicants in V The Hierophant.

5 LEMNISCATE

The lemniscate or infinity symbol signifies cycles and renewal; the two loops represent the continual flow of energy. In this card, the lemniscate appears above the maiden's crown to illustrate her connection with ever-flowing divine energy.

See this symbol on I The Magician, Two of Pentacles and in the arm position on the figure in the Nine of Cups.

6 YELLOW SKY

The color yellow stands for conscious awareness, support, and clarity—this is also reassurance that we, as readers, clearly see its relevance in our life.

7 MOUNTAINS AND PASTURE

The green pasture symbolizes fertility and growth, while the blue mountain symbolizes challenges overcome and challenges to come.

Strength and Justice—VIII and XI

In earlier tarots, Justice took number VIII and Strength, XI—but A. E. Waite, co-creator of the Rider Waite Smith deck, swapped their position. The reasoning was that Justice needed to become XI to align with the zodiac sign of Libra (and its common symbol of the scales) and Strength needed to align with Leo, to share the symbol of the lion. The zodiac signs were applied to each card in sequence beginning with Aries for IV The Emperor and ending with Pisces for XVIII The Moon (the other cards have associated planets). So, the card sequence was changed to accommodate the order of zodiac signs. The associated Hebrew letters were also applied in order, from Aleph for 0 The Fool to Tau for XXI The World. Having Justice as XI linked the card with Lamed, meaning fairness, while Strength as VIII meant it became associated with Teth, which means "courage."

FINDING RESILIENCE

When you need to draw on your energy reserves to stay strong and focused, try this little spread.

Take out the Strength card and place it face up as shown to oversee the reading. Then shuffle the remainder of the deck and lay three cards face down as shown. When you are ready, turn all the cards face up and begin your interpretation.

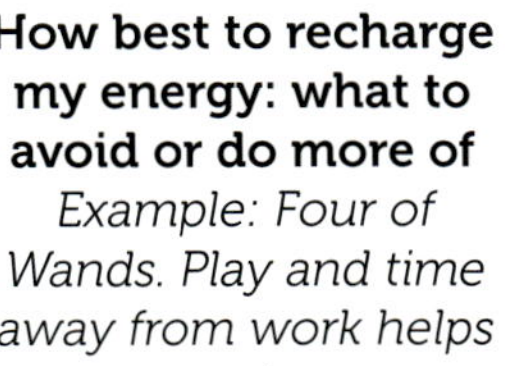

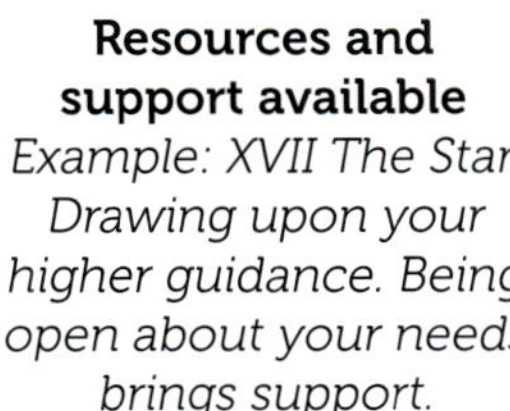

1

How best to recharge my energy: what to avoid or do more of
Example: Four of Wands. Play and time away from work helps you recharge.

2

Resources and support available
Example: XVII The Star. Drawing upon your higher guidance. Being open about your needs brings support.

3

Likely outcome
Example: I The Magician. Learning a lesson: how to work with your natural cycles—when best to create and when to conserve your strength.

IX THE HERMIT

Other Names: The Old Man, The Poor Man, Time, The Monk, Father Time

Esoteric Titles: The Magus of the Voice of Light, The Prophet of the Gods

Number: Nine

Numerology Link: XVIII The Moon

Astrological Sign or Planet: Virgo the Virgin

Day of the Week: Wednesday

Element: Earth

Hebrew Letter: Yod

- **Symbol:** The hand
- **Meaning:** Prudence

Tree of Life Pathway: Tenth, between Chesed and Tiphareth

Chakra: Heart seed, for soul remembrance

Crystals: Tugtupite

DESCRIPTION

An elderly man in a monk's habit reaches a snowy mountaintop. He carries a staff and a lamp containing a shining star to light his way in the growing darkness.

KEY MEANINGS

Reflection, retreat, esoteric learning, wisdom, patience, slowness, a spiritual journey, healing, quietude

UPRIGHT MEANING

The Hermit reveals a quiet time of contemplation and reflection, so you find space to gather your thoughts and consider your next step. The card also signifies a new path—this may take the form of a spiritual retreat, a physical pilgrimage, or other learning journey you are now ready for; you may be drawn to research, reading, and in general delving into esoteric and cerebral subjects. In relationships, the Hermit shows you going your own way or at the least, taking time out. Overall, this is a time for self-discovery and healing, and importantly, making space for your needs and interests. As a card of wisdom, you draw yours from within or find the right adviser or mentor to guide you.

REVERSED MEANING

When reversed, the Hermit can show enforced but temporary solitude. See this as an opportunity to please yourself and trust your inner wisdom.

THE HERMIT'S SYMBOLS

1	**Number IX**	Links with XVIII The Moon
2	**The Hermit**	Soul's path
3	**The lamp**	Time and guidance
4	**Staff**	Support
5	**Monastic attire**	Protection
6	**Snowy mountains**	Isolation

What the Symbols Mean for You

When you are drawn to a particular symbol or feature of a card, it's because it holds a special meaning for you. Here is a guide to interpreting your symbols.

1 NUMBER IX

The Hermit's number IX links with XVIII The Moon (XVIII = 18; 1 + 8 = 9). Both the Hermit and the Moon are cards of twilight, a liminal time of enchantment and possibility; they are also introspective, calling for soul-searching. Nine is the number of culmination—it carries the experiences represented by all the preceding cards—before the completion and revelation signified by number ten. The Hermit sees that there is a world beyond his own mind; a greater, more expansive universe is symbolized by the next card in the sequence, X The Wheel of Fortune.

As the tenth card in the major arcana sequence, Strength takes the tenth letter of the Hebrew alphabet, Yod, meaning prudence. Yod is also associated with the Fire element—perhaps as the star in the Hermit's lamp, and the light within him. Placed upon the tenth Tree of Life pathway, the card is positioned between Chesed, for love and peacefulness, and Tiphareth, for beauty and rebirth, or salvation—qualities we associate with living a religious life.

2 THE HERMIT

The hermit appears as a monk, dressed simply with no possessions other than his staff and lamp. The monastic aspect aligns with the card's astrological sign of Virgo, the Virgin. Elderly, the Hermit has a white beard, symbol of wisdom—perhaps he is the Fool, born in light, grown old: here he is in darkness, looking down from where he has come. In this way, number 0 to IX is its own chapter in the major arcana—as the hermit is about to leave behind the first phase of the material world to follow his soul's path.

3 THE LAMP

The lamp holds a six-pointed star, symbol of divine guidance. The Hermit lights his own path and is a guiding light for others making their journey through this barren terrain. In earlier tarots the lamp was an hourglass and the Hermit was known as Father Time, a personification that became associated with Saturn, Roman god of time and agriculture (the Greek Cronus). Saturn believed a prophecy that said one of his sons would grow up to overthrow him, so he ate his children at birth in attempt to stop time (one of his children did escape, so Saturn was not successful); time, after all, cannot be stopped.

4 STAFF

The Hermit's staff symbolizes support, travel, and self-determination as he guides himself through the mountains.

See the staff on 0 The Fool and VII The Chariot.

5 MONASTIC ATTIRE

The simple robe resembles a monk's habit, a symbol of humility. A further meaning is protection from the influences of the material world and a way to hide our identity until we are ready to show ourselves.

6 SNOWY MOUNTAINS

The snowy mountains signify isolation; this is a barren, inhospitable place, but the Hermit's lamp light will guide him. The card's element of Earth represents the physical aspects of his journey and its challenges.

The Hermit as the Wounded Healer

The Hermit is often linked with Chiron, known as the wounded healer. In mythology, Chiron was a centaur, half horse and half man, an oracle and wise healer who lived apart from his tribe, just like the Hermit. He was accidentally shot by an arrow from Heracles, son of Zeus—and discovered he could not heal himself. As an immortal he could not die but gave up his immortality to save the life of fire-god Prometheus; and as a result, Chiron is in pain all his life. Zeus takes pity on him and places him among the stars in the Centaurus constellation. This archetype of the wounded healer—one who helps others' suffering due to their own experiences of pain—expresses the meanings of healing and reflection that are traditional Hermit attributes.

HEALING WITHIN

In this spread, we look at healing and what we may need to soothe in ourselves.

First, take out IX The Hermit and place the card face up as shown to oversee the reading. Then shuffle the remainder of the deck and lay three cards face down, in positions 1, 2, and 3. When you are ready, turn over the cards and begin your interpretation.

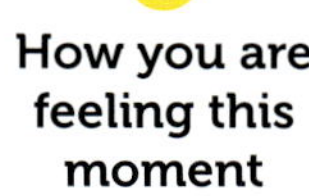

1 How you are feeling this moment

2 What aspect of your life needs care and attention

3 How this approach can benefit you going forward

X WHEEL OF FORTUNE

Other Names: Fate, Destiny, The Wheel

Esoteric Title: The Lord of the Forces of Life

Number: Ten

Numerology Links: I The Magician and XIX The Sun

Astrological Sign or Planet: Jupiter

Day of the Week: Thursday

Element: Fire

Hebrew Letter: Kaph

  Symbol: The palms of the hand, or cup

  Meaning: Destiny

Tree of Life Pathway: Eleventh, between Chesed and Netzach

Chakra: Soul star, for soul connection

Crystal: White topaz

Animal Symbols: Eagle, bull, lion, snake, jackal, sphinx

DESCRIPTION

A wheel in the clouds is inscribed with esoteric symbols. In the card's corners are four winged creatures, along with a sphinx, snake, and jackal-headed figure toward the center.

KEY MEANINGS

Fate, destiny, change, intuition, luck, cycles, consequences, chance, synchronicities, spirit helpers

UPRIGHT MEANING

The Wheel of Fortune means a change for the better. Synchronicities, from chance meetings to angel numbers and other messages offer confirmation that you are moving in the right direction. It's also a card of good fortune, so be ready to be open to receive what you need; money luck is on the cards, too. The Wheel can also show psychic ability, as you open up to higher wisdom and spiritual guidance. As this is the card of cycles and change, you find that people from the past come back into your life—particularly former partners and old friends. At home, you feel ready to make changes to your environment.

REVERSED MEANING

When reversed, the Wheel shows the end of a cycle. A further meaning is delay and feeling disconnected; trust your inner knowing.

WHEEL OF FORTUNE'S SYMBOLS

1	**Number X**	Links with I The Magician and XIX The Sun
2	**The Wheel**	Rebirth
3	**The wheel's rings**	Life's phases
4	**Latin letters**	The hidden message
5	**Hebrew letters**	Divinity

6	**Alchemical symbols**	Four elements
7	**Sphinx**	Mystery and wisdom
8	**Anubis**	Cycles
9	**The snake Typhon**	The downside
10	**Corner figures**	Elements of life

What the Symbols Mean for You

When you are drawn to a particular symbol or feature of a card, it's because it holds a special meaning for you. Here is a guide to interpreting your symbols.

1 NUMBER X

Number ten is the number of completion. In the major arcana sequence, it marks the end and beginning of a cycle of experience—the youthful Fool has grown into IX The Hermit, the old man, so X marks the culmination of a phase; it is also the halfway point of the major arcana cycle. As ten contains number 1, the meaning of beginnings is embedded in the ending. We see beginnings in the Wheel's numerological relations, I The Magician and XIX The Sun (XIX = 19; 1 + 9 = 10; 1 + 0 = I).

As the eleventh card in the major arcana sequence, the Wheel takes the eleventh letter of the Hebrew alphabet, Kaph, meaning destiny; the card's astrological association is Jupiter, planet of luck. Placed upon the eleventh Tree of Life pathway, the Wheel comes between Chesed, for love and Netzach, for the forces of nature. The counsel of these two spheres is to accept the flow of life with grace.

2 THE WHEEL

In many traditions, the wheel is a symbol of the sun and its journey through darkness and rebirth. The Wheel of Fortune with its attendant creatures is an image from antiquity that meant the rise and fall of fortune, as it does for us today; a further meaning is karma and consequences (see sidebar, opposite).

3 THE WHEEL'S RINGS

The outer ring is the material world, the middle ring is the formative world—or what is emergent—while the center of the wheel symbolizes creation. The eight spokes in the center circle of the wheel also appear as a motif in the first card of the major arcana, the newly created Fool.

See the wheel motif on the Fool's tunic in 0 The Fool.

4 LATIN LETTERS

The Latin characters are T A R O. By reading these letters forward and backward, we get these words: ROTA TAROT ORAT TORA ATOR. According to Paul Foster Case, author of *The Tarot: A Key to the Wisdom of the Ages*, Ator is an old Latin form of Egyptian goddess Hathor, so the translation is "The Wheel of Tarot speaks the Law of Hathor (Law of Nature)."

5 HEBREW LETTERS

The Hebrew letters YHVH are the tetragrammaton, the name of God in Judaism.

6 ALCHEMICAL SYMBOLS

The alchemical symbols are salt, left, Mercury, top, sulfur, right, and water, below. Each has an element—salt is Earth, Mercury at the top of the wheel is Air, sulfur on the right is Fire (the card's element), and water is of course Water.

7 SPHINX

In ancient Egypt, the sphinx represented the sun god and royalty—hence its position at the top of the wheel. On the card, the sphinx is a unified symbol of the corner figures (see Corner Figures, opposite)—it has a lion-like body, a bull's tail and the human face of the angel. The eagle is represented by a sword rather than wings. The legendary winged sphinx of Thebes symbolized terrifying wisdom, posing the famous riddle, "What has one voice yet becomes four-footed and two-footed and three-footed?" If anyone gave the wrong answer, she ate them; only Oedipus succeeded, saying the answer was man—a child crawling on all fours, a man standing on two legs then walking with a stick, the third foot, in old age. In this way, the sphinx has been long associated with mysteries—just like the wheel of fortune.

The Wheel and Justice

While the Wheel is a symbol of luck and cycles, there is also an element of justice and karma at work, too—in that "what goes around, comes around." We see XI Justice represented as the sphinx's sword on the top of the wheel, signifying that justice strives always for balance; success must be offset by ruin, creation by endings. We can see this, too, in the positioning of the Wheel in the major arcana sequence. It falls between VII The Chariot (which also shows the sphinx) and XIII Death. The Chariot is the ego riding forth, as Death is the death of the ego. The moral message is to be mindful of what we give out, as it may return.

8 ANUBIS

The red jackal-headed figure is Anubis, god of the afterlife. He is wrapped around the wheel, fixed in place to oversee the full turn of the wheel—the whole cycle of birth, death, and rebirth.

9 THE SNAKE TYPHON

The snake is the mythological monster Typhon, bringer of storms and volcanic eruptions. Pointing downward toward the Underworld where Typhon dwelled, the snake represents the downside of the wheel: a time of ill-luck, darkness, and struggle.

See the snake on VI The Lovers and in the Magician's belt in card I.

10 CORNER FIGURES

The corner figures denote the four evangelists of the New Testament and the fixed signs of the zodiac—the angel corresponds to Aquarius, the bull to Taurus, the eagle to Scorpio and the lion to Leo. Each sign also brings its associated element—Air, Earth, Water, and Fire, respectively, to represent life on earth.

See the four evangelists on XXI The World.

UPS AND DOWNS

This simple spread takes its inspiration from the Wheel's cycles of fortunes. To begin, take out X The Wheel of Fortune and place the card face up as shown to oversee the reading. Then shuffle the remainder of the deck and lay three cards face down, in positions 1, 2, and 3. When you are ready, turn over the cards and begin your interpretation.

The upside of your present situation
Example: Page of Pentacles. The beginning of a learning journey.

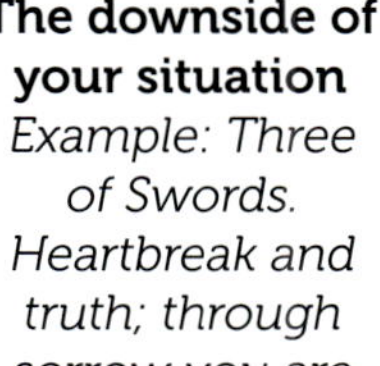

2

The downside of your situation
Example: Three of Swords. Heartbreak and truth; through sorrow you are learning the truth of a situation.

The outcome
Example: Ace of Cups. An overflow of emotion; a release of past hurt and a new lease on life.

XI JUSTICE

Other Name: Adjustment

Esoteric Titles: The Daughter of the Lord of Truth, The Holder of the Balances

Number: Eleven

Numerology Link: II The High Priestess

Astrological Sign or Planet: Libra the scales

Day of the Week: Friday

Element: Air

Hebrew Letter: Lamed

Symbol: The whip

Meaning: Fairness

Tree of Life Pathway: Twelfth, between Tiphareth and Geburah

Chakra: Earth star, for spiritual grounding

Crystals: Hematite, obsidian, bloodstone

Compositional Affinity: II The High Priestess, V The Hierophant

DESCRIPTION

A judge in red robes and crown sits in judgement between two pillars. She holds the scales in her left hand and the sword in right.

KEY MEANINGS

Justice, fairness, integrity, decisions, balance, objectivity, positive outcomes, consequences, karma

UPRIGHT MEANING

Justice, card of the law, represents legal issues and formal agreements. It brings successful conclusions—so decisions go in your favor.; this positivity also applies to interviews and applications. Justice also says that your financial situation is about to improve after a time of instability. As one of the virtue cards, there is naturally a moral dimension here too: you must be deserving of justice. For this reason, the card reminds us to have integrity in all our dealings and relationships, and to make wise choices that are fair to ourselves and others. A further message of the card is finding work-life balance.

REVERSED MEANING

The reversed card suggests intolerance and a lack of integrity. A decision or accusation may be unjust.

JUSTICE'S SYMBOLS

1	**Number XI**	Links with II The High Priestess
2	**The mural crown**	Authority
3	**The figure of Justice**	Justice in action
4	**Sword**	Retribution

5	**Scales**	Mercy
6	**Veil**	Hidden futures
7	**Pillars**	Boundaries
8	**Cloak and clasp**	Growth and status
9	**Yellow section**	Illumination

What the Symbols Mean for You

When you are drawn to a particular symbol or feature of a card, it's because it holds a special meaning for you. Here is a guide to interpreting your symbols.

1 NUMBER XI

Number XI reduces to 2 (XI = 11; 1 + 1 = 2), number of II The High Priestess. Both cards deal with duality, the meaning of 2—The High Priestess walks between the earthly realm and the spirit world, and Justice deals with rights and wrongs. Symbolically, this is shown by the veil on both cards. Justice's 11 also suggests balance, as the female figure—the personification of justice—holds the scales by which she weighs the matter at hand.

As the twelfth card in the major arcana, Justice is placed on the twelfth Tree of Life pathway between Tiphareth and Geburah. Tiphareth is associated with beauty and rebirth—in terms of Justice, mercy, and second chances; Geburah, sphere of power and destruction, evokes Justice's sword of retribution.

2 THE MURAL CROWN

The crown is known as a mural crown because it has crenelations like a city wall. In mythology, the Greek goddess Tyche is depicted with the mural crown to show she protected the wealth of a city. Justice likewise protects and controls money. The stone decoration on the front of the crown symbolizes order, in its square shape for the element of Earth; its blue color symbolizes clarity.

See the mural crown on the Four of Pentacles.

3 THE FIGURE OF JUSTICE

Traditional depictions of Justice as a personification of the law show a female figure, blindfold. Our Justice without her blindfold denotes immediate action (as opposed to the blindfolded Two and Eight of Swords, which are about procrastination and restriction). Justice wears the robes of office—and the flowing robes of red, color of energy and the material world, emphasize the idea of action and immediacy.

4 SWORD

Justice holds the sword of retribution upright as a symbol of successful retribution, or punishment for past misdeeds. It is also associated with Air, the card's element, for the mind—Justice's decisions rely on logic.

See the upright sword of victory on the Ace of Swords.

5 SCALES

The scales symbolize mercy and balance. The scales are a symbol of Libra, the zodiac sign association with Justice; literally, they embody the idea of balance and weighing, as the judge must weigh up the evidence in a case. This also links with the card's associated Hebrew letter, Lamed, which means "fairness."

6 VEIL

The veil symbolizes hidden futures; we cannot know the impact of the decision in hand, only that it will change the future.

7 PILLARS

The pillars symbolize strength, tradition, and boundaries—the judge is protected by law as tradition and her judgements fall within the law's boundaries.

8 CLOAK AND CLASP

The green cloak is a symbol of growth, while the ruby inset into the brooch denotes status, wealth, and vitality.

9 YELLOW SECTION

The yellow section symbolizes illumination—the process of judgement—but also echoes the lower portion of the sun in card VI The Lovers, another card of decisions.

See the sun on VI The Lovers.

Justice and Archangel Michael

A white foot peeks out beneath the robe of Justice. On some Marseilles tarot cards, we see the foot and leg of Justice, clad in armor—like that of IV The Emperor. The armor suggests Archangel Michael, the warrior angel. Michael was once associated with XX Judgement, as it was believed he judged which souls went to heaven on Judgement Day (see The Angel on XX Judgement, page 100). This is relevant to XI Justice, because some earlier Justice cards were numbered XX (the position of Judgement in the sequence); this may account for shared associations. Also, some Marseilles tarot Justice cards and those from later nineteenth-century decks such as the Milanese Tarot show the Justice figure with wings—again, a memory of Archangel Michael.

MAKE THAT DECISION

Use this three-carder when you have a decision to make. If minor arcana cards come up, pay attention to their suit as well as individual card meanings for an extra level of insight. For example, a Swords card in the Advantage position says that a logical approach is best, whereas Cups would mean follow your intuition.

Take out the Justice card and lay it face up to oversee your reading, helping you take a balanced view in your interpretation. Then shuffle the remainder of the deck and lay down three cards face down as shown. When you are ready, turn all the cards face up, and begin.

Strengths

Weaknesses

Advice

XII THE HANGED MAN

Other Names: The Traitor, The Lone Man

Esoteric Title: The Spirit of the Mighty Waters

Number: Twelve

Numerology Link: III The Empress

Astrological Sign or Planet: Neptune

Day of the Week: Friday

Element: Water

Hebrew Letter: Mem

Symbol: Water and the oceans

Meaning: Transition

Tree of Life Pathway: Thirteenth, between Hod and Geburah

Chakra: Third eye, for intuition

Crystals: Amethyst, sapphire

DESCRIPTION

From a T-shaped tree, a haloed man hangs upside down, tied by the ankle. Wearing red and blue, one knee is bent, and his hands rest behind his back.

KEY MEANINGS

Waiting, decisions, perspective, sacrifice, compromise, spiritual transformation, protection, trust, prophecy, divine connection

UPRIGHT MEANING

The Hanged Man literally means waiting around, so you may be in limbo just now, waiting for a decision. Your unusual position presents an opportunity to see the situation differently, gaining a new perspective. However, to create momentum you may need to make a compromise or sacrifice rather than remain in a state of suspense (or suspension). The card often applies to house moves and work offers, so negotiation may be in order—if the time is right. Spiritually, this is a very positive card as you sense a shift in energy and feel oneness. Your external life may be slower just now, but your internal world is deeply fulfilling.

REVERSED MEANING

When reversed, the card can show martyrdom. This may be way to avoid certain decisions and if so, it is time to make the changes you need.

THE HANGED MAN'S SYMBOLS

1	**Number XII**	Links with III The Empress
2	**The Hanged Man**	Sacrifice
3	**Halo**	Enlightenment
4	**Fylfot cross**	The cosmos
5	**Blue and red attire**	Inner work
6	**The tether**	Trust
7	**Tree**	Salvation
8	**Neutral background**	Openness

What the Symbols Mean for You

When you are drawn to a particular symbol or feature of a card, it's because it holds a special meaning for you. Here is a guide to interpreting your symbols.

1 NUMBER XII

The Hanged Man's number XII reduces to III The Empress (XII = 12; 1 + 2 = 3). The Empress through her pregnancy incubates life, a physical form, whereas the Hanged Man represents a state of spiritual incubation.

Comprising ten and two, both numbers are stable and passive. The ten symbolizes a stage of completion we see with X The Wheel of Fortune, while the II takes us to the High Priestess, which, like the Hanged Man, reveals altered forms of consciousness and the duality of presence in the material world and the spiritual world. This also links with the card's planet, Neptune, for mysticism and the imagination.

As the thirteenth card in the major arcana sequence, the Hanged Man takes the thirteenth letter of the Hebrew alphabet, Mem, which means "transition." On the Tree of Life pathway, the Hanged Man is suspended between the spheres of Hod for insight and the mind, and Geburah, sphere of power and destruction. This expresses his status as the spiritual initiate, suspended between life and ego-death.

2 THE HANGED MAN

The Hanged Man is very much alive; hanging around, he waits for what comes. Upside down, he has a unique perspective on the world. He represents the Norse god Odin who hung from Yggdrasil the World Tree; he may also be seen as a Christ figure (see Tree, at right). In this way, the Hanged Man represents sacrifice for the higher good.

3 HALO

The halo is a symbol of enlightenment and the Hanged Man's initiation into the mysteries of life, death, and rebirth. The halo also symbolizes the bliss that he experiences during this ritual of self-sacrifice.

4 FYLFOT CROSS

The Hanged Man's legs form a fylfot cross, a symbol of the cosmos. The leg position also suggests a mirror-image number 4. The number represents the four elements, which represent stability and balance in his current state of flux.

5 BLUE AND RED ATTIRE

The figure's blue tunic symbolizes the element of Water, the card's element. His leggings are red, for action, but this is internal rather than external. Red is also the color of the Fire element, which clashes with Water—hence the card's meaning of suspension. Neither element can dominate, so action is on hold.

6 THE TETHER

The Hanged Man is tethered to the tree by his right ankle; his hands are behind his back in a position of surrender. He trusts the gods, the Universe, to keep him where he should be.

7 TREE

The tree represents Yggdrasil the World Tree from which Odin hung for nine days and nights, after which he could read the runes. The tree here also suggests the Tree of Life, the central motif of Kabbala. The T-shape represents the Tau cross. *Tau* is the last letter of the Hebrew alphabet, and it also symbolizes the cross on which Christ was crucified.

8 NEUTRAL BACKGROUND

The neutral background represents the liminal world the Hanged Man inhabits. This may be a place of uncertainty, but he is open to creative possibilities.

The Hanged Man in the Minors

As the Hanged Man reveals a time of suspension, several minor arcana cards relay a similar message:

- The Two of Swords means limbo—either due to a temporary truce or because of procrastination
- The Two of Pentacles reveals a choice, usually between two known options
- The Seven of Cups is the card of fantasy, choices, and confusion. Like the Hanged Man, the Seven features a Christ symbol in it central cup (see page 120).
- When these cards arise in a reading, we are neither here nor there—and seek a way forward.

TRUST ISSUES

As the figure on the card hangs by a thin tether, he trusts he will not fall. This spread looks at what or whom you can trust, the area of doubt, and advice going forward.

First, take out XII The Hanged Man and place the card face up as shown to oversee the reading. Then shuffle the remainder of the deck and lay three cards face down, in positions 1, 2, and 3. When you are ready, turn over the cards and begin your interpretation.

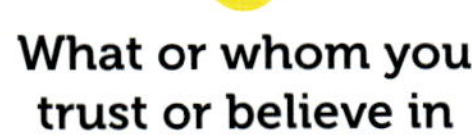

1 **What or whom you trust or believe in**

2 **Doubt: what to commit to or walk away from**

3 **Advice going forward**

XIII DEATH

Other Names: Mortality, Transformation, Thirteen; sometimes unnamed

Esoteric Titles: The Child of the Great Transformers, Lord of the Gates of Death

Number: Thirteen

Numerology Link: IV The Emperor

Astrological Sign or Planet: Scorpio the Scorpion

Day of the Week: Tuesday

Element: Water

Hebrew Letter: Nun

Symbol: The fish

Meaning: Decline and rebirth

Tree of Life Pathway: Fourteenth, between Netzach and Tiphareth

Chakra: Alta major, for the past and past lives

Crystal: Blue moonstone

Animal Symbol: Pale horse

DESCRIPTION

Beyond the city gates, Death appears on his pale horse holding a black and white flag. A king is dead; a bishop, child, and maiden kneel before him.

KEY MEANINGS

Change, transformation, endings, beginnings, necessity, randomness, cycles, rebirth, renewal

UPRIGHT MEANING

Death brings necessary endings. This may apply to work, relationships, a fledgling idea or project, or your living situation. There is no ambiguity here, and you may have sensed this ending all along. If not, be prepared to let go rather than resist; know that this change is inevitable and will bring in new opportunities. Financially, this may be a challenging time as you feel cut off—but your fortunes will turn around. Note that XIII Death does not mean physical death; rather, it is a transition that is needed for your personal growth. For some, the card comes as a relief after a time of confusion or upheaval.

REVERSED MEANING

Death reversed emphasizes the upright meaning, so the ending may be accompanied by disbelief or drama. The message is the situation is settled, and to move on.

DEATH'S SYMBOLS

1	**Number XIII**	Links with IV The Emperor
2	**Death**	The human condition
3	**The pale horse**	Prediction
4	**Flag**	Harvest
5	**Gates**	Transition

6	**The bishop and the fallen**	Equality
7	**Sunset**	Cycles and endings
8	**Red feather**	Life force
9	**River and boat**	Continuing life

What the Symbols Mean for You

When you are drawn to a particular symbol or feature of a card, it's because it holds a special meaning for you. Here is a guide to interpreting your symbols.

1 NUMBER XIII

Death's number XIII links with card IV, The Emperor (XIII = 13; 1 + 3 = 4); The Emperor, card of authority and security, is the return of stability after the upheaval that XIII Death may bring. Thirteen has been thought of as an unlucky number since antiquity when King Philip of Macedon placed his own statue with those of the twelve Olympic gods and was assassinated shortly afterward. According to some numerologists, thirteen is unlucky because its constituent numbers mean demise. Three is outnumbered by ten, hence the meaning of an ending.

Death's astrological sign of Scorpio is associated with sex and death, while its Hebrew letter Nun, means decline and rebirth—all of which describe stages of transformation, Death's primary meaning. As the fourteenth card of the major arcana, Death stands on the fourteenth pathway of the Tree of Life between the spheres of Netzach, for endurance and desire, and Tiphareth, for beauty and rebirth.

2 DEATH

Skeletal Death has many iterations, from one of the four horsemen of the apocalypse to the Grim Reaper who appeared in Europe during the fourteenth century—the time of the pandemic Black Death. This Death card combines the image of the pale horseman with the Danse Macabre, an allegory of Death from the late Middle Ages in which skeletons dance to the grave, calling a pope, emperor, king, child, and laborer to dance with them (see The Bishop and the Fallen, at right). The message of the Danse and the card is the eternal presence of death—and that we must accept its universality and power to change our lives.

3 THE PALE HORSE

The horse is a pale lunar white, rather than bright, solar white, which echoes Death's association with coming darkness (see Sunset, opposite). The horse has red eyes, which may be a reference to the Irish warrior Cuchulainn's horse the Macha Gray, which wept tears of blood because it knew Cuchulainn would die in battle. This story also associates the horse with prediction; as the horse comes before the rider, the horse is the first indictor that Death, or transformation, is coming.

See the solar-white horse on XIX The Sun.

4 FLAG

The flag's rose motif symbolizes life. The five ears of corn within the emblem signify harvest. Death is the Grim Reaper, harvester of souls.

5 GATES

The two towers represent the gates of heaven and the gates of the city; in medieval times, people were buried beyond the city gates, well away from the living. Gates define physical territory and mark the transition from one state to the next.

See the two towers on XVIII The Moon.

6 THE BISHOP AND THE FALLEN

The figures on the card illustrate that no one—even a bishop—can defy Death. We also see Death's triumph over other cards: the bishop as V The Hierophant, the maiden as VII Strength, and the King with his fallen crown as one of the four kings of the minor arcana. Note the tiny burial crosses nearby, a reminder that Death has been here before.

Death as Transition

The transition to the next stage of being, or next phase of life involves a symbolic death, a letting go of some past experiences. As a snake sheds its skin in cycles, we often sense when it is our time to shed something. This may be a relationship, a way of working, or a way of thinking; Death can come up in readings to show a deep shift in attitudes or beliefs, and the ending of certain commitments. As the card does not mean physical death, it is to be welcomed: at last, you get to see the truth of your situation. Death's personification as a skeleton reveals what you know in your bones—that it is time for change.

7 SUNSET

Sunset signifies the end of the day, or a cycle, and the beginning of night. Death as the fourth horseman of the apocalypse (see Death, opposite) brought pestilence, or deadly disease. As the body is most vulnerable during the small hours, in the past many people feared that Death would take them in the night—hence Death's approach at sunset.

8 RED FEATHER

The red feather symbolizes the life force. As plumage on Death's helmet, it is wilted to mirror the ebbing life of the human figures on the card.

See the red feather on 0 The Fool, XIX The Sun, Nine of Cups, and the Page and Knight of Wands.

9 RIVER AND BOAT

The river and boat symbolize the mythological river Styx and the journey of the soul over the river to the afterlife. An alternative reading is normality; life, or the river, must go on regardless. Water also represents the card's ruling element.

WHAT'S ON THE HORIZON?

This spread looks at what may be ending in your life, how best to manage it, and what comes next. First, take out XIII Death and place the card face up as shown to oversee the reading. Then shuffle the remainder of the deck and lay three cards face down, in positions 1, 2, and 3. When you are ready, turn over the cards and begin your interpretation.

PAGE OF WANDS

What is to be transformed
Example: Page of Wands. A new situation may not develop—it may need to be abandoned or completely rethought.

What you need to move forward
Example: King of Cups. Emotional intelligence and being able to manage many demands. This card also explains card 1—that a new situation cannot progress because there is already much to contend with.

What's on the horizon?
Example: IV The Emperor. A new-found stability and self-determination; the confidence to take control.

XIV TEMPERANCE

Other Name: Art

Esoteric Titles: Daughter of the Reconcilers, The Bringer Forth of Life

Number: Fourteen

Numerology Link: V The Hierophant

Astrological Sign or Planet: Sagittarius the Archer

Day of the Week: Thursday

Element: Fire

Hebrew Letter: Samekh

- **Symbol:** Support or crutch
- **Meaning:** Patience

Tree of Life Pathway: Fifteenth, between Yesod and Tiphareth

Chakra: Solar plexus, for self-empowerment

Crystals: Citrine, amber, yellow topaz

Archangel: Archangel Michael

DESCRIPTION

A white-robed angel with fiery red wings stands in a pool. He holds two chalices, with water flowing between them. To his left is a pathway and a radiating golden crown.

KEY MEANINGS

Balance, negotiation, pressure, diplomacy, adaptation, solutions, priorities, reconciliation, peace, miracles, angelic guidance

UPRIGHT MEANING

Temperance reveals the need for peaceful balance. In your work relationships and projects, the card shows careful negotiation as you deal with demanding individuals or deadlines. Be willing to make adjustments, and you will find the perfect solution; this applies to creative projects, too. Broadly, the card shows managing your time so you prioritize tasks and look after work, family, and home as efficiently as you are able. In finances, you have the resources you need. A further meaning of the card is spiritual guidance—such as receiving angel signs—and even a miracle.

REVERSED MEANING

Reversed Temperance can show pressure and imbalance in relationships and finances. It may be difficult to reconcile warring demands.

TEMPERANCE'S SYMBOLS

1	Number XIV	Links with V The Hierophant
2	The angel	Guidance
3	The two chalices	Miracles
4	Flowing water	The flow of life
5	Solar crown	The future

6	Irises	Hope
7	The pool	The unconscious mind
8	The sun symbol	Spiritual illumination
9	Triangle and square	Union
10	The Tetragrammaton	Divine connection

What the Symbols Mean for You

When you are drawn to a particular symbol or feature of a card, it's because it holds a special meaning for you. Here is a guide to interpreting your symbols.

1 NUMBER XIV

Temperance's number XIV reduces to V, the number of the Hierophant (XIV = 14; 1 + 4 = 5). As the card's Archangel Michael is a messenger of God, the Hierophant or High Priest communicates God's words to man: both connect humanity with the divine. Fourteen is comprised of ten and four—ten for completion and four for stability. This is the goal of Temperance: to temper, or balance competing needs to create steady progress and flow. This aligns with the card's Hebrew letter Samekh, which means "patience."

As the fifteenth card in the major arcana sequence, Temperance appears on the fifteenth pathway on the Tree of Life between the spheres of Yesod and Tiphareth, bringing together the idea of the flow of the unconscious mind as continual rebirth.

2 THE ANGEL

Michael is the archangel of courage and powerful protection. Here, he signifies guidance during the quest for balance that Temperance represents. He has one foot in the pool, symbol of the unconscious mind, and one foot on a rock, the conscious mind; he mediates both. His vast red wings symbolize his element of Fire, which is also the card's element (see sidebar, opposite).

3 THE TWO CHALICES

The chalice on the left signifies the past and the lower subconscious, whereas the higher chalice (on the right) symbolizes the future and the unconscious, so the present is life in this moment—represented by the water (see Flowing Water, at right). The chalices also look like those used in religious ceremonies, so we are witnessing a divine action. The water between the cups is poured at an angle and appears to flow both ways, symbolizing magic and miracles. Not a drop is spilled—this careful attention aligns with the card's sign of Sagittarius the archer, whose aim is precise.

See the water poured from two vessels in XVII The Star.

4 FLOWING WATER

Water in general symbolizes the unconscious mind, the emotions, and life itself; the water flowing between the cups signifies not just the flow of life but the power of the mind in the present moment (see The Two Chalices, at left).

5 SOLAR CROWN

The solar crown with its corona, or rays, symbolizes the power of the sun; this is seen in antiquity in images of sun god Helios, who wears the solar or radiate crown. In our card, the solar crown rises over the mountains, symbolizing renewal—a new day is dawning.

6 IRISES

The Irises signify Iris, Greek goddess of rainbows and hope. The meaning of hope also foreshadows XVII The Star, card of hope and inspiration.

7 THE POOL

Water symbolizes the unconscious mind, emotions, and life itself. Water can also signify memories, so past issues may surface.

See the pool on XVII The Star and XVIII The Moon.

8 THE SUN SYMBOL

The dotted circle signifies the sun and spirit; it is also the alchemical symbol for gold. The symbol appears on Archangel Michael's forehead near his third eye and crown, the chakra points associated with insight and spiritual connection. Here, it suggests spiritual illumination.

Temperance as a Gateway

As card XIV, Temperance appears as the last card of the second stage of the major arcana journey and acts as a gateway to the cards of higher awareness that fall toward the end of the sequence, as follows:

- Cards 1 The Magician—VII The Chariot. The body. The Fool's formative encounters.
- Cards VIII Strength—XIV Temperance. The mind. Innocence to experience.
- Cards XV—XXI The World. The spirit. Evolution and ascension.
- Note that 0 The Fool is not included, as he travels through every card (see page 18).

In this way, Temperance is a gatekeeper to the third stage of the journey. The Fool meets Archangel Michael as part of his evolution toward spiritual awareness; he discovers a higher form of consciousness. This angelic influence will help him deal with the next card in the sequence—XV The Devil.

9 TRIANGLE AND SQUARE

The triangle and square motif mean Fire (the triangle) and Earth (the square). Fire is the card's element, which is contained safely within the boundaries of the square, symbolizing fire energy that is carefully directed and grounded. This is the way of Temperance—to manage heated demands. The triangle also represents the integration of mind, body, and spirit; we need every part of us to negotiate change and be resilient under pressure.

10 THE TETRAGRAMMATON

Divine connection. The letters IHVH appear on the neckline of the angel's robe. This is the tetragrammaton, the name of God in the Hebrew Bible. The four letters, reading from right to left are Yod, He, Waw, and He.

1

The situation now

BALANCING OPPOSITES

This spread reveals how you might find a way forward when dealing with opposing demands. Take out XIV Temperance and place the card face up in position 1 to oversee the reading. Then shuffle the remainder of the deck and lay three cards face down as shown. When you are ready, turn all the cards face up and begin your interpretation.

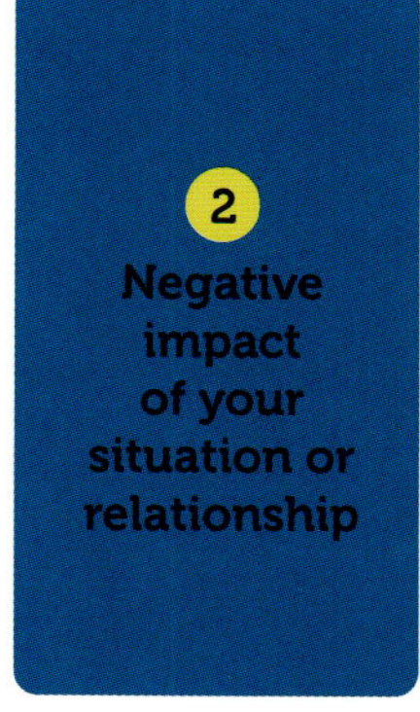

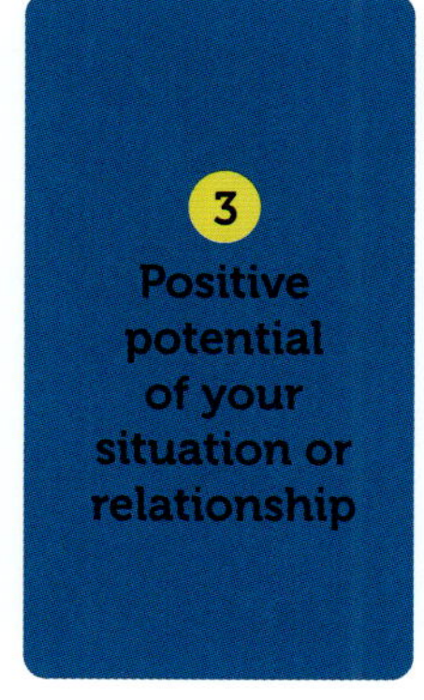

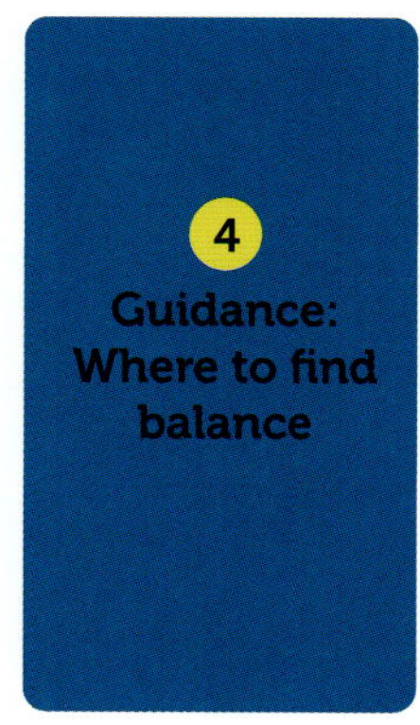

If you have a minor arcana card for card 4, interpret it by looking at the suit. For example, if you had the Five of Wands, you'll need all your drive and Fire energy to push through the pressure. If you had a Cups card, the advice is gentle negotiation. Swords reveals an intellectual solution, while Pentacles asks you to do only what is practical—and protect your boundaries.

XV THE DEVIL

Other Names: Pan, Temptation

Esoteric Titles: Lord of the Gates of Matter, Child of the Forces of Time

Number: Fifteen

Numerology Link: VI The Lovers

Astrological Sign or Planet: Capricorn the Goat

Day of the Week: Saturday

Element: Earth

Hebrew Letter: Ayin

- **Symbol:** Eye
- **Meaning:** Clear vision

Tree of Life Pathway: Sixteenth, between Hod and Tiphareth

Chakra: Base, for base instincts

Crystals: Red carnelian, ruby

Animal Symbol: Goat

Archangel: Archangel Uriel

DESCRIPTION

Crowned with an inverted pentagram, a devil sits with one hand raised and the other lowered, holding a flaming torch. Two demons appear to be chained to his black altar.

KEY MEANINGS

Control, bonds, restriction, excess, affairs, lust, dependency, addictions, temptation, debt, materialism

UPRIGHT MEANING

The Devil signifies restriction. This manifests as contracts and personal arrangements that keep you trapped, feeling oppressed by people or authorities who have power over you. It is also the card that reveals materialism, greed, addictions, and negative behaviors that block personal growth and inhibit good relationships. Financially, you may be overcommitted; in love, the card means temptation, revealing affairs and lust. In business and creative projects, you may feel obliged to do work that brings you little pleasure. However, some of this feeling of enslavement is perception—you do have the power to walk away from toxic situations.

REVERSED MEANING

The reversed Devil is more positive than the upright card, as the darkness is nearly over; you begin to see clearly what must be done and can embrace a new freedom.

THE DEVIL'S SYMBOLS

1	**Number XV**	Links with VI The Lovers
2	**The Devil**	Base instincts
3	**The open hand**	The outcast
4	**The two demons**	Enslavement

5	**Tails**	Transgression
6	**Inverted pentagram**	Materialism
7	**The chains**	Habit
8	**Darkness**	Limitation

What the Symbols Mean for You

When you are drawn to a particular symbol or feature of a card, it's because it holds a special meaning for you. Here is a guide to interpreting your symbols.

1 NUMBER XV

The Devil's number XV reduces to VI, the number of the Lovers. Both cards share a similar composition, with a male and female figure overseen by an otherworldly being—an angel and a devil. As a card of love and free will, VI The Lovers is the opposite of the Devil's lust and control. Fifteen also comprises number five, the number of V The Hierophant. Like the Devil and the Lovers, The Hierophant card features with a central figure above two supplicants.

As the sixteenth card of the major arcana, the Devil is associated with the sixteenth pathway on the Tree of Life, between the spheres of Hod and Tiphareth. Hod is for the mind, while Tiphareth is beauty and rebirth—which says we can determinedly release ourselves from binds and agreements and start afresh. This accords with the card's Hebrew letter, Ayin, which means "clear vision." When we see the truth of a situation, we become empowered.

2 THE DEVIL

Goat-face, horns, clawed feet, and bat's wings—this is the archetypal devil: he may be Pan, god of excess, Satan, symbol of evil, or Baphomet, the idol that the Knights Templar were accused of worshiping. The occultist Éliphas Lévi's 1854 drawing of Baphomet for his book *Dogme et Rituel de la Haute Magie* is the likely basis for the card we see here—the sketch shows a bearded, goat-like devil with the same hand positions and inverted pentagram on his forehead. The devil's half-animal form, which links with the card's sign of Capricorn the goat, also signifies a descent into baseness.

The Devil may also be associated with Archangel Uriel, angel of wisdom, truth, and light—the attribution of "light" with Uriel links to the Devil as Lucifer, or "light-bringer," before his fall from grace.

3 THE OPEN HAND

The devil's open palm is the opposite to the partly concealed palm of the hierophant. The card's co-creator A. E. Waite describes this as "the reverse of the benediction which is given by the Hierophant." The opposite of a benediction, or blessing, defines the Devil as the outsider who denounces the church.

See the symbol of blessing on V The Hierophant and on the left hand of the figure on the Ten of Swords.

4 THE TWO DEMONS

The male and female figures are demons, shown by their horns. They are the lovers from card VI in the grip of the dark aspect of their own nature or the situation that finds them; love flips to lust, autonomy to enslavement. However, their chains are loose; they can walk away if they choose.

5 TAILS

The tails show the couple's animal nature. Further, the woman's tail appears with ripe fruit, symbol of temptation, a reference to the forbidden fruit that Eve ate in the Garden of Eden. The man's tail is alight, close to the devil's torch, which symbolizes negative influences and potential corruption.

See forbidden fruit on VI The Lovers.

6 INVERTED PENTAGRAM

The upright pentagram, symbol of protection, also signifies the correct hierarchy of the material and spiritual, with the spiritual aspect of humanity in charge. When reversed, the material world dominates, hence the card's element of Earth—and the orderliness associated with the upright pentagram descends into disorder and chaos. The inverted pentagram is associated with Baphomet (see The Devil, at left).

The Devil and the Minor Fives

The Fives of the minor arcana relate directly to XV The Devil. As we have seen, he presents as a reversal of VI The Lovers and V The Hierophant, yet is closely tied to the four minor Fives, too. Each Five presents us with a challenge. The Five of Wands reveals a test of will; the Five of Cups, the journey through grief; the Five of Pentacles, for the stress of poverty or isolation; and the Five of Swords, the humiliation of defeat. And yet, as with all cards, it is how we manage these experiences that often define our future. If we struggle to recover from the impact of a Five, we may end up dealing with the Devil, trapped in a situation we did not see coming and/or accepting poor treatment. If we can care for ourselves and find support during the tests of the Fives, we become VI The Lovers, able to choose our futures.

7 THE CHAINS

The chains are symbols of control and enslavement. However, they are loose—so the demons may stay trapped out of habit; they could walk free and take charge of their lives again.

8 DARKNESS

The darkness in the Devil's lair symbolizes limitation and hidden issues; we are "in the dark" without the truth, or facts.

HIDDEN TRUTH

In the darkness lays a hidden truth that unlocks a stuck situation. This spread asks you to find the hidden truth in the card on the bottom of the deck and place it as card 3, as shown.

First, take out XV The Devil and place the card face up as shown to oversee the reading. Then shuffle the remainder of the deck and lay down two cards face up; now take the card from the bottom of the deck and place it face up, too. Begin your interpretation.

1 The reason for this situation

2 What needs to change

3 Hidden truth to help you move forward

XVI THE TOWER

Other Names: The House of God, The Fire of Heaven, The Lightning-struck Tower, House of Falsehood, The Blasted Tower

Esoteric Title: Lord of the Hosts of the Mighty

Number: Sixteen

Numerology Link: VII The Chariot

Astrological Sign or Planet: Mars

Day of the Week: Tuesday

Element: Fire

Hebrew Letter: Peh

Symbol: Mouth

Meaning: Chaos

Tree of Life Pathway: Seventeenth, between Hod and Netzach

Chakra: Crown and base, for heaven and earth

Crystals: Clear quartz, red carnelian, red jasper

DESCRIPTION

A lightning bolt strikes the top of a flaming tower, its gold crown falling into the black air. Two figures, a male and female, fly headlong toward the rock below.

KEY MEANINGS

Revelation, destruction, enlightenment, pride, breakdown, breakthrough, release, shock, endings, change, expansion

UPRIGHT MEANING

The Tower's meaning is indisputable: here is sudden destruction, without warning—so you may deal with shock endings. In money matters and relationships there may be exposure and revelation as certain truths, once hidden, come to light. This is the tower of the ego, too, so old ways of thinking and living collapse as you let go of what you have constructed. You can only surrender to the tower's fall, accepting this destruction without blame before you recover and build anew. The positive aspect of the Tower, however, is spiritual illumination and creative breakthroughs; at home, the card can reveal structural issues with a property.

REVERSED MEANING

The reversed Tower can show victimhood and an unwillingness to let go. A further interpretation is taking needless blame.

THE TOWER'S SYMBOLS

1	**Number XVI**	Links with VII The Chariot
2	**The tower**	Old structures; ego
3	**Blasted crown**	Lost authority
4	**Lightning bolt**	Illumination, truth

5	**Falling figures**	Force of nature
6	**Golden droplets**	Hand of God
7	**Darkness**	Limitation

What the Symbols Mean for You

When you are drawn to a particular symbol or feature of a card, it's because it holds a special meaning for you. Here is a guide to interpreting your symbols.

1 NUMBER XVI

The Tower's number XVI reduces to VII, the number of The Chariot. The Chariot is progress after recovery from the tower's collapse. The sunlit Chariot is all about willpower and control; the dark tower is the reverse in its meaning of chaos and destruction. Both concern the ego—the charioteer must control his in order to progress, while XVI The Tower shows us how the human ego is no match for divine power.

Sixteen comprises numbers ten and six. Like XVI The Tower, X The Wheel of Fortune also deals with a higher power and the workings of fate and cycles. Card VI The Lovers shows us paradise before the Fall, whereas XVI The Tower depicts a fall from grace.

As the seventeenth card in the major arcana sequence, the Tower is placed between Hod and Netzach, or the mind and nature; no amount of willpower can control nature's power.

2 THE TOWER

In Genesis, the tower was abandoned, and God made the Babylonians speak in different languages so they could not understand one another. In the rabbinic text the Midrash, the tower of Babel is burned down by God as retribution for our sins. In psychology, the tower in its phallic form represents the ego, our personal identity.

3 CROWN

The falling crown symbolizes the downfall of material structures and hierarchies. This violent displacement links the card with its ruling planet of Mars, planet of war. As the crown also signifies the mind, the crown hit by lightning reminds us that permanency is an illusion.

4 LIGHTNING BOLT

In Christianity, the lightning bolt is a symbol of divine retribution for man's sins. In Buddhism, the lightning bolt or dorje signifies the purification of the mind. Both interpretations share the idea of clarity: when the tower falls, we see the truth. In Kabbala, the lightning bolt is the tenfold emanation of the spirit, which moves between the ten spheres of the Tree of Life (see page 228). The card's Hebrew letter, Peh, means chaos—the destructive impact of lightning.

5 FALLING FIGURES

Their identity remains mysterious: the card's co-creator A. E. Waite says, "The one is the literal world made void and the other its false interpretation." The figure on the left may be the literal world—the world of human pride and assumptions of power personified by I The Magician in his red cloak. The woman on the right is the false rendering. Wearing a jester's hat she becomes 0 The Fool, who this time falls from the cliff top to his death. In this way, the falling figures symbolize the Tower's victory over the Magician and Fool: however much we manifest our reality and set out on our own adventures, nature—and God—have the ultimate power.

6 GOLDEN DROPLETS

Twenty-two flame-like droplets mirror the number of letters in the Hebrew alphabet. Each droplet is in the shape of the Hebrew letter Yod, for fire, the card's element; Yod also means the divine hand of God, which encapsulates the card's meaning. One of the card's old titles is Maison Dieu, or House of God.

7 DARKNESS

Night-time symbolizes a limited view. Through the two "night" cards of the major arcana—XV The Devil and XVI The Tower—we experience the dark night of the soul, a time of crisis. Rebirth and renewed hope comes with XVII The Star, the next card in the sequence.

The Tower: Majors and Minors

Towers in the tarot are gateways to other worlds, and symbols of ambition, ego, or protection. On this card, XVI The Tower, the meaning is ego and the man-made world; in XIII Death, two towers appear as the gates of heaven, while on XVIII The Moon, the two towers represent the gates of Hades. These are portals to other states of being—life to death, the conscious mind to the realm of the subconscious, and the past to the present. In the minor arcana, the meaning is less profound, as towers here often signify protection and home—such as the loving Six of Cups and Four of Wands—along with material matters and materialism. The Four, Six, Eight, Nine, Ten, and King of Pentacles all feature towers, a reminder of the earthly, material world that the suit of Pentacles represents.

SURRENDER AND REFLECTION

As XVI The Tower is about acceptance rather than action, we work with two face up cards and add just two new cards to create the spread.

First, take out XVI The Tower and VII The Chariot as card positions 1 and 4. Then shuffle the remainder of the deck and lay down two face down, in positions 2 and 3. Begin your interpretation.

The Tower: Destruction

What to surrender to
Example: Ten of Pentacles. After the impact of card 1, finding abundance and support through family connections and friendship.

What to reflect on
Example: Justice. Contemplating what is in and out of balance in life, and how to be fairer to yourself as a way to embrace the new energy represented by card.

The Chariot: Moving on

XVII THE STAR

Other Names: Hope, The Stars

Esoteric Titles: Daughter of the Firmament, Dweller between the Waters

Number: Seventeen

Numerology Link: VIII Strength

Astrological Sign or Planet: Aquarius the Water-Carrier

Day of the Week: Wednesday

Element: Air

Hebrew Letter: Tzaddi

- **Symbol:** The fishhook
- **Meaning:** Hope

Tree of Life Pathway: Eighteenth, between Yesod and Netzach

Chakra: Higher heart, for universal love

Crystals: Kunzite, dioptase, red tourmaline

Animal Symbol: Ibis bird

DESCRIPTION

A maiden kneels by a pool at twilight, the sky illuminated by eight stars. From two pitchers she pours water into a pool and onto fertile earth.

KEY MEANINGS

Hope, inspiration, wishes, guidance, creativity, healing, renewal, nourishment, wholeness, self-care, beauty

UPRIGHT MEANING

The Star brings hope and inspiration. After a period of darkness, the brightest Star guides us back to peace, to freedom, and to ourselves as life begins to flow again. This is a time not only for recovery and self-care but for self-expression and creativity, too, as you feel inspired to share your talents with others. In relationships, you feel appreciated, and you may be guided toward a soul mate. The Star also represents spiritual connection and luck, and can represent a healer in a reading.

REVERSED MEANING

The reversed Star may indicate disappointment and lack of fulfillment. The message is not to give up; you can find your way.

THE STAR'S SYMBOLS

1	**Number XVII**	Links with VIII, Strength
2	**Eight stars**	Hope and guidance
3	**Star maiden**	Eternal youth
4	**Pool**	The unconscious

5	**Pitchers**	Resources
6	**Pouring water**	The flow of life
7	**Rivulets**	Growth and healing
8	**Bird**	Soulful expression

What the Symbols Mean for You

When you are drawn to a particular symbol or feature of a card, it's because it holds a special meaning for you. Here is a guide to interpreting your symbols.

1 NUMBER XVII

Number XVII, or 17, reduces to 8 (XVII = 17; 1 + 7 = 8), the number of VIII Strength. Both XVII The Star and VIII Strength feature a maiden who emanates peace and grace.

As the Star is the eighteenth card in the major arcana sequence, it takes the eighteenth letter of the Hebrew alphabet, Tzaddi, which means "hope"—the card's key meaning. The Star also appears on the eighteenth Tree of Life pathway between the spheres of Yesod and Netzach, which are associated with light and shadow; the Star's twilight world embraces both.

2 EIGHT STARS

The stars are a sign of spiritual guidance. The largest of the eight stars may be Venus, the Morning Star, considered the brightest in the sky, or Sirius, depending on how we identify the star maiden—as Venus/Aphrodite, or the Egyptian Isis, goddess of magic. Each star has eight points, which is the sum of the Star's number, 17. The cards' co-creator A. E. Waite says the star is the Flamboyant Star, an emblem of faith in Freemasonry. The seven smaller stars have been linked to the seven classical planets (Mercury, Mars, Venus, Saturn, Jupiter, the Moon, and Sun), the seven Pleiades, and the seven principal chakras, or energy centers of the body.

See the star in the lantern of IX The Hermit, the star crown and canopy of stars on VII The Chariot, and the diadem of stars on III The Empress.

3 STAR MAIDEN

The star maiden symbolizes awakening to life. A symbol of eternal youth and beauty, the maiden's nakedness denotes purity and her close connection to nature and the world. She may be Venus/Aphrodite or Isis (see Isis Bird, at right); also, Nut, goddess of the sky who was depicted nude, making an arc shape across a starry sky. The symbol for Nut's name is a water pot, an echo of the Star maiden's pitchers.

4 POOL

The pool symbolizes depth of feeling, memory, the unconscious mind, and/or the collective unconscious.

See the pool on XIV Temperance and XVIII The Moon.

5 PITCHERS

The pitchers denote our relationship with our physical body. The pitchers are vessels, like the body, that hold our life experience and contain our spirit. The pitchers also relate to the Star's astrological sign of Aquarius, the water-carrier.

See the pitchers as chalices on XIV Temperance.

6 POURING WATER

The flowing water symbolizes the flow of life, along with wholeness and healing. Water also represents baptism and rebirth, signified by octagonal baptismal fonts in churches—the eight being the sum of the card's number, 17.

See the flow of water between chalices on XIV Temperance.

7 RIVULETS

The rivulets signify growth and healing our past issues; the maiden pours the water to her left, which in tarot usually represents the past. The five rivulets have been associated with the five senses and the quintessence, the fifth element of spirit.

8 IBIS BIRD

The bird is a soul symbol, here also a symbol of the element of Air, the card's element. The bird is likely the ibis, used in ritual worship to the Egyptian goddess Isis, and also appears as the head of the god Thoth. Some readers see the ibis as the dove, symbol of Venus/Aphrodite. If you are drawn to the bird, this is also a broader message about personal freedom and spiritual communication.

Temperance and the Star: Miracles

Card XIV Temperance and XVII The Star both depict a figure with two vessels. Temperance's chalices are ceremonial, like those used in religious services, whereas the star maiden's pitchers are domestic earthenware: she represents the inner, personal world. The Star is all about flow, while Temperance is exact measure (see page 74). Both cards have the feel of a miracle: the Star, the miracle renewal—the maiden's foot hovers above the pool as if she could walk on water—while Temperance's water appears to flow upward, against gravity. Both cards bring us the possibility of miracles.

STAR POWER

When you have a wish, this spread helps you check your focus and pull in a little starlight.

Take out XVII The Star and place the card face up as shown. Then shuffle the remainder of the deck, asking, "What do I need to see about this situation?" Draw three cards, placing them face down from left to right. Turn all the cards face up and begin your interpretation.

1

What you're creating or manifesting now
Example: Three of Cups. A celebration!

2

What to release to allow your wish to manifest
Example: Four of Swords. Given the work needed for the celebration, release the idea that rest is possible just now.

3

Star power: cosmic guidance
Example: Six of Cups. A reunion; also, forgiveness. The event brings a key person back into your life.

XVIII THE MOON

Other Names: Luna, Illusion

Esoteric Titles: Ruler of Flux and Reflux, Child of the Sons of the Mighty

Number: Eighteen

Numerology Link: IX The Hermit

Astrological Sign or Planet: Pisces the Fish

Day of the Week: Monday

Element: Water

Hebrew Letter: Qoph (Kuf)

  Symbol: The back of the head

  Meaning: Hidden problems

Tree of Life Pathway: Nineteenth, between Netzach and Malkuth

Chakra: Third eye, for intuition

Crystals: Moonstone, amethyst, lapis lazuli

Animal Symbols: Dog, wolf, crayfish

DESCRIPTION

A crayfish appears from a moonlit pool. A path ahead stretches into unknown lands; the crayfish may move forward or retreat.

KEY MEANINGS

Illusion, dreams, mystery, deception, disturbance, hidden issues, the past, the unconscious, doubt, crisis of faith, risk, psychic work

UPRIGHT MEANING

All is not as it seems; moonlight both enchants and distorts the picture. This is a time of soul-searching and uncertainty, when you may doubt what you see; you may be unsure whom or what to trust, or whether a risk is worth taking. If so, your intuition and your dreams—the language of the unconscious mind—will guide you forward. The card also offers an opportunity to overcome fears, which may involve facing an issue from the past. The Moon can also show psychic potential and psychic work.

REVERSED MEANING

When reversed, the card can show a struggle to move forward. An old dilemma or relationship issue may need revisiting.

THE MOON'S SYMBOLS

1	**Number XVIII**	Links with IX, The Hermit
2	**Sun-moon**	Confusion
3	**Twilight**	The liminal world
4	**Watchtowers**	Gateways
5	**Golden droplets**	Element of fire

6	**Blue mountains**	Aspiration and reality
7	**Dog and wolf**	Fear
8	**Path**	The unknown
9	**Crayfish**	Instinct, vulnerability
10	**Pool**	The unconscious

What the Symbols Mean for You

When you are drawn to a particular symbol or feature of a card, it's because it holds a special meaning for you. Here is a guide to interpreting your symbols.

1 NUMBER XVIII

Number XVIII, or 18, reduces to 9 (XVIII = 18; 1 + 8 = 9), the number of IX The Hermit. Like the Moon's crayfish, the Hermit also faces a lone journey into unknown territory.

As the Moon is the nineteenth card in the major arcana sequence, it takes the nineteenth letter of the Hebrew alphabet, Qoph, for hidden problems. Qoph is associated with the back of the head, for the things behind us that we cannot see. This reflects the Moon's meaning of hidden issues and mystery. The Moon appears on the nineteenth Tree of Life pathway between the spheres of Malkuth and Netzach; Netzach is emotion whereas Malkuth is the logical mind: the Moon sits uncomfortably between the two, hence the card's meaning of doubt. A further interpretation of Malkuth is learning lessons.

2 SUN-MOON

The sun is the sleeping conscious self while the moon represents the hidden or unconscious self. Here, we are troubled by what our moon-self—our heart—is trying to communicate, as awakening intuition brings unrest.

See the sun-moon on the Eight of Cups.

3 TWILIGHT SKY

A time of magical possibility, twilight denotes liminality, the in-between. After the sun dips beneath the horizon the remaining sunlight turns blue. Our view of the world is changing, expanding.

See twilight on XVII The Star.

4 WATCHTOWERS

The watchtowers represent the edge of the known world; they are gateways to another realm of consciousness or experience. A further interpretation is that the towers represent the mythological gates of Hades guarded by the goddess Hecate (see Dog and Wolf, below).

See the towers on XIII Death.

5 GOLDEN DROPLETS

Fifteen golden droplets each form the Hebrew letter Yod. One of its meanings is fire or flame. (Yod is also the Hebrew letter associated with the Moon's numerological twin, IX The Hermit.) A. E. Waite calls these Yods "the dew of thought." These thoughts, as fire, may create conflict with the water of emotion beneath the sun-moon.

See the Yods on XVI The Tower and the Ace of Cups, Ace of Wands, and Ace of Swords.

6 BLUE MOUNTAINS

The mountains are symbols of goals and higher consciousness. There may be tension between dreams and reality, revealed by the celestial blue peaks and ordinariness of the green fields in the mid- and foreground.

See the blue mountains on the Ace and Ten of Swords.

7 DOG AND WOLF

These creatures represent our instinctual animal nature and our natural fear of the unknown. A French saying for dusk is *entre chien et loup*—between dog and wolf. The dog is tame, and the wolf, wild: between them, they tell us something profound is evolving. Another reading of the animals is that they represent the companions of the dark deity Hecate, guardian of the gates of Hades, who was often shown with two dogs and two towers.

See the dog on 0 The Fool and the Ten of Pentacles.

What's in the Number?

The Moon's number XVIII contains VIII, for card VIII Strength. Both cards deal with animal instinct, symbolized by Strength's lion and the Moon's crayfish. The maiden signifies higher consciousness, like the Moon's blue mountains—which stand for the idea or goal, provided we can embrace the fearful animal within. The number XVIII also contains the number X, for the Wheel of Fortune and life's cycles and phases, which forges another link with the moon.

8 PATH

The path reveals what is new and unknown. As it dips and meanders, it disappears then reappears—so the journey ahead is unclear. The path also connects with the feet, the body part linked with the card's sign of Pisces.

See the path on XIV Temperance and the Ace of Pentacles. The path also suggests journey cards 0 The Fool, IX The Hermit, the Moon's numerological twin (see 1).

9 CRAYFISH

The crayfish is instinct, the primordial self that needs attention so we can move forward. Emerging from the safety of the pool, the crustacean tells us that an old, buried need or truth is about to surface.

10 POOL

The pool represents the depths of emotion and the unconscious mind, just like the card's element of Water. Rippling beneath the moon, which controls the tides, the pool also symbolizes phases, cycles, and regeneration.

See the pool on XIV Temperance, XVII The Star, and the Ace of Cups.

MOON WISDOM

Use this spread inspired by the ocean's tides to see the benefits and the challenges in any situation of your choosing. Take out XVIII The Moon and place the card face up as shown. Then shuffle the remainder of the deck, asking, "What do I need to see about this situation?" Draw three cards (see page 15) placing them face down from left to right. Then turn all the cards face up and begin your interpretation.

XIX THE SUN

Other Name: The Children

Esoteric Title: Lord of the Fire of the World

Number: Nineteen

Numerology Links: X The Wheel of Fortune and I The Magician

Astrological Sign or Planet: The Sun

Day of the Week: Sunday

Element: Fire

Hebrew Letter: Resh

- **Symbol:** The front of the head, or face
- **Meaning:** Success

Tree of Life Pathway: Twentieth, between Yesod and Hod

Chakra: Solar plexus, for physical health and soul wisdom

Crystals: Citrine, golden topaz

Animal Symbol: Horse

DESCRIPTION

A smiling child rides a white horse, holding a red flag. He is safe in his walled garden and is warmed by a huge sun.

KEY MEANINGS

Growth, optimism, success, protection, inner child, confidence, healing, fulfillment, higher consciousness

UPRIGHT MEANING

The sun brings joy into your love life, family, work, and projects—and is one of the most optimistic cards in the deck, canceling out any negative cards nearby. If you need recharging, the sun says that rest is coming. Your experience feels like a blessing as you are appreciated, loved, and rewarded. Spiritually, you access the integrated wisdom of collective consciousness, feeling at one with the world. More literally, the card shows holidays and time with children. The card is a "yes" to any question and, in a spread, cancels out any negative cards that fall beside it.

REVERSED MEANING

The Sun is so positive that the upright meaning holds; the only issues may be slight delay or temporary disappointment.

THE SUN'S SYMBOLS

1	**Number XIX**	Links with X The Wheel of Fortune and I The Magician
2	**The sun**	Optimism
3	**Child**	Innocence
4	**Child's pose**	Perfect balance
5	**White horse**	Progress
6	**Red feather and flag**	Life and vitality
7	**Four sunflowers**	Growth and optimism
8	**Wall**	Protection

What the Symbols Mean for You

When you are drawn to a particular symbol or feature of a card, it's because it holds a special meaning for you. Here is a guide to interpreting your symbols.

1 NUMBER XIX

Number XIX or 19, reduces to 10 (XIX = 19; 1 + 9 = 10), the number of X The Wheel of Fortune, which reduces further to I The Magician. All three cards have in common the idea of universal energy or consciousness—the Magician harnesses it to bring heaven to earth, the Wheel shows us its cycles, while the Sun expresses collective consciousness.

As the twentieth card in the major arcana, the Sun takes the twentieth letter of the Hebrew alphabet, Resh, which means "success"—one of the card's interpretations. The Sun comes out on the twentieth Tree of Life pathway between Yesod and Hod. Yesod is associated with the unconscious mind; Hod is the sphere the logical mind, so together, they bring the meaning of fulfillment and growth, the gifts of the Sun.

2 THE SUN

The sun on the card is a symbol of conscious awareness and positivity. Naturally, it is the card's ruling planet, associated with the element of Fire. Traditionally masculine, the sun is associated with the sun god Helios (the Greek Apollo). There are two types of ray, straight and wavy, symbolizing the positives of the sun's warmth for growth and healing, and the negative aspect of drought; this offers the characteristics of gentleness and humility as opposed to harshness and arrogance.

3 CHILD

The child represents purity and innocence and, according to Jung, is a representation of the Divine Child (see sidebar, opposite). The sunflower garland with its seven small flower heads signifies celebration and civility—so this child is not wild but safely contained. S/he is also our inner child, happy and hopeful. A further meaning of the flower garland is harvest—which says we are nearing the end of the Fool's journey through the major arcana.

See the flower garlands on the Two and Three of Cups.

4 CHILD'S POSE

With outstretched arms and legs—and no saddle—the child as rider signifies perfect balance. The cards' co-creator A. E. Waite attributes this balance to the child's outstretched right hand, symbol of self-consciousness. We can interpret this as being fully aware and present within ourselves.

5 WHITE HORSE

The horse signifies the human body with its innate soul. Because the horse moves, it symbolizes transitional states of being: in the Sun card, the child is riding toward a higher awareness that culminates in spiritual ascension with XXI The World, the final card of the major arcana sequence.

See the white horse on XIII Death, the Knight of Cups, and Knight of Swords.

6 RED FEATHER AND FLAG

The red flag and the red feather are symbols of the life force.

See the red feather on 0 The Fool, the Nine of Cups, and the Page and Knight of Wands. On XIII Death, the red feather is withered.

7 FOUR SUNFLOWERS

The sunflowers represent the sun and stand for growth and optimism. Their number, four, signifies the element of Earth. Further interpretations include the four suits of the minor arcana and the four kingdoms of nature—human, animal, mineral, and vegetable.

See the sunflower on the Queen of Wands.

8 WALL

The wall symbolizes protection and strong personal boundaries.

The Sun and the Pages: Divine Children

The child on the Sun card is Jung's archetype of the Divine Child, symbol of a new beginning and hope against the odds. According to Jun, the Sun card is "The completion of the long path" as we near the end of the major arcana cycle. We can see how the four Pages—the tarot's other children or young people—might interact to create the garden of the Sun:

- The Page of Pentacles, suit of Earth, provides mortar for the wall
- The Page of Cups, suit of Water, provides water for the sunflowers
- The Page of Swords, suit of Air, defends the wall
- The Page of Wands is the gardener, as gardening is the work of the soul, representing Wands' element of Fire and the fire of the Sun itself.

SUN LIGHT

When you need time to recharge and grow creatively, let these cards illuminate the way.

Take out XIX The Sun and place the card face up as shown. Then shuffle the remainder of the deck, thinking about your situation and asking, "What do I need to see clearly now?" Draw three cards (see page 15) placing them face down from left to right. Turn all the cards face up and begin your interpretation.

What can't grow?
Example: Five of Swords. Walk away from a no-win situation.

What should I sow?
Example: Two of Wands. Planning adventures; reaching out to others to discuss new ideas.

What will manifest as a result?
Example: IX The Hermit. Time for contemplation; spiritual quest or study.

XX JUDGEMENT

Other Names: The Angel, Fame, Time, Awakening, The Last Judgement

Esoteric Title: The Spirit of the Primal Fire

Number: Twenty

Numerology Link: II The High Priestess

Astrological Sign or Planet: Pluto

Day of the Week: Tuesday

Element: Fire

Hebrew Letter: Shin

Symbol: The tooth

Meaning: Renewal

Tree of Life Pathway: Twenty-first, between Malkuth and Hod

Chakra: Alta major, for the past and past lives

Crystal: Blue moonstone

Archangel: Archangel Gabriel

DESCRIPTION

With their arms raised in praise, six gray figures awaken and rise from their graves. Archangel Gabriel sounds his bannered trumpet, a call to judgement.

KEY MEANINGS

Revelation, assessment, call to service, memories, spiritual awakening, release, second chances, forgiveness, acceptance

UPRIGHT MEANING

Judgement brings a key decision about the future and asks that you assess your past actions and experiences before making that choice and moving on. You may feel pleased with your achievements and relationships so far—and look back with pride and love—or realize that forgiveness is in order. This is an opportunity to go back and give a relationship, place, project, or job a second chance. In finances, the news is positive, and spiritually, the card means awakening to a higher consciousness, so you sense a deeper connection with yourself and with your spirit guides. A further meaning of Judgement is mediumship.

REVERSED MEANING

When reversed, Judgement can show a need to learn past lessons and work on self-acceptance and releasing guilt. A further meaning is delay.

JUDGEMENT'S SYMBOLS

1	**Number XX**	Links with II The High Priestess
2	**The angel**	Message from spirit
3	**Trumpet**	Awakening
4	**Flag**	Unity
5	**Rising dead**	Rebirth
6	**Sea and mountains**	Ascension

What the Symbols Mean for You

When you are drawn to a particular symbol or feature of a card, it's because it holds a special meaning for you. Here is a guide to interpreting your symbols.

1 NUMBER XX

Number XX or 20 reduces to 2 (XX = 20; 2 + 0 = 2), number of II The High Priestess. Both cards deal with duality, the meaning of two—The High Priestess walks between the earthly realm and the spirit world, whereas Judgement calls us to investigate the tension between the past and the present. The two XXs as identical forms also signify balance, and ask us if, on balance, we are satisfied with our past behaviors and decisions.

As the twenty-first card in the major arcana sequence, the Hanged Man takes the twenty-first Shin, which means "renewal"—the outcome of the ritual of self-judgement. On the Tree of Life pathway, Judgement appears between the spheres of Malkuth for the material world and Hod, for the rational mind, offering the meaning of assessment—one of the card's interpretations.

2 THE ANGEL

One of four angels of the tarot, Archangel Gabriel brings God's messages to humanity. Archangel Michael is present too, in Gabriel's flag—Michael is the spiritual manifestation of Saint George (see Flag, at right). Archangel Michael's element is Fire, in keeping with the card's element whereas Gabriel's is Water, symbolized by his blue flowing robe and the sea of consciousness below.

See Archangel Raphael on VI The Lovers and Archangel Michael on XIV Temperance.

3 TRUMPET

The seven lines radiating from the trumpet bell represent the seven tones of the musical scale and, in turn, the seven classical planets, the Moon, Mercury, Venus, Sun, Mars, Jupiter, and Saturn. (In Pythagorean thinking, the ratios of the planets' speed of orbit created tones of energy resulting in sound, hence the term "the music of the spheres.") The trumpet's sound is a universal call of awakening—when we judge the truth of our relationships and actions.

4 FLAG

The flag or banner is that of Saint George, patron saint of England, who is linked with Archangel Michael (see The Angel, at left). The flag was associated with the Knights Templar—the red stood for martyrdom, and the white, faith. More generally, the flag is a symbol of unity and identity.

5 RISING DEAD

The man, woman, and child represent all human life. The six figures are a mirror image for the duality of the past and present, earth and spirit, the living and the dead—the card's planet, Pluto, is the planet of the dead. Their gray skin signifies their unearthly status; at this moment of resurrection they exist between worlds.

6 SEA AND MOUNTAINS

The sea represents consciousness and the white mountains, spiritual aspiration. The figures rise from their coffins leaving behind their past selves on their journey to ascension.

Body Language: Arm Gestures

Four of the card's figures have both arms raised to the side, a gesture of wonder—"Behold!"—that echoes the ancient Egyptian symbol of the Ka, for the life force or spirit. A further interpretation comes from the American occultist and writer Paul Foster Case (1884–1954), who theorizes that all the gestures represent the Latin noun LVX, or LUX, meaning "light": the woman makes the L-shape, the V is in the raised arms and, on his own illustration of the card, the X is in the crossed arms of the male figure. In the Rider Waite Smith card shown here, we see the X not in the figure but in the card's number.

ANGEL MESSAGES

This spread brings through messages from the tarot's four angels, based on the element associated with each archangel.

Take out the four angel cards and place them face up in a row as shown: VI The Lovers, XIV Temperance, XX Judgement and XV The Devil. Then shuffle the remainder of the deck and lay down a card under each angel, facedown, completing a second row as below. When you are ready, turn all the cards face up and begin your interpretation.

1
Archangel Raphael, element of Air: *What in your life needs your close attention now.*

2
Archangel Michael, element of Fire: *What is in or out of balance.*

3
Archangel Gabriel, element of Water: *What hidden truth is to be revealed.*

4
Archangel Uriel, element of Earth: *The higher lesson. How to proceed.*

XXI THE WORLD

Other Name: The Universe
Esoteric Title: The Great One of the Night of Time
Number: Twenty-one
Numerology Link: III The Empress, XII The Hanged Man
Astrological Sign or Planet: Saturn
Day of the Week: Saturday
Element: Earth
Hebrew Letter: Tav (Tau)
  Symbol: The cross
  Meaning: Completion
Tree of Life Pathway: Twenty-second, between Yesod and Malkuth
Chakra: Stellar gateway, the cosmic portal
Crystals: Lemurian seed quartz
Compositional Affinity: The Wheel of Fortune
Animal Symbols: Eagle, bull, lion

DESCRIPTION

Up in the clouds, a human face, eagle, bull, and lion surround a dancer within an oval laurel wreath. The dancer holds two double-ended wands.

KEY MEANINGS

Completion, success, celebration, travel, reward, joy, harmony, togetherness, expansion, acknowledgment

UPRIGHT MEANING

The World signifies success and expansion. It often reveals the completion and celebration of a life stage, predicting anniversaries and passing tests, or enjoying rewards in your career or personal projects. This is a time for travel and expanding your vision, too, and in creative ventures you sense the potential ahead. Relationships thrive under the World's influence as you plan your next chapter and appreciate your time together. A further meaning of the World is acknowledgment, so you feel appreciated beyond your usual circles. Overall, the card brings optimism for the future. The world is rich with possibility.

REVERSED MEANING

The reversed World often shows delay and frustration. You may need to wait a little longer for the result you wanted, or revise your goal.

THE WORLD'S SYMBOLS

1	**Number XXI**	Links with III The Empress and XII The Hanged Man
2	**Double-ended wands**	The Collective
3	**Corner figures**	Elements of life

4	**The world dancer**	Oneness
5	**Red ribbon**	Infinity
6	**Mandorla wreath**	Conception
7	**Scarf**	Renewal

What the Symbols Mean for You

When you are drawn to a particular symbol or feature of a card, it's because it holds a special meaning for you. Here is a guide to interpreting your symbols.

1 NUMBER XXI

XXI The World is related to III The Empress (XXI = 21; 2 + 1 = 3) and XII The Hanged Man (XII = 12; 1 + 2 = 3). The World represents the physical goal of the Empress—the birth of the new, symbolized by the egg-shaped wreath—and the spiritual goal of the Hanged Man, who awaits illumination and evolved consciousness.

XXI also marks the end and beginning of the major arcana cycle; X, the Wheel of Fortune, is the halfway point. The Wheel of Fortune, like the World, also includes symbols of the four evangelists (see Corner Figures, below).

As the twenty-second card in the major arcana sequence, the World is associated with the twenty-second letter of the Hebrew alphabet, Tav, which means "completion"—a central meaning of the World card. On the Tree of Life pathway, the World lies between the spheres of Yesod, for change, and Malkuth, for the material world, or Earth—the card's ruling element.

2 THE WANDS

The wand, a symbol of power and purpose, is double-ended. It signifies balance and the Hermetic maxim "as above, so below"—so what happens in heavenly or spiritual realms manifests on earth. The dancer holds a wand in each hand as they are the opposite of the singular magician—this is about embracing a multitude, the whole world.

See the double-ended wand on I The Magician.

3 CORNER FIGURES

The angel and three animals depicted in the card corners are the four evangelists of the New Testament: The angel is Matthew. The lion is Mark. The bull is Luke, and the eagle is associated with John. They also symbolize the fixed signs of the zodiac and the four elements, the building blocks of life.

See these symbols on X The Wheel of Fortune.

4 THE WORLD DANCER

The world dancer is the animus mundi, or "soul of the world," dancing in celebration. The figure is a symbol of self-integration—the point at which all the Fool's experiences through the major arcana become a part of him. The dancer also embodies different forms of consciousness—the conscious self, the subconscious, and the higher self that connects to collective consciousness. The dancer has breasts and allegedly male genitalia hidden behind the scarf, which refers to the previous two cards XIX The Sun (masculine) and XVIII The Moon (feminine), and together signify wholeness. Yet the dancer is also genderless—the summit of human experience reached, we go beyond the body and beyond gender, existing purely in soul form before rebirth.

5 RED RIBBON

The ribbon ties at the top and base of the wreath make the shape of the lemniscate or infinity symbol, for eternal life and energy.

See the lemniscate on I The Magician and VIII Strength.

6 MANDORLA WREATH

The laurel wreath is a symbol of success. This success is deserved—the card's planet, Saturn, says we have learned lessons and worked hard. The mandorla symbolizes heaven on earth (the mandorla often frames images of holy figures in religious art). As it has the form of an egg, the mandorla also signifies successful conception; it is the egg ready to be born as 0 The Fool.

7 SCARF

The scarf may reference the Staff of Asclepius, an ancient symbol of healing and resurrection traditionally depicted as a snake coiled around a staff. The clue lies in the fluidity of the shape—on older versions of the card the scarf is given texture, like snakeskin.

The Mandorla in the Minors

The mandorla, the wreath at the heart of XXI The World also appears on the Ace of Pentacles: the symbol is created by the archway in the flowering hedge. Through a field of lilies, a path leads to the arch that frames the mountains beyond. The arch is a portal, like the World's mandorla, through which we travel to gain the experience our soul needs. We also see a partial stone arch on the Ten of Pentacles; this divides the outer and inner spaces of the house's grounds. In this way, the arch marks the shift between our public persona and inner, private lives.

RECURRING SITUATIONS

As the World marks the completion and beginning of a new cycle, this spread reveals a recurring situation in your life and the lesson it brings.

To begin, take out XXI The World and place the card face up as shown to oversee the reading. Then shuffle the cards, asking, "Show me my recurring situation," and choose three. Place them face down below the World as shown. Turn the cards face up and begin your interpretation.

1

The recurring situation
Example: Four of Pentacles. Self-dependency and/or materialism; clinging to money and the idea of stability.

2

Advice
Example: Eight of Swords. Do not let fear keep you trapped in this cycle; without negative thoughts, you can connect with the guidance in card 3.

3

Guidance for healing this cycle
Example: XII The Hanged Man. A spiritual lesson is coming; you find the perspective you need.

MINOR ARCANA SYMBOLS

CHAPTER 3

ACE OF CUPS

Esoteric Title: Root of the Powers of Water
Number: One
Astrological Associations: The Water signs—Cancer, Scorpio, and Pisces
Element: Water
Major Arcana Link: I The Magician
Season: Summer
Tree of Life Position: Kether the crown, sphere of divine light
Compositional Affinity: All minor arcana Aces
Animal Symbol: Dove

DESCRIPTION

From a cloud, a hand presents a golden chalice that overflows with five rivulets flowing into a lily pond. A dove with a communion wafer is about to descend into the chalice.

KEY MEANINGS

Beginnings, love, joy, empathy, relationships, fertility, pregnancy, creativity, spiritual connection, healing, wisdom

UPRIGHT MEANING

A new love begins. Expect deep, and potentially overwhelming, emotions—this is a card of conception, pregnancy, birth, and falling in love with something or someone new. In established relationships love flows, and in projects, creativity shines as you explore a new passion and birth ideas. Spiritually, you find a new calling.

REVERSED MEANING

The reversed card shows blocks in creative projects including potential fertility issues; also, disappointment and trust issues in a new relationship.

THE ACE OF CUPS' SYMBOLS

1	**Number I**	Beginnings and oneness
2	**Chalice**	Faith and fertility
3	**M/W symbol**	Wisdom
4	**Dove and Host**	Divine spirit
5	**Hand**	Invitation
6	**Rivulets**	Flow of emotion
7	**Water lily**	Purity and rebirth
8	**Droplets**	Divine grace
9	**Bells**	News

What the Symbols Mean for You

When you are drawn to a particular symbol or feature of a card, it's because it holds a special meaning for you. Here is a guide to interpreting your symbols.

1 NUMBER I

One, or Ace, is the number of beginnings and oneness (feeling "at one" within and with the divine). All Aces also relate to card I The Magician in the major arcana, who displays each suit symbol on his altar (see page 22). As the first card of its suit, the Ace holds the essence of the Water element for emotion and spiritual connection, shown by the card's Tree of Life sphere of Kether, for divine light.

2 CHALICE

The chalice or ceremonial cup is used perform the Eucharist, the Christian ceremony honoring the blood and body of Jesus. It is also a symbol of the womb, so in this card takes the meaning of faith and fertility.

See the chalice on the Queen of Cups and XIV Temperance.

3 M/W SYMBOL

The meaning of M/W is unknown. The initial M may stand for mother—for the chalice as womb symbol—or the Hebrew letter Mem, which means "waters" and represents wisdom.

4 DOVE AND HOST

The dove is a symbol of love and peace. In its beak is the Host—the communion wafer marked with the symbol of the cross—which is the spark of divinity. The spirit is about the enter the cup, symbol of the body or womb: this is the moment of conception.

5 HAND

The hand offering the chalice represents an invitation and a gift. Traditionally, the right hand is the hand of giving and the left the hand of receiving.

See the giving hands on the Ace of Pentacles, Wands, and Swords.

6 RIVULETS

The five streams symbolize the five senses—through which we experience feeling, which relates to the Water element of the card. A symbol of high sensitivity; emotion flows.

See the five streams on XVII The Star.

7 WATER LILY

Along with its general meaning of purity and rebirth, specifically the water lily symbolizes the resurrection (of Christ), so the flower also signifies spiritual connection.

8 DROPLETS

The twenty-six droplets are formed in the shape of the Hebrew letter Yod, which means "the divine hand of God" and the element of fire. Yod is the first letter of Y, H, V, H, the name of God in Hebrew: the values of each letter add up to 26. A further meaning of the droplets is tears—an emotional outpouring—or even semen, in alignment with the card's meaning of fertility.

See the droplets on the Ace of Swords, XVI The Tower, and XVIII The Moon.

9 BELLS

The tiny bell decorations just under the bowl of the chalice symbolize good news.

TWO OF CUPS

Esoteric Title: Love
Number: Two
Astrological Associations: Venus in Cancer
Element: Water
Season: Summer
Tree of Life Position: Chockmah, the sphere of wisdom
Compositional Affinity: VI The Lovers
Animal Symbols: Lion, snake

DESCRIPTION

A young man and woman offer one another a golden cup. Above them is a caduceus and winged lion and, in the distance, a country home.

KEY MEANINGS

Love, partnerships, soul mates, commitment, creative partnerships, forgiveness, harmony, healing, support

UPRIGHT MEANING

This is a card of love and harmony, which extends to all forms of relationship—romantic, family, chosen family, friends, and colleagues. It favors partnerships, so new love grows and in existing relationships there is more commitment, such as an engagement, marriage, or moving in together. In your career, study, or creative projects, you find the right person to work with, as ideas flow. A further meaning is forgiveness and reconciliation, so past hurts are healed.

REVERSED MEANING

When reversed, the card shows a relationship under stress or on hold. There may be practical reasons for this, but if not, let your intuition speak: follow the thread.

THE TWO OF CUPS' SYMBOLS

1	**Number II**	Partnership and duality
2	**Cups**	Faith in love
3	**Caduceus**	Balance and peace
4	**Winged lion**	Passion and protection
5	**Female figure**	The High Priestess: Intuition
6	**Male figure**	The Fool: Risk
7	**House and fields**	Aspiration

What the Symbols Mean for You

When you are drawn to a particular symbol or feature of a card, it's because it holds a special meaning for you. Here is a guide to interpreting your symbols.

1 NUMBER II

Two, number of duality, is reflected in the two cups and two people. The design of the card is almost symmetrical, mirroring balance in the relationship. This is a meeting of hearts and of equals, so the message is love and support, which reflects the card's astrological association of Venus in Cancer.

2 CUPS

The chalice or cup is a symbol of emotion, as it holds water; as the cup resembles the womb, it also means fertility and transformation. The couple are about to exchange cups as an act of faith; they trust the love they will receive from one another.

3 CADUCEUS

The two entwined snakes and winged lion form the caduceus, meaning "herald's staff." It is a symbol of Mercury, the messenger-god (the Greek Hermes) and means balance and peace.

4 WINGED LION

The winged lion is a symbol of passion and protection. Associated with the element of Fire, the creature also represents the spark of physical attraction between the couple. This Two is similar in composition to VI The Lovers, which also shows a couple plus a winged protector. In this way, the lion echoes the Lover's Archangel Raphael as a symbol of spiritual protection, too.

5 FEMALE FIGURE

The female figure wears an olive crown for peace and success. Her blue and white robes are like those of the intuitive High Priestess. As the walker between the spirit world and material world, the High Priestess brings a sense of altered reality, which, for the two lovers, is the headiness of being in love. The High Priestess is also associated with wisdom, the meaning of the card's Tree of Life sphere of Chockmah.

6 MALE FIGURE

The male figure wears a crown of red flowers, for love and success. He is dressed in a similar way to that of 0 The Fool in a patterned tunic with yellow leggings and boots. He tentatively reaches out to the woman's cup, a gesture of sexual intent.

7 HOUSE AND FIELDS

The country scene, with the house on the hill, could be the forerunner of the dream house in the Ten of Cups. In this card, it represents the domestic life they might aspire to.

THREE OF CUPS

Esoteric Title: Abundance
Number: Three
Astrological Associations: Mercury in Cancer
Element: Water
Season: Summer
Tree of Life Position: Binah, the sphere of compassion and understanding

DESCRIPTION

Three women, two wearing garlands, dance together and raise their cups in a toast. Around them are the ripened fruits of summer.

KEY MEANINGS

Happiness, parties, weddings, Christenings and naming ceremonies, anniversaries, friendship, socializing, flirtation, hedonism, indulgence, creativity, healing

UPRIGHT MEANING

This is the celebration card of the tarot, bringing happy occasions, reunions, and new people into your life: you reignite friendships and form new, undemanding romantic relationships. It's also a time for sensuality and feeling rather than thinking, so you find emotional replenishment, healing, and nourishment, particularly through friends, family, and chosen family. The Three also brings creativity, so you may feel aligned with arts and other personal projects now that bring you fulfillment.

REVERSED MEANING

When reversed, the card reveals imbalance, which can manifest as overindulgence or inappropriate responses. This may mean distance in some relationships and too much intensity in others.

THE THREE OF CUPS' SYMBOLS

1	**Number III**	Creative power
2	**Toasting cups**	Celebration
3	**Three women**	Unity
4	**Fruits**	Abundance
5	**Blue sky**	Optimism and clarity

What the Symbols Mean for You

When you are drawn to a particular symbol or feature of a card, it's because it holds a special meaning for you. Here is a guide to interpreting your symbols.

1 NUMBER III

Number Three is expressed as three women and three cups. Three is the number of creative fulfillment—the beginning, middle, and end, or completion. A dynamic number associated with the element of Fire, three activates the card's element of Water, so feelings and conversation flows. Mercury in Cancer, the cards' astrological association, also expresses light-hearted enjoyment and new social adventures, while Binah, the Three's Tree of Life sphere, brings the qualities of compassion and understanding—the basis of strong friendship.

2 TOASTING CUPS

Three cups raised in a toast signify celebration and express bonds of friendship. The toast also brings the women physically close, emphasizing their connection. The card's composition may be based on Raphael's painting *The Three Graces*: three women stand together just like those on our card, offering an apple to one other rather than a cup. The apple is a symbol of love, so also signifies a bond. Offering with the right hand is significant, too, as in tarot the right side denotes what is to come: holding up their cups, the trio makes a toast to the future.

3 THREE WOMEN

The women echo the Three Graces of antiquity. The daughters of Zeus or Dionysus, they represented grace, beauty, and charm—attributes of the card's astrological association, Mercury in Cancer. This Three card also links to the major arcana: the woman in white is the maiden from VIII Strength; the woman in red is XI Justice; the woman in yellow has similar coloring to Archangel Gabriel on Temperance, card XIV. These are the virtue cards in the deck that guide us to find balance—physically with Strength, spiritually and emotionally with Temperance, and mentally with Justice. In this way the virtue cards—and the three dancing women—symbolize body, mind, and spirit, dancing in unity.

See the maiden on VIII Strength.
See the judge on XI Justice.
See the angel on XIV Temperance.

4 FRUITS

On the ground we see ripe fruits and a pumpkin, symbols of harvest, abundance, and generosity of spirt. The purple grapes are also symbols of Dionysus (Roman Bacchus) god of vegetation, wine, and ecstasy. Dionysus (or in some sources, Zeus) was the father of the Three Graces (see Three Women, above). Overall, the fruits tell us it is time for life's sensual pleasures.

5 BLUE SKY

The cloudless sky signifies no doubt or confusion; this is clearly a time of optimism and happiness.

FOUR OF CUPS

Esoteric Title: Blended Pleasure

Number: Four

Astrological Association: Moon in Cancer

Element: Water

Season: Summer

Tree of Life Position: Chesed, the sphere of love and mercy

Compositional Affinity: Ace of Cups

DESCRIPTION

A young man sits beneath a tree, his arms and legs crossed. A hand from a cloud offers a golden cup; three more cups stand before him on the grass.

KEY MEANINGS

Boredom, flatness, restlessness, disillusion, static situations, retreat, avoidance, despondency, emotional risks

UPRIGHT MEANING

This Four is the card of despondency; it shows flat situations and boredom, particularly in love and work. If a relationship has become stuck, it is time to try new ways forward; in work, trust yourself and take a risk rather than be worn down by disappointment. If you are hoping to meet someone new, don't let the past skew your expectations. The card can also show that you're waiting for a clear sign—or intuitive hit—before you commit or recommit to an enterprise or relationship. This card is that sign.

REVERSED MEANING

The upright meaning becomes acute in the reversed card, so there is even more need to be open to change and create your own opportunities.

THE FOUR OF CUPS' SYMBOLS

1	**Number IV**	Stability
2	**The offered cup**	An invitation
3	**Crossed arms**	Emotional retreat
4	**Hebrew letter Tet**	Hidden goodness; potential
5	**Attire**	Suppression
6	**Young tree**	Youth

What the Symbols Mean for You

When you are drawn to a particular symbol or feature of a card, it's because it holds a special meaning for you. Here is a guide to interpreting your symbols.

1 NUMBER IV

Four is the number of stability and the element of Earth. Earth is slow energy—but Water, the card's element, needs to flow, so the combination of Earth and Water equals stagnation. The card's Tree of Life sphere is Chesed, for loving kindness; its astrological association of Moon in Cancer also brings love and sensitivity, along with intuition. However, Moon in Cancer conjunction also means nostalgia: holding on to the past, there's a reluctance to embrace change, shown by the man's crossed arms.

2 THE OFFERED CUP

A hand holds out a cup, an invitation to the seated figure, who does not look up: he has no curiosity to see what the cup might contain, as if he has already decided it will be of no benefit. Unless he looks up and engages with the cup—symbol of the emotions involved—little can change.

See the offered cup on the Ace of Cups.

3 CROSSED ARMS

The figure's crossed arms and legs indicate self-protection. The crossed arms constitute a broken infinity symbol, which represents blocked energy.

See the crossed arms on the Nine of Cups.

4 HEBREW LETTER TET

Hidden within the tree foliage is a symbol that resembles the Hebrew letter Tet, or Teth, meaning hidden goodness. Tet's symbol is the serpent, which we see in the serpent belt of I The Magician; the Four of Cups' man is the unrealized magus, yet to discover his power. We also see this similarity physically—both figures have a similar look, with their dark straight hair and fringes.

5 ATTIRE

The male figure wears a vibrant red tunic partially covered by a long tunic, symbolizing suppressed desire—red is color of action and passion. The fabric of the tunic appears rough like sackcloth, a symbol of martyrdom.

6 YOUNG TREE

Trees denote wisdom, longevity, and protection—here, the male figure appears to seek refuge beneath its canopy. Trees have long been associated with the body and representing the life of a young person, so this young oak signifies the man's youth.

FIVE OF CUPS

Esoteric Title: Loss in pleasure

Number: Five

Astrological Association: Mars in Scorpio

Element: Water

Season: Summer

Tree of Life Position: Geburah, the sphere of power and destruction

DESCRIPTION

A cloaked figure in black stands by a river. Three cups before him are overturned, their contents spilled on the ground; two cups behind him remain upright.

KEY MEANINGS

Sadness, grief, shame, loss, departure, past sorrows, memories, imbalance, support, options

UPRIGHT MEANING

This is undoubtedly a card of loss and sadness, and there is little you can do but honor your feelings. The loss is around what you love and value, and this card applies particularly to relationships and can indicate grief due to bereavement (note that the card does not predict bereavement, however, but relates to the aftermath). A further meaning is shame and feeling you have somehow failed. However, this will pass; support is available from close friends and family when you are ready to receive it.

REVERSED MEANING

When reversed, the card is more positive because it says the dark days are nearly over; you recover and come to a place of acceptance.

THE FIVE OF CUPS' SYMBOLS

1	**Number V**	Tests
2	**Five cups**	Imbalance
3	**Blood and water**	Sacrifice and hope
4	**River**	Separation
5	**Cloaked figure**	Protection
6	**Bridge**	Transitions
7	**Double arches**	Healing

What the Symbols Mean for You

When you are drawn to a particular symbol or feature of a card, it's because it holds a special meaning for you. Here is a guide to interpreting your symbols.

1 NUMBER V

Five is the number of imbalance and disruption; as an odd number, nothing is even or settled. Five in the sensitive suit of Cups with its element of Water means unsettled emotions. As the number of fingers on the hand, five is associated with human experience—and all of life's attendant tests and challenges. In the Five of Cups Mars, planet of war meets Scorpio, sign of death and the past, so intense emotions surface.

2 FIVE CUPS

Five's meaning of imbalance is demonstrated here in the three overturned cups (what has been lost) and two upright cups (a symbol of hope). Life is out of balance—all the cloaked figure can see are what has been spilled rather than what remains.

3 BLOOD AND WATER

Two cups have spilled blood, a symbol of vitality, sacrifice, and death. This is confirmation that a situation or relationship that has taken much energy is over, which also links with the card's Tree of Life association of Geburah, sphere of power and destruction. However, from a third cup comes water, pooled like tears. Tears bring release and understanding; as the earth is watered, there is hope for new life.

See the pooled water in XVII The Star, the card of hope.

4 RIVER

The flowing river is a reference to the fabled Styx, the river that divided the living from the dead. On the far bank is a structure—it may be the home the mourner has left behind or a church, symbol of faith and stability; either way, he has become separated from the comfort of home and religion. The river is a reminder that sorrow can create feelings of isolation.

See the river as a separation symbol on the Knight of Cups.

5 CLOAKED FIGURE

On early editions of the cards, the figure has a red face, for shame and embarrassment. The figure is shrouded in black, the color of mourning and of self-protection, and his head is tucked into his wing-like shoulders like a sleeping crow. Not everything is black, though—his boots are an everyday brown, so we know the cloak is not his usual attire. When mourning is over, he will put it aside.

6 BRIDGE

Bridges are symbols of change, moving from one place to another. Here, the meaning is states of mind. The mourner could walk the bridge and take in the view from the tower, but he is not ready for this broader perspective. The two arches under the bridge symbolize the duality we feel when in recovery from loss—living in the past and the present at once.

7 DOUBLE ARCHES

The two arches of the bridge divide the river; this may show how it is possible to separate grief for a time while staying in the flow of everyday life.

See the double arches on the Four of Wands.

SIX OF CUPS

Esoteric Title: Pleasure
Number: Six
Astrological Association: Sun in Scorpio
Element: Water
Season: Summer
Tree of Life Position: Tiphareth, the sphere of beauty and rebirth

DESCRIPTION

Two children meet in the garden of a manor house. The larger figure holds a cup; five more surround them, all filled with white flowers and leaves.

KEY MEANINGS

Memories, nostalgia, reunion, the past, visitors, grown-up children, affection, forgiveness, harmony, peace

UPRIGHT MEANING

This is a happy time of reconnection and memories as you reminisce about the past or meet up with old friends and family in person. This reaffirms your bond, bringing peace and sweetness into your life. The Six is also a card of reconciliation, reassuring you that all will be well. There's a childhood influence, too, as you remember the freedom of your early years or spend time with children. A traditional meaning of the card is "the visitor," so expect surprise visits—a former partner or old love interest may just reappear.

REVERSED MEANING

The reversed card can reveal sentimentality and living too much in the past to avoid current challenges.

THE SIX OF CUPS' SYMBOLS

1	**Number VI**	Harmony
2	**The six cups**	Peace
3	**Two figures**	Development and play
4	**White flowers**	Pure intentions
5	**The red hood**	A blessing in disguise
6	**Another face**	Hidden feelings
7	**The manor house**	High status
8	**Retreating figure**	Trust
9	**Family crest**	The number ten

What the Symbols Mean for You

When you are drawn to a particular symbol or feature of a card, it's because it holds a special meaning for you. Here is a guide to interpreting your symbols.

1 NUMBER VI

Six is the number of harmony and completion. With the card's element of Water, harmonious feelings flow. Sun in Scorpio, the card's astrological expression, brings together Scorpio's association with the past in the Sun's positive light—which means "to remember the past with fondness and contentment." The card's Tree of Life sphere of Tiphareth for beauty and rebirth also links with the idea of the renaissance of a friendship, familial bond, or romance.

2 THE SIX CUPS

Four cups appear in the foreground; one rests on a plinth, like a trophy, and the other is held as a gift. The trophy cup is behind the hooded figure, which represents past happiness; the offered cup symbolizes friendship and affection in the present, while the four cups signify emotional stability. As a group of six, they symbolize harmony, or, if forgiveness is in order, a peace offering.

3 TWO FIGURES

The two figures may represent a child and parent—a grown child comes home to find his mother in her garden (she is wearing gardening gloves), or even two children at play. However, the figure who looks most childlike in his red hood is much larger than the smaller female, so his size indicates his development and growth in the world beyond the manor house.

4 WHITE FLOWERS

The cups hold white flowers, signifying spiritual growth. White is the color of purity; as the white flowers are an offering, this says that the giver has pure intentions toward the recipient. The white flower may be datura, apple-thorn flower, or the white balloon flower—all have healing properties and are annuals. As the card means "visits," the flowers suggest people who make an annual or seasonal appearance.

5 THE RED HOOD

The red hood evokes fairy tales and childhood, expressing the card's meaning of happy memories. The hood is a symbol of disguise; as red signifies positivity and action, the red hood means a blessing in disguise.

See the hood on the Three of Pentacles.

6 ANOTHER FACE

Look closely at the woman's hair and you see another face turning away from the figure in red. This can signify that there is more to this relationship than meets the eye; perhaps she has feelings she keeps to herself.

7 THE MANOR HOUSE

We see a manor house here and a tower that might be part of a chapel. Along with the heraldic shield below the plinth, this suggests that this is the domain of an important family who had their own chapel and lands. The shield with its X-shaped saltire cross has multiple meanings, including protection and endurance.

See the manor house on the Ten of Pentacles.

8 RETREATING FIGURE

The retreating figure appears to be a guard with a lance. He is no longer needed to guard the perimeter of the house because the visitor is welcome; the house is open to him.

9 FAMILY CREST

The crest is the saltire cross—its X is the number 10, so foreshadows the happiness we see in the Ten of Cups.

See other family emblems on the Two of Wands and Ten of Pentacles.

SEVEN OF CUPS

Esoteric Title: Illusionary Success
Number: Seven
Astrological Association: Venus in Scorpio
Element: Water
Season: Summer
Tree of Life Position: Netzach, the sphere of endurance, instinct, and desire
Animal symbols: Snake, salamander/dragon

DESCRIPTION

Seven gold cups appear to hover in clouds, each one bearing an object. In the foreground is a man in shadow with his back to us, his right hand raised.

KEY MEANINGS

Fantasy, imagination, creative choices, illusion, opportunities, confusion, choices, idealism

UPRIGHT MEANING

This Seven is the card of confusion, delusion, and choices. Positively, a situation or relationship has potential, but these are early days. And, while wild ideas may be captivating, what you contemplate may not materialize. The danger is losing yourself in a fantasy rather than examine the offer in the cup—and even then, it is likely that you will need more information before you can decide. Tune into your intuition, too, to find your way through the clouds. In creative work, the seven cups often reveal a choice of techniques or forms.

REVERSED MEANING

The reversed card can reveal obsessions, avoidance of the facts, and potential deception, particularly in romantic relationships.

THE SEVEN OF CUPS' SYMBOLS

1	**Number VII**	Number of potential
2	**The arrangement of cups**	Heaven or earth
3	**Shroud**	What is awakening
4	**Snake**	Wisdom or flattery
5	**Forked tongue**	Truth or lies
6	**Wreath**	Fame or its shadow
7	**Jewels**	Reward
8	**Castle**	Imagination and ambition
9	**Angel**	Guidance
10	**Shadow figure**	Being in the dark

What the Symbols Mean for You

When you are drawn to a particular symbol or feature of a card, it's because it holds a special meaning for you. Here is a guide to interpreting your symbols.

1 NUMBER VII

Seven is the number of potential. Sevens are traditionally associated with mysteries—including the mysteries of the unseen future—along with luck, divinity, and magic. The combination of mystery and the emotional element of Water leads to great leaps of imagination—hence the fantastical nature of the card. The combination of Venus in Scorpio means extreme passions, which relates to the cards' upright meaning of illusion and delusion, and the reversed meaning of obsession. The Tree of Life sphere of Netzach brings in the element of desire—in that the cups symbolize the material things we might crave.

2 THE ARRANGEMENT OF CUPS

The cups are arranged into two groups, a three and a four. Three means heaven while four signifies earth and together, heaven on earth. We wish that potential translates into reality.

See heaven on earth on I The Magician.

3 SHROUD

The shroud signifies what is hidden and symbolizes Christ and awakening consciousness.

4 SNAKE

The snake is a symbol of wisdom, healing, and transformation. In Christian belief it signifies flattery and betrayal; the snake is dangerously close to Christ's cup, suggesting the betrayal of Christ by Judas.

See the snake on VI The Lovers and X The Wheel of Fortune.

5 FORKED TONGUE

The cup holds a salamander or dragon with a forked tongue, which signifies lies. Next to the victory wreath, it also tells of the pitfalls of fame: confidantes may not be trustworthy.

6 WREATH

The cup holding the wreath, symbol of victory, is etched with a faint skull. There are two interpretations: First, that reputation outlives death, and second, that the fame has a shadow side.

See the wreath on the Six of Wands and Two of Cups, VII The Chariot, and XXI The World.

7 JEWELS

This is the treasure we hope to find: the reward that comes with fame, symbolized by the wreath. We need to discern if the jewels are genuine.

8 CASTLE

The castle may be the "castle in the air," a symbol of fairy tales and fantasy; it also signifies ambition.

9 ANGEL

The face of the angel means spiritual guidance. He appears like Archangel Michael, overseeing what is about to unfold.

See Archangel Michael on XIV Temperance.

10 SHADOW FIGURE

Like the shadowy figure, we are also in the dark, trying to discern what is true and what is false.

EIGHT OF CUPS

Esoteric Title: Abandoned Success
Number: Eight
Astrological Association: Saturn in Pisces
Element: Water
Season: Summer
Tree of Life Position: Hod, the sphere of majesty and the mind

DESCRIPTION

A traveler, his back to us, is already on his journey. Walking a coastal path toward rocky mountains under a waning moon, he leaves behind eight standing cups.

KEY MEANINGS

Departure, endings, travel, search, quest, change, emotional intelligence, right timing, cycles

UPRIGHT MEANING

This card reveals a change of heart. You may no longer want what you have, so need to move on. There is no drama in this decision, which may be long overdue; this is a quiet departure that will be easier than anticipated. The card often comes up to signal the end of a relationship, a change in your working life, or walking away from a position you hold. You need more than is available to you, and now is the time to find it. More literally, the card shows journeys and, overall, moving toward what you heart desires.

REVERSED MEANING

What reversed, the meaning is to find the right time to act and acknowledging when change is needed. A further interpretation is a situation ending before you are ready.

THE EIGHT OF CUPS' SYMBOLS

1	**Number VIII**	Cycles and renewal
2	**The missing cup**	The quest
3	**Sun-moon**	Heart's pain
4	**The red cloak**	Action and energy
5	**Low tide**	Exposure

What the Symbols Mean for You

When you are drawn to a particular symbol or feature of a card,
it's because it holds a special meaning for you. Here is a guide to interpreting your symbols.

1 NUMBER VIII

Eight, number of fulfillment and renewal, is also the lemniscate (infinity symbol) for the infinite flow of energy. Eight in the card's element of Water suggests a baptismal font, which has eight sides. This expresses the card's meaning of change and rebirth, as a new cycle is about to begin. The astrological association for the Eight is Saturn in Pisces, which places tough-minded Saturn with idealistic Pisces. Perhaps this is why the Eight feels like a relief: all the work of thinking has been done, and now we can follow our own flow. The card's Tree of Life association is Hod, sphere of majesty and the mind. Hod's virtue is truthfulness—a reminder that when we leave a position or relationship, we ideally so do to seek our own truth.

See the lemniscate in I The Magician and VIII Strength, and in the arm position of the figure on the Nine of Cups.

2 THE MISSING CUP

Looking at the two rows of cups in the foreground, their spacing is uneven—this shows that something is missing; emotionally, there is a gap to be filled. Maybe the retreating figure has taken the ninth cup and carries it under his cloak. The cup is a symbol of faith and the Holy Grail—the cup from which Christ drank during the Last Supper, which is associated with rebirth and miracles. In this way, our cloaked figure begins his quest to find his own Holy Grail.

3 SUN-MOON

The sun signifies the sleeping conscious self, while the moon represents the hidden or unconscious self. We can see this as head and heart, and the heart, or moon leads—as the sun sits inside the moon crescent. The moon is also waning, denoting decrease and endings.

See the sun-moon on XVIII The Moon.

4 THE RED CLOAK

Red stands for action, passion, and energy. The traveler is focused just on what is ahead of him and does not look back. He knows he has the strength to make his journey, and his path, away from the rockpools, is well lit.

See the turned back as a symbol of focus on the Three of Wands.

5 LOW TIDE

At low tide, we see what has been hidden from view—all the hope that lives in the ocean of wisdom and all the fear, too. The rocks, therefore, symbolize emerging issues or truths that feel dangerous. A further meaning of low tide is waiting, or feeling trapped until the tide comes in, but our traveler is not dependent on the cycles of the sea; he must walk now, as this is his time for departure.

See low tide on the Two and Eight of Swords.

NINE OF CUPS

Esoteric Title: Happiness

Number: Nine

Astrological Association: Jupiter in Pisces

Element: Water

Season: Summer

Tree of Life Position: Yesod, the sphere of foundation and the unconscious

DESCRIPTION

A man in a red hat sits on a bench before a table lined with nine golden cups. His arms crossed, he has an expression of satisfaction.

KEY MEANINGS

Manifestation, abundance, prosperity, generosity, luck, happiness, social occasions, fulfillment, romance, spirituality

UPRIGHT MEANING

One of the happiest cards in the deck, this Nine brings joy, abundance, and connection. This is the time to appreciate and share what you have, and manifest more of what you desire. It is a card of wishes come true and feeling fulfilled in life—so it reveals joyful relationships, romance, spiritual connection, close friendships, and celebration; you share your good fortune. In work and projects, you find instant support and input, such as a dream collaborator or finance angel. The Universe delivers what you need right now.

REVERSED MEANING

When reversed, there is much ego on show, and you may be dealing with narcissism; a further interpretation is delay and miscommunication.

THE NINE OF CUPS' SYMBOLS

1	**Number IX**	Number of integration and intensity
2	**Crossed arms**	Give and take
3	**The nine cups**	Security
4	**The blue cloth**	Flow
5	**Feathered hat**	Success
6	**Striped tunic**	Humility

What the Symbols Mean for You

When you are drawn to a particular symbol or feature of a card, it's because it holds a special meaning for you. Here is a guide to interpreting your symbols.

1 NUMBER IX

Nine is the number of integration and intensity. In the minor arcana, nine carries the weight of all the number cards that precede it, holding that energy until the release and expression of the Ten. All the lessons of the previous cards integrate at this stage, so in the emotional, imaginative suit of Cups, we see an abundance of love and joy—the culmination of the suit's journey through love, loss, forgiveness, and change. Nine in the suit's element of Water intensifies what is dear to us, while the astrological association of Jupiter in Pisces, for luck and ideals, gives the card's meaning of sharing good fortune. The card's Tree of Life sphere of Yesod represents hidden forces and mysteries—such as signs from the Universe that answer prayers and wishes.

2 CROSSED ARMS

The man's arms form the lemniscate, or infinity symbol, for energy-flow and renewal. This signifies that he understands the flow of love and money—that when we give to others unconditionally, we will continue to receive all we need.

See the lemniscate on I The Magician and VII Strength.

3 THE NINE CUPS

Cups are symbols of faith and emotion and as a womb symbol, fertility. According to the cards' co-creator A. E. Waite, the vessels are filled with wine left after a banquet, which indicates that the future will be abundant and secure. We can also sense this stability through the positioning of the cups on the table; some appear to be touching, a sign of intimacy and connection. A further meaning is that the cups appear as trophies, displayed to be admired and celebrated. The cups make a partial arc, foreshadowing the rainbow of hope on the next card in the suit.

See the rainbow on the Ten of Cups.

4 THE BLUE CLOTH

The drape and color of the cloth link with the card's element of Water, for the heart and relationships. Relationships prosper and feelings flow.

5 FEATHERED HAT

The red hat and red feather symbolize vitality and joie de vivre. The feather also links with the idiom of having a feather in one's cap. Traditionally this feather was a hunting trophy, and now a symbol of achievement; the man who wears it on the Nine is proud of his success.

See the red feather on 0 The Fool, XIII Death, and XIX The Sun.

6 STRIPED TUNIC

The striped tunic does not match the luxurious look of the man's feathered hat—it is workwear, suggesting he comes from humble beginnings.

TEN OF CUPS

Esoteric Title: Perfected Success
Number: Ten
Astrological Association: Mars in Pisces
Element: Water
Season: Summer
Tree of Life Position: Malkuth, the Kingdom, the sphere of experience

DESCRIPTION

A man and woman behold a rainbow with an arc of golden cups. Two children play nearby, the family home just upstream.

KEY MEANINGS

Love, bliss, family, fulfillment, happiness, dream home, prosperity, love, commitment, perfect friendship, appreciation

UPRIGHT MEANING

The Ten is the ultimate expression of love, stability, and positivity: the card brings harmony in relationships and stronger family bonds. A romantic relationship is blissful and leads to deeper love and commitment. Everything comes together in all life aspects, so you find success in business partnerships, career, and creative projects, too. It is a particularly auspicious card for group activities and closeness, so expect weddings, parties, and other social opportunities. Further meanings include spending time with children and finding your dream home.

REVERSED MEANING

When reversed, the card's meaning is largely positive, but there may be unsettling changes in family dynamics and friendships; communication will improve in time.

THE TEN OF CUPS' SYMBOLS

1	**Number X**	Number of completion
2	**The ten cups**	Happiness
3	**Rainbow**	Miracles and reward
4	**House**	Kingdom
5	**Family groups**	Unity and containment

What the Symbols Mean for You

When you are drawn to a particular symbol or feature of a card, it's because it holds a special meaning for you. Here is a guide to interpreting your symbols.

1 NUMBER X

Ten, the first double number, marks the ending of one cycle and the beginning of another; the number 10 comprises 1 for beginnings and the zero, with its circular form, is a symbol of completion. The meaning of the Tens, whether positive or negative, arises from the nature of the suit: a multitude of Cups brings bliss and love. The card's astrological association is Mars in Pisces—Mars may be warlike, but Pisces brings softness and intuition: together, they signify the powerful emotion of the Ten of Cups.

2 THE TEN CUPS

Cups are symbols of faith and emotion and as a womb symbol, fertility. Four of the cups are touching, symbolizing the close relationship between the two adults and two children. The Ten also signifies completeness; here, a complete family of four.

3 RAINBOW

The rainbow is a sign of miracles and reward—hence the idea of treasure at rainbow's end. The rainbow does not have seven colors, but creates the effect with pastel shades—pink, blue/green and yellow; the simplified rainbow denotes the pleasure we gain from life's simple pleasures: love, nature, and home.

4 HOUSE

The house symbolizes security. The red roof signifies life and vitality, so this is a lively, productive home; nestling in trees by a brook, it also denotes the ideal place to live. The card's Tree of Life sphere of Malkuth, the kingdom, is a sign that our own kingdom or piece of heaven is within reach.

5 FAMILY GROUPS

The couple have their backs to us, and there are almost a mirror-image of one another, making the same gesture of wonder and of a similar height and build; a symbol of togetherness and completion. The children play together, in their own world. They may symbolize the inner child, and the return of childhood happiness.

PAGE OF CUPS

Other Names: Princess, Knave, or Jack of Cups

Esoteric Titles: The Princess of the Waters and the Lotus

Element: Earth of the suit of Water

Animal Symbol: Fish

DESCRIPTION

A young person appears by the sea. He bears a golden cup and, inside it, a live fish—which appears to be communicating with him.

KEY MEANINGS

Beginnings, news, new relationships, socializing, partnerships, playfulness, creativity, psychic work

UPRIGHT MEANING

As an influence: The card brings beginnings in the form of friendships and other key relationships. It's also a time for playfulness and letting your intuition guide you toward a new creative pathway. There is also good news about relationships, from family or chosen family to work relationships, too. As an individual, the Page is a younger person who is sensitive, friendly, empathic—and in some instances, potentially psychic.

REVERSED MEANING

When reversed, it's a time of extremes—you discard your dreams too readily or retreat into a dream world. Otherwise, there may be disappointment in relationships.

THE PAGE OF CUPS' SYMBOLS

1	**The Page**	Young person or situation
2	**Head tilted left**	Dream world
3	**The cup**	Offer of a relationship
4	**Talking fish**	Psychic communication
5	**Sea and walkway**	Balance
6	**Water-lily tunic**	Pure emotion
7	**Pink and blue attire**	Sensitivity
8	**Blue hat and scarf**	True intentions

What the Symbols Mean for You

When you are drawn to a particular symbol or feature of a card, it's because it holds a special meaning for you. Here is a guide to interpreting your symbols.

1 THE PAGE
Pages are messengers, bringing us news of future events. They also describe young people and young situations. This Page is Earth of the suit of Water. This is a harmonious combination, as Water feeds Earth, creating growth.

2 HEAD TILTED LEFT
The Page looks a little to our left, which represents the past, although his stance is centered. He appears to be in dream world, neither in the past nor the present.

3 THE CUP
The cup holds water, symbol of the flow of emotions, and is offered with the right hand, the hand of giving (the left hand is associated with receiving). A new relationship is on offer.

4 TALKING FISH
It's as if the Page is in conversation with the fish, a multilayered symbol meaning wealth, wisdom, fertility (associated with female genitalia) and as the ichthys, an emblem of Christianity. Talking animals also signify altered states of consciousness and psychic ability, so here, the fish is also a symbol of otherworldly experience.

See the fish on the Queen and King of Cups.

5 SEA AND WALKWAY
The sea represents the element of Water and the walkway, Earth. They are shown in equal proportion—there is roughly equal water to ground, symbolizing balance.

6 WATER-LILY TUNIC
The water-lily design is in keeping with the Water element of the card, for emotions. Lilies are symbols of purity, telling us that the Page's heart runs true: his feelings are genuine.

7 PINK AND BLUE ATTIRE
Pink is the color of the heart and blue, truth and spiritual purpose. The Page is unafraid to show his sensitivity.

8 BLUE HAT AND SCARF
The scarf makes a scallop shape on the left, and flows like a stream on the right to represent the card's Water element. Blue is for truth, so this emphasizes the Page's true intentions.

See the hat and flowing scarf on the Page of and Six of Pentacles.

KNIGHT OF CUPS

Esoteric Title: The Prince of the Chariot of the Waters
Element: Fire of the suit of Water
Major Arcana Link: VII The Chariot
Astrological Associations: Aquarius and Pisces
Animal Symbols: White horse, fish

DESCRIPTION

In a bright valley, a knight on a dainty white horse holds out a golden chalice. He looks toward a person or place unseen.

KEY MEANINGS

Invitations, proposals, promises, dreams, romance, new friends, time in nature, kindness

UPRIGHT MEANING

As an influence: The card means proposals and opportunities and, in particular, new friendships, and new love. A further meaning is enjoying creative pursuits and time in nature. Spiritually, the card says that what you desire is coming, but to be sure this offer comes from the right place or person; time will tell. As a person, the Knight appears to offer exactly what you want, but it is best to judge them by actions rather than words.

REVERSED MEANING

Disappointment: an offer does not materialize, at least in the way you expect. A further meaning is commitment issues.

THE KNIGHT OF CUPS' SYMBOLS

1	**The Knight**	Change
2	**Facing right**	The future
3	**White horse**	Beauty
4	**The cup**	An offer
5	**Riverbank**	Safety
6	**Red fish**	Passion
7	**Winged armor**	A love message

What the Symbols Mean for You

When you are drawn to a particular symbol or feature of a card, it's because it holds a special meaning for you. Here is a guide to interpreting your symbols.

1 THE KNIGHT

Always on horseback, the Knights are the tarot's agents of change. The Knight of Cups is an aspect of card VII The Chariot, and they have the astrological sign of Aquarius in common (Scorpio and the other fixed signs are represented by the sphinx on The Chariot). The card's elements are Fire and Water, which extinguish each other—so there may be conflict.

2 FACING RIGHT

The Knight's whole body is turned to us in profile, to the right; the right means the future, so his thoughts are firmly fixed ahead. The horse's head is down, so they are not in alignment: this can indicate stop-start relationships and projects.

3 WHITE HORSE

A knight in shining armor on a white horse is the epitome of the romantic dream. It's all about appearance; the rider is beautifully presented, expressing the concept of beauty in the card's Tree of Life association, the sphere of Tiphareth. The color white stands for innocence and purity of intention. This horse and rider might intend to travel, but the horse seems to dance rather than leap toward his goal.

See the white horse as a purity symbol on XIX The Sun.

4 THE CUP

The cup holds water, symbol of the flow of emotions, and is offered with the right hand, the hand of giving (the left hand is associated with receiving). A new relationship is on offer. As this is the Knight rather than the Page, this symbol—and the card—can mean a serious proposal.

5 RIVERBANK

The valley river flows through the center of the card, which tells us that water, or emotion, is at the heart of its meaning. However, the knight makes his offer from a comfortable position on the riverbank. He is yet to walk into the water, or the emotion of the situation. In this way, the river acts as a boundary; he keeps emotional distance.

6 RED FISH

The red fish is a water symbol, shown as a motif with a blue wave as a tunic design. These are the card's Fire (red) and Water (fish) elements. The red fish symbolizes passion.

7 WINGED ARMOR

The wings at the Knight's ankles evoke the winged sandals of the Greek god Hermes (Roman Mercury), deity of luck and travel. As a messenger of the Olympian gods, he has a message about love.

QUEEN OF CUPS

Esoteric Title: The Queen of the Thrones of the Waters

Element: Water of the suit of Water

Major Arcana Link: III The Empress

Astrological Associations: Gemini and Cancer

Animal Symbols: Fish, scallop

DESCRIPTION

By the sea at the foot of the cliffs, a Queen sits on a throne at the edge of the water. Her throne is decorated with carved water babies, and she holds up an elaborate closed chalice.

KEY MEANINGS

Empathy, sensitivity, faith, kindness, a love relationship, compassion, imagination, intuition, parenthood and children

UPRIGHT MEANING

As an influence: A time for heart-centeredness—being in love, enjoying nurturing relationships with friends and family, and honoring your sensitivity. The card also reveals imagination and intuition, so this is a time for creativity. Your dreams hold messages now, and you notice synchronicities. As a person, the Queen traditionally represents the ideal romantic partner and an individual with high emotional intelligence and empathy.

REVERSED MEANING

Jealousy, pressure, and potentially financial setbacks. A person or situation needs too much attention.

THE QUEEN OF CUPS' SYMBOLS

1	**The Queen**	Empowerment
2	**Facing left**	The past
3	**Scallop throne**	Fertility
4	**Flowing robes**	Pure intention
5	**Water babies**	Motherhood
6	**The chalice**	Faith and fertility
7	**Ocean**	The unconscious
8	**Pebbles**	Intuition
9	**Pearls**	Wisdom

What the Symbols Mean for You

When you are drawn to a particular symbol or feature of a card, it's because it holds a special meaning for you. Here is a guide to interpreting your symbols.

1 THE QUEEN
Queens signify empowerment. As the Queen of Cups' suit is Water, she represents the heart, or emotions of card III The Empress (see page 30). The Queen's elements are Water of Water—so, like Cancer, one of her zodiac signs, this is a card of deep emotion and high sensitivity. Relationships and connection with others are central.

2 FACING LEFT
The Queen sits to the left, which symbolizes the past. Her focus is on what she has created so far.

3 SCALLOP THRONE
The scallop, sign of fertility, evokes Botticelli's painting *The Birth of Venus*—with love goddess Venus emerging from the sea on a scallop shell. The scallop design is echoed in the pink scallop clasp of the Queen's cloak.

4 FLOWING ROBES
The Queen's white robe signifies purity of intention, while blue is truth; we see both colors on the wave design on her cloak. Her dress and cloak flow like water right to the sea's edge, a symbol of feelings flowing naturally.

5 WATER BABIES
Two water babies flank the scallop shell on the Queen's throne, symbols of motherhood and the family. A third baby at the base holds a fish, for fertility and prosperity.

6 THE CHALICE
The Queen's cup is ceremonial rather than domestic: a jeweled gold chalice with angel figurines used to perform the Eucharist—the Christian ceremony honoring the blood and body of Jesus. The chalice or cup is also a symbol of the womb, and it is closed to suggest that what is inside is sacred: together, they give us the meanings faith and fertility.

See the cup as chalice on the Ace of Cups.

7 OCEAN
In psychology, water is seen as a symbol of the unconscious and dreams. As a symbol on this card, the ocean signifies unlimited possibility.

8 PEBBLES
The pebbles appear at the Queen's feet, washed up by the tide. The ocean (see above) as the unconscious brings to shore little pieces of our inner knowing. The message is to notice and appreciate your intuition and its messages.

9 PEARLS
A pearl cluster decorates the top of the chalice, and there are pearl-shaped motifs on the Queen's crown: pearls symbolize knowledge, as in "pearls of wisdom."

KING OF CUPS

Esoteric Titles: The Lord of the Waves and the Waters, The King of the Hosts of the Sea
Element: Air of the suit of Water
Major Arcana Link: IV The Emperor
Astrological Associations: Libra and Scorpio
Animal Symbols: Fish, jellyfish

DESCRIPTION

Holding a cup and scepter, a calm King sits on his throne in the middle of a choppy sea. A red ship rides the waves in the distance.

KEY MEANINGS

Emotions, balance, sensitivity, understanding, wisdom, transformation, cycles and change, care, listening

UPRIGHT MEANING

As an influence: The King represents managing emotions, offering steadiness when life is in flux. The card represents sensitive communication, so intuition rather than logic, will help you navigate—you can trust what unfolds and embrace change. As an individual, this is a kind person who, while sociable, also needs space and private time to process feelings. The King can also represent the ideal romantic partner.

REVERSED MEANING

Creative and emotional blocks; vulnerability showing up as defensiveness. An additional meaning is destructive behaviors.

THE KING OF CUPS' SYMBOLS

1	The King	Authority
2	The cup and scepter	Balance of power
3	Fish amulet	Attraction
4	Leaping fish	Optimism
5	Ship	Changing fortunes
6	Jellyfish crown	Trust
7	Green slippers	Magic
8	Primary colors (yellow, blue, red)	Origins
9	Scroll throne	Knowledge

What the Symbols Mean for You

When you are drawn to a particular symbol or feature of a card, it's because it holds a special meaning for you. Here is a guide to interpreting your symbols.

1 THE KING
Kings signify authority. As the King of Pentacles' suit is Water, he represents the heart and emotions of IV The Emperor (see page 34). The King's two elements are Air and Water for the mind and the heart. When in alignment, everything flows beautifully. Out of balance, feelings are suppressed or feel out of control.

2 THE CUP AND SCEPTER
The cup represents the Water element of love and the heart. In the King's left hand is the scepter, symbol of sovereign authority. The left is the receiving hand, so the scepter is the power bestowed upon him, or received, from God. He holds out the cup with his right hand, the hand of giving. The King must be mindful of his responsibilities while staying true to his values.

3 FISH AMULET
The golden fish amulet is a symbol of wealth and good fortune; further meanings include faith and fertility (see also the Talking Fish, the Page of Cups, page 128). As this is worn as jewelry, a further meaning of the amulet is physical attraction.

4 LEAPING FISH
This fish might have jumped from the Page's Cup into the sea, a symbol of fun and enjoyment—a reminder that there are always ups to counter the downs.

See the fish on the Page of Cups.

5 SHIP
The ship is a symbol of fortune, good and ill. Its listing movement signifies how it adapts to change; its red color denotes action and energy.

6 JELLYFISH CROWN
The jellyfish on the King's crown links with his sign of Scorpio the scorpion, which also has its sting. The jellyfish guides us to trust the flow of life.

7 GREEN SLIPPERS
The King's slippers resemble fish scales—he dips a toe toward the water as if at home in the sea, like a merman. Green is traditionally a color not only of fertility but the supernatural; magic is afoot.

8 PRIMARY COLORS
The Kings wears the three primary colors in his cloak, collar, and robe. The word "primary" leads us to origins: all life began in the water. In this way, the King's colors say that through the sea—our emotions—we are connected to all of life.

9 SCROLL THRONE
The throne says afloat, held by the King's self-belief and faith. Wise, he knows that tides come and go. The back of the throne is curved into a scroll—a symbol of knowledge—which also echoes a spiral shell. The shell-shape, with its resemblance to ears, offers the meaning of listening.

ACE OF PENTACLES

Esoteric Title: Root of the Powers of Earth

Number: One

Astrological Associations: The Earth signs—Taurus, Virgo, and Capricorn

Element: Earth

Major Arcana Link: I The Magician

Season: Autumn/Fall

Tree of Life Position: Kether the crown, sphere of divine light

Compositional Affinity: All minor arcana Aces

DESCRIPTION

A hand in profile appearing from a cloud proffers a golden coin. Below is a paradise landscape: a garden of lilies and roses, and a pathway running through an archway to mountains beyond.

KEY MEANINGS

Beginnings, money, property, success, prosperity, values, new ventures, wealth potential, opportunity

UPRIGHT MEANING

The Ace means the potential for abundance, in terms of finances to rich opportunities that will bring you what you desire. This may translate as new income, finding a new property or seeding a new business, or being offered a route to achieving these goals. It is up to you to decide how to maximize this good fortune for the future; everything is possible.

REVERSED MEANING

The reversed card shows materialistic attitudes. Also, false starts—the need to wait for the right time to begin.

THE ACE OF PENTACLES' SYMBOLS

1	**Number I**	Beginnings and oneness
2	**Coin**	Material world
3	**Pentagram**	Perfection and protection
4	**Hand**	Invitation
5	**Lilies and roses**	Purity and love
6	**Rose arch**	Transitions
7	**Mountains**	The future
8	**Neutral sky**	Potential

What the Symbols Mean for You

When you are drawn to a particular symbol or feature of a card, it's because it holds a special meaning for you. Here is a guide to interpreting your symbols.

1 NUMBER I

One, or Ace, is the number of beginnings and oneness (feeling "at one" within and with the divine). All Aces relate to card I The Magician in the major arcana, who displays each suit symbol on his altar (see page 22). As the first card in its suit, the Ace holds the essential power of the suit element; in playing-card games such as Whist, aces count highest and outrank even the king. The Ace, here, is a golden opportunity to begin whatever you desire.

2 THE COIN

The Ace's coin symbolizes the element of Earth: the material world. The coin is double ringed, which suggests importance and differentiates it from the other coins shown in the suit. Its size and position in the sky also suggests a radiating sun, symbol of joy, growth, and success. This also echoes the card's Tree of Life position of Kether, the sphere of divine light.

3 THE PENTAGRAM

The pentagram is an ancient symbol of protection and perfection. It has many meanings across different cultures; in Pythagorean philosophy and Pagan belief, it signifies the unity of the elements: Earth, Water, Fire, Air, and the fifth element of Ether. Five is also the number of humanity, representing the five fingers of the hand—which is also dominant in the card image.

4 HAND

The super-sized hand offering the pentacle represents and invitation and a gift. Traditionally, the right hand is the hand of giving and the left, the hand of receiving. (This is why in tarot we choose cards for a reading with our left, or receiving, hand.)

See the giving hands on the Ace of Cups, Wands, and Swords.

5 LILIES AND ROSES

Lilies stand for purity of purpose and roses, love—so together, they symbolize love directed in its purest (or highest) form.

See these flowers on I The Magician and on the gowns of the supplicants on V The Hierophant.

6 ROSE ARCH

The rose arch is a portal in the shape of the mandorla, a symbol of heaven on earth. To move through the arch is to experience earthly paradise.

See the arch on the Ten of Pentacles and the double arches on the Four of Wands and Five of Cups.

See the mandorla on card XXI The World.

7 MOUNTAINS

Through the rose-arch portal are mountains, symbols of future experience. The peaks may stand for protection and shelter, or challenges, depending on our choices.

8 NEUTRAL SKY

The sky is almost a blank, like paper waiting for color. This neutrality symbolizes potential and creative space to develop ideas.

TWO OF PENTACLES

Esoteric Title: Harmonious Change

Number: Two

Astrological Association: Jupiter in Capricorn

Element: Earth

Season: Autumn/Fall

Tree of Life Position: Chockmah, the sphere of wisdom

DESCRIPTION

A young man in a tall red hat juggles two coins on green rope in the shape of a figure-eight, the infinity symbol. Behind him is the sea, with two ships riding precarious waves of fortune.

KEY MEANINGS

Decisions; juggling finances, cashflow, overthinking, balancing two options, choosing where to live or what to study, finding resources

UPRIGHT MEANING

Weighing up your options, it is time to make a decision, particularly relating to material concerns: money, work, education, and property. The card can also show the need to manage money very carefully as there may be little to go round just now, but this is a familiar cycle. Pay close attention to where your money—and your heart—goes.

REVERSED MEANING

Money worries and overall imbalance, feeling life is out of kilter now. You may be adversely affected by other's irresponsible spending or expectations.

THE TWO OF PENTACLES' SYMBOLS

1	**Number II**	Number of duality
2	**Moving figure**	Uncertainty
3	**The two coins**	Balance and tension
4	**The infinity symbol**	Flow and energy
5	**The red hat**	Overthinking
6	**Oak-leaf fringe**	Wisdom
7	**Two ships**	Tides and fortunes

What the Symbols Mean for You

When you are drawn to a particular symbol or feature of a card, it's because it holds a special meaning for you. Here is a guide to interpreting your symbols.

1 NUMBER II

Two, number of duality, is reflected in the two coins and two ships. One is up, one down; they cannot sit comfortably together. The Roman numeral II also represents a narrow portal. There is little room for maneuver.

2 MOVING FIGURE

The man could be juggling—an entertainer, even—but his expression is tense and his hesitant stance, with one half-raised knee, implies uncertainty.

3 THE TWO COINS

Within the green rope, the two coins represent the tension of opposite forces, or options. Here, the separate coins symbolize division within the self: literally, being in two minds.

4 THE INFINITY SYMBOL

The infinity symbol is green, for growth, but the coins don't yet flow along its looping pathway. The man may be holding too tightly to his coins, potentially narrowing his options. Equally, this symbol can show repetitive actions and feeling stuck in a loop.

See this symbol on I The Magician, VIII Strength, and in the arm position on the figure in the Nine of Cups.

5 THE RED HAT

The elongated acorn hat is a symbol of overthinking, or of too much ego. Its phallic shape relates to the card's Tree of Life sphere of Chockmah, for wisdom and the male principle. The youth's legs and hat are red, the color of action—but his thoughts and actions are not yet aligned. He is yet to act, and to do so, needs to be clear in his intentions.

6 OAK-LEAF FRINGE

The man's tunic hem is cut into the shape of oak leaves. Oak is a symbol of wisdom and longevity.

See the oak-leaf fringe on the Two of Pentacles, Page of Wands, and the King of Wands' cowl.

7 TWO SHIPS

The sea and ships represent fortune. Will our ship come in? We need a firm footing rather than a half-dance to weather the tides. The advice is to remember you have tenacity and resourcefulness—the qualities of Jupiter in Capricorn, the card's astrological association.

See this symbol on the King of Cups.

THREE OF PENTACLES

Other Name: The Architect
Esoteric Title: Material Works
Number: Three
Astrological Association: Mars in Capricorn
Element: Earth
Season: Autumn/Fall
Tree of Life Position: Binah, the sphere of compassion and understanding

DESCRIPTION

In a church crypt, a master stonemason is at work. A monk and a hooded figure appear to discuss an architectural plan.

KEY MEANINGS

Skill, mastery, work, enterprise, early success, practical outcomes, working together, foundations, growth

UPRIGHT MEANING

A new enterprise is successful, bringing respect and material rewards. In projects, the card shows solid work that's in alignment with your spiritual values, and ideas to build upon. Auspicious for creative projects and, literally, building work, the card also indicates teaching and learning.

REVERSED MEANING

Missed opportunities due to lack of commitment or planning issues. The need for a meaningful project, pursuit, or career.

THE THREE OF PENTACLES' SYMBOLS

1	**Number III**	Number of creativity
2	**The three coins**	Progress and artistry
3	**The quartered circle**	Grounded ideas
4	**The stonemason**	Mastery
5	**Uncarved stone**	Future potential
6	**The crypt**	Foundations
7	**The monk**	Spiritual direction
8	**The hooded figure**	A blessing
9	**The bench**	Support

What the Symbols Mean for You

When you are drawn to a particular symbol or feature of a card, it's because it holds a special meaning for you. Here is a guide to interpreting your symbols.

1 NUMBER III

Three, number of creativity, is echoed in the triad of pentacles and the three figures—mason, monk, and architect—who between them transform an idea into reality. Three also symbolizes creative fulfillment—the beginning, middle, and end, so the number also expresses a stage of completion.

2 THE THREE COINS

The three coins are symbols of secure progress and building a future. The tracery window of pentacles shows talent on display, and your accomplishments are unmistakable—as if set in stone. The pentacle is a symbol of Earth, the card's element, while the upward-pointing triangle is the symbol for fire; together they represent Mars (Fire) in Capricorn (Earth), the card's astrological associations.

3 QUARTERED CIRCLE

The cross within a circle is a sun symbol, known as the solar wheel or sun cross. It suggests the ancient sun gods' chariot-wheels, spinning across the sky during daylight hours. Its four quarters signify the card's element of Earth, bringing the meaning of light, or ideas/energy, made visible (earth).

4 THE STONEMASON

The stonemason denotes developed skills and talents—he holds a chisel and a mallet, symbol of the Master Mason. The spiritual dimension of the card is shown by the purple of his tunic, and his link with Freemasonry, which is based on the concept of temple-building (after King Solomon's Temple) as a template for building a better world. This idea also aligns with the card's Tree of Life sphere of Binah, for compassion and understanding.

5 UNCARVED STONE

The unhewn stone represents the future or what is being shaped. The mason works with stone, or Earth, the card's element.

6 THE CRYPT

The crypt means strong foundations for an enterprise, working from the ground up.

7 THE MONK

A symbol of spiritual guidance, the monk oversees the work, ensuring the mason's design is aligned with the values of the church.

8 HOODED FIGURE

Hoods can mean hidden approval or gifts. The hooded figure is either the church architect with his plan or a patron who will give the stonemason's work his blessing.

See the hooded figure in the Six of Cups.

9 THE BENCH

Support and uplift. The mason stands above the other two figures, showing how his expertise supports him financially.

See the bench on the Eight of Pentacles.

FOUR OF PENTACLES

Other Name: The Miser

Esoteric Title: Earthly power

Number: Four

Astrological Association: Sun in Capricorn

Element: Earth

Season: Autumn/Fall

Tree of Life Position: Chesed, the sphere of love and mercy

DESCRIPTION

A figure sits on a stone plinth before a city. He has four coins—under each foot, one on his crown and one held in an awkward pose of display.

KEY MEANINGS

Financial stability, holding on to money, finding security and value, recovery after upheaval, the material world, self-improvement, control and order, smugness

UPRIGHT MEANING

Stability, particularly in finance and property. This is a time to conserve energy, money, and resources. More generally, taking a fixed position on a matter; holding your ground. The downside is materialism—holding too tightly to possessions rather than letting abundance flow.

REVERSED MEANING

When reversed, there is stubbornness and in some instances, clinging to what you have due to fear of change.

THE FOUR OF PENTACLES' SYMBOLS

1	**Number IV**	Number of stability
2	**The four coins**	Balance and order
3	**The nobleman's attire**	Making an impression
4	**The cloak**	Self-protection
5	**Hand position**	Money at heart
6	**Stone plinth**	Solidity
7	**The crown**	Authority
8	**The city towers**	Ambition

What the Symbols Mean for You

When you are drawn to a particular symbol or feature of a card, it's because it holds a special meaning for you. Here is a guide to interpreting your symbols.

1 NUMBER IV

Four is the number of Earth, the card's element. It also stands for stability; the card's Tree of Life sphere of Chesed, for love, brings a love of the security that money can provide. The Four's astrological association of Sun in Capricorn means taking responsibility, solving problems and, in the true spirit of the element of Earth, getting things done.

2 THE FOUR COINS

The coins held over the heart, above the crown, and under the feet suggest feeling (heart), thinking (crown), and doing (feet). The coins are arranged symmetrically, to express the idea of balance and order.

3 THE NOBLEMAN'S ATTIRE

The unusual colors of the garments suggest expensive dyes, denoting his noble status: it also appears that the deep purple cloak and a russet tunic with a lavender trim have been carefully chosen to wear in public, so the man is fully aware of the impression he makes.

4 THE CLOAK

The dark cloak symbolizes protection. Its red lining stands for action—red is the color of energy—but here we see just a small flash of fabric. It is time to conserve energy and resources rather than take on new projects.

See the dark cloak on the Five of Cups as a symbol of emotional self-defense.

5 HAND POSITION

The hands appear awkward—as if they could roll the coin like a bowling ball. The pose is tight and protective, and the coin is held over the heart: money, at heart, is what's important just now.

See the two hands and coin in a relaxed position of offering on the Queen of Pentacles.

6 STONE PLINTH

The plinth could be in a town square, and the nobleman a statue. In this sense, the man becomes a person to look up to: like the orderly Emperor, another IV, he sets an example to others. The additional meaning of stone, however, is being immovable—and determined to hold on to his coin.

7 THE MURAL CROWN

The square crenelations are symbols of earth, the card's element. The crown has crenelations like a city wall, so is known as a mural crown (from the French *mur*, for *wall*). In mythology, the Greek goddess Tyche is depicted with the mural crown to show she protected the wealth of a city. The crown, therefore, may also suggest having control over money.

See the mural crown on XI Justice.

8 THE CITY TOWERS

The towers show us what has been built. Skyscrapers are symbols of ambition; the higher the building, the greater the dream. A further interpretation is surfeit of ego.

See the city towers on the King of Pentacles.

FIVE OF PENTACLES

Esoteric Title: Material Trouble

Number: Five

Astrological Association: Mercury in Taurus

Element: Earth

Season: Autumn/Fall

Tree of Life Position: Geburah, the sphere of power and destruction

DESCRIPTION

Two beggars brave a freezing night in the snow. They are so locked into their hardship that they do not see the potential sanctuary represented by the stained-glass window.

KEY MEANINGS

Hardship, isolation, disempowerment, vulnerability, poverty consciousness, insularity, social exclusion, tests, friendship in adversity

UPRIGHT MEANING

In readings this card often comes up to show poverty consciousness—fear of poverty—rather than actual lack. In social situations, there's a sense of being ostracized or not being able to find kindred spirits. Rather than tread the same path in darkness, look for the window of light; change your approach. Support, and other social and financial options, are available.

REVERSED MEANING

Traditionally, the reversed card can mean debt, money loss, or potentially loss of a friendship. More positively, your position is clear—it is time to re-evaluate and rebuild.

THE FIVE OF PENTACLES' SYMBOLS

1	**Number V**	The number of tests
2	**Two beggars**	Poverty and frustration
3	**Facing right**	The future
4	**Beggar's attire**	Vulnerability
5	**Bell**	The outcast
6	**The five coins**	Available resources
7	**Window**	Sanctuary
8	**Night**	Dark times
9	**Crutches**	Need for support

What the Symbols Mean for You

When you are drawn to a particular symbol or feature of a card, it's because it holds a special meaning for you. Here is a guide to interpreting your symbols.

1 NUMBER V

The number of humanity. As five relates to the five fingers of the hand, this number represents our actions and the experience this brings. Poverty, whether financial or social, is a test, and part of our earthly existence—which also links with the card's element of Earth, for the material world.

2 TWO BEGGARS

This pair clearly communicate poverty—after the Four, or Miser, we are shown those on the underside of fortune's wheel. Their journey is slow due to the man's disability and, for both, the physical discomfort of walking in freezing conditions. They look despondent; as far as they can see, they have no place to go. This is reflected in the conflictual energies of fast Mercury in heavy Taurus, the card's astrological association. However, as the pair are not alone in adversity, an additional meaning is support.

See the beggars on the Six of Pentacles.

3 FACING RIGHT

The beggars walk to our right; the right means the future, but as their heads are down, they can think only of how they might survive the immediate future.

4 BEGGAR'S ATTIRE

The female figure's shawl and skirt are ragged, and she has no shoes. The male has no coat or cloak and has a bandaged foot while the other has only a stocking. This clothing is not fit for purpose—there's a need for protection from the elements, so their poor clothing symbolizes vulnerability.

5 BELL

Once worn by lepers to warn others of their approach, the bell is a symbol of the outcast.

6 THE FIVE COINS

In a stained-glass window, five coins are arranged on a tree, a symbol of growth and abundance.

7 WINDOW

The beggars do not look up to the window because they have their heads down against the cold; it offers the light and warmth they need. Hardship narrows their view of the world when they could find sanctuary in the church-like window full of light and hope. The card's Tree of Life association is Geburah, for power and destruction, which suggests that the pair do have options, if only they can see them.

See the stained-glass window in the Four of Swords.

8 NIGHT

Darkness symbolizes challenging, and potentially painful experiences. Other cards of dark times include the Nine and Ten of Swords, XV The Devil, and XVI The Tower.

9 CRUTCHES

The male figure has an injured foot, so his progress is slow. The crutches symbolize the need for support.

SIX OF PENTACLES

Esoteric Title: Material Success

Number: Six

Astrological Association: Moon in Taurus

Element: Earth

Season: Autumn/Fall

Tree of Life Position: Tiphareth, the sphere of beauty and rebirth

Compositional Affinity: V The Hierophant

DESCRIPTION

Two beggars plead for alms from a wealthy man. He gives one of them four coins; we do not know if the other will receive anything. The man holds the scales in his left, as if carefully weighing up how much to give.

KEY MEANINGS

Gifts, generosity, a benefactor, donations, agreements, charity, success, care, mercy, receiving or giving money, accepting help

UPRIGHT MEANING

This is welcome card, particularly after the poor Five, as it brings wealth and appreciation. You may be the one giving to others, or be the lucky recipient. The card also represents donations, charity work, and gifts of all kinds. There is also compassion and self-care here; looking after yourself and others in practical ways.

REVERSED MEANING

The reversed card shows money running through your fingers; a gift may be squandered or otherwise used unwisely. It is also a sign that whoever gives the gift seeks control.

THE SIX OF PENTACLES' SYMBOLS

1	**Number VI**	Number of harmony
2	**The six coins in the sky**	Heaven-sent money
3	**Falling coins**	Gifts
4	**Wealthy man**	Generosity
5	**Facing left**	The past
6	**Standing and kneeling**	Social position
7	**The hand gesture**	A blessing
8	**The red cloak**	Justice in action
9	**The scales**	Mercy and precision
10	**The city towers**	Ambition

What the Symbols Mean for You

When you are drawn to a particular symbol or feature of a card, it's because it holds a special meaning for you. Here is a guide to interpreting your symbols.

1 NUMBER VI

Six, number of harmony and completion, meets Earth, the suit's element. Happiness comes from substance, or the material world in the form of the merchant's coin. The card's astrological association is Moon in Taurus, for the ability to put feeling into action; in this instance, as an act of charity.

2 THE SIX COINS IN THE SKY

The coins represent heaven-sent money. The Six and Ten of Pentacles are the only cards that show coins floating alone in the sky; this expresses the idea of heaven-sent money or help that comes from a good (or divine) source. The arrangement of coins suggests the form of the Hebrew letter Kaph, which represents the palm. The beggar's open palms are about to be filled with coins.

3 FALLING COINS

There are four coins—four is the number of stability, which is also a quality of steady Taurus. Ideally, the money will bring the beggar future stability—symbolized by the cards' Tree of Life association of Tiphareth, sphere of beauty and rebirth. The falling coins represent windfalls and gifts, and say that money flows.

4 WEALTHY MAN

From his fringed cloak to the matching fancy hat and green boots, the man's attire, along with his ready money, signals wealth. He is comfortable to show his success and share his gains with others. He makes the gesture of blessing with his right hand. Two fingers are extended, and the others folded into the palm, a symbol of the known and unknown worlds—or as the song goes, pennies from heaven.

5 FACING LEFT

The man looks to our left; the left means the past, so his money symbolizes his past achievements.

6 STANDING AND KNEELING

The composition of the image is like that of V The Hierophant—with the priest giving counsel to two kneeling supplicants. Here, it's a demonstration of social standing: the person who stands above the other has power over them.

7 THE HAND GESTURE

The man's right hand makes the gesture of a blessing as the coins fall toward the beggar's palms.

See this gesture on V The Hierophant.

8 THE RED CLOAK

Red is the color of action, and the man's red attire also suggests the figure of Justice—here, meaning justice in action.

See the prominent red cloak on XI Justice, I The Magician, IV The Emperor, and V The Hierophant.

9 THE SCALES

Scales signify mercy and careful decisions. The rich man may only give to one beggar rather than both, enacting the idea of the "deserving" poor—that one deserves more help than the other—or he may intend to give to both beggars. In this way, the scales tell us to look at priorities.

See the scales of justice on XI Justice.

10 THE CITY TOWERS

The city towers in the distance suggest future ambition and what he has already built; his achievements and goals are visible. His wealth is on display.

SEVEN OF PENTACLES

Esoteric Title: Success Unfulfilled
Number: Seven
Astrological Association: Saturn in Taurus
Element: Earth
Season: Autumn/Fall
Tree of Life Position: Netzach, the sphere of endurance, instinct, and desire

DESCRIPTION

A young person rests on his garden hoe, gazing upon a grapevine as if taking a break from the work of tending it. Behind him are distant hills and fields.

KEY MEANINGS

Potential, attention, self-belief, decisions, midpoints, commitment, time, endurance

UPRIGHT MEANING

A situation has great potential but needs consistent effort and investment of time, money, or other resources. As card seven out of fourteen in the suit, it symbolizes the halfway point: when doubt sets in. However, it's time to recommit to a project or relationship, as the rewards will come in the future. An additional meaning is deciding what to do with existing resources, such as building savings or spending it.

REVERSED MEANING

The reversed card says you may be giving up too soon. A situation needs more time to mature.

THE SEVEN OF PENTACLES' SYMBOLS

1	**Number VII**	Number of potential
2	**The seven coins**	Fruits of labor
3	**Facing left**	The past
4	**The garden hoe**	Work and support
5	**The orange tunic**	Hope and patience
6	**The grapevine**	Legacy and riches
7	**Neutral sky**	Creative space
8	**Purple mountains**	Goals and intuition

What the Symbols Mean for You

When you are drawn to a particular symbol or feature of a card, it's because it holds a special meaning for you. Here is a guide to interpreting your symbols.

1 NUMBER VII

Sevens are traditionally associated with mysteries—including the mysteries of the unseen future—along with potential, luck, and magic. The card's Tree of Life sphere of Netzach gives advice on maximizing this potential: to be resilient and pursue what you desire.

2 THE SEVEN COINS

Seven coins stand for the unripe fruit of the vine. Six coins are on the vine, while one stands alone in a new row. It may be planted to seed a new vine, symbol of future growth, or taken now as income. The coins appear at different levels from the ground up to elbow height, signifying different stages of development. To care for each unripe fruit, at each level, takes work—hence the card's element of Earth, for physical action.

3 FACING LEFT

The gardener looks to our left; the left means the past, so his thoughts are about what he has achieved so far.

4 THE GARDEN HOE

The hoe signifies work still to do. The card's planet, Saturn denotes responsibility—and in the heavy earth energy of Taurus, the workload feels heavy, just as he turns the soil with his hoe over and again hoping to further his enterprise. The hoe, like a staff, is also his support. His work now will support him financially in the future.

5 THE ORANGE TUNIC

The youth's tunic and boots are orange, the color of creativity associated with fall and harvest. The gardener hopes for harvest, but the leaves of the vine are still green. Will more fruit, or money come if he waits? This is a test of resilience.

See this in the lion of VIII Strength, also a card of endurance.

6 THE GRAPEVINE

Grapevines represent growth, legacy, and potential riches. Vines need regular tending and feeding if the fruit is to ripen without tasting sour. In our projects, finances and relationships, there's a need to embrace the work of caring without resentment. Then, the rewards are sweet.

7 NEUTRAL SKY

The huge neutral sky says that the future is not set, and there is plenty of space for expansion.

8 PURPLE MOUNTAINS

The figure is focusing purely on his potential crop, yet behind him are fields and purple mountains—a huge terrain. Purple is a symbol of intuition. If the young man can trust his intuition and wider goals, he will succeed.

EIGHT OF PENTACLES

Esoteric Title: Prudence
Number: Eight
Astrological Association: Sun in Virgo
Element: Earth
Season: Autumn/Fall
Tree of Life Position: Hod, the sphere of majesty and the mind

DESCRIPTION

Within sight of a city, an apprentice craftsman works at his bench. He displays his finished pieces—the pentacle coins—on a tree trunk.

KEY MEANINGS

Learning, apprenticeship, perfectionism, dedication, goals, duty, commitment, educational wins, exhibition, cycles, productivity

UPRIGHT MEANING

Your commitment and skill bring rewards, as money comes in and you gain ground in your career. In education, the Eight stands for dedication to study and achievement in examinations and tests. The effort may be repetitive, but practice makes perfect. Overall, careful attention to detail and to high standards.

REVERSED MEANING

Feeling trapped in a routine that doesn't serve you, money may be the only consolation. It's time to embrace a new cycle and brighter opportunities.

THE EIGHT OF PENTACLES' SYMBOLS

1	**Number VIII**	Cycles and renewal
2	**The eight coins**	Measurable progress
3	**The tree**	Growth
4	**The apprentice's pose**	Dedication
5	**Facing right**	The future
6	**Red leggings**	Action; ideas materialized
7	**Blue tunic**	True purpose
8	**The distant city**	Society
9	**The bench**	Support
10	**The dark apron**	Protection

What the Symbols Mean for You

When you are drawn to a particular symbol or feature of a card, it's because it holds a special meaning for you. Here is a guide to interpreting your symbols.

1 NUMBER VIII
Eight, number of fulfillment and renewal, is expressed as the total of limbs and legs—the apprentice's four limbs and the four legs of his bench. Positioned here, the young man will do sustainable and rewarding work; he is learning the art of replication and production cycles—also symbolized by the sideways number eight or lemniscate. The card's Tree of Life association of Hod for the mind also brings the meaning of focus and dedication. Number 8 and the lemniscate are also seen in VIII Strength, the card of patience and tenacity.

2 THE EIGHT COINS
The coin is the symbol of the element of Earth, for the material world. As each coin is perfected, it is displayed for us to evaluate. The identical coins show measurable skill—knowledge is manifest as object. However, one coin has been cast aside. While the apprentice is learning quality control, there may be perfectionism, too, which links with the card's association with Virgo, the sign that prizes attention to detail.

3 THE TREE
The tree is a universal symbol of growth, wisdom, and legacy. The apprentice may hope to use his skills to support others financially or pass on his trade to future generations.

4 THE APPRENTICE'S POSE
Bent to his task, the apprentice holds a hammer and chisel, the tools of his trade. He must cut fine, accurate lines into the disks to create a perfectly balanced pentagram. His pose reveals careful attention (this is the "Prudence" in the card's esoteric meaning) and dedication to his task.

See this pose in card XVII The Star; the cards' number 17 adds up to 8.

5 FACING RIGHT
The apprentice faces to our right, which signifies the future. The work the apprentice does now assures his future security.

6 RED LEGGINGS
Red is the color of action and energy. The apprentice's red shoes and leggings show that important work is being done.

7 BLUE TUNIC
The blue tunic represents workflow—blue is the color of the element of Water, which must flow to bring in positive energy and experiences. The color also signifies truth, so in combination, the apprentice's blue stands for his true purpose.

8 DISTANT CITY
The apprentice is willing to do what is needed to qualify him to enter the city—the image of the tower and city walls stands for society. His skills will be his passport, and the path to the city awaits.

9 THE BENCH
Support and uplift. The apprentice's skills will raise him up in society.

See the bench in the Three of Pentacles.

10 THE DARK APRON
Craftsmen's aprons were made of leather to protect the clothes and the body, so the apprentice in his apron signifies strong protection—almost like body armor. In this practical suit of Pentacles, the apron, or skills learned, guards against future poverty. Black, traditionally, is the color of protection.

See the black cloak as a symbol of protecting existing money on the Four of Pentacles and in the Five of Cups as a symbol of emotional self-defense.

NINE OF PENTACLES

Esoteric Title: Material Gain	
Number: Nine	
Astrological Association: Venus in Virgo	
Element: Earth	
Season: Autumn/Fall	
Tree of Life Position: Yesod, the sphere of foundation and the unconscious	
Animal Symbols: Bird of prey, snail	

DESCRIPTION

We see a woman in a sun-filled garden with ripened grapes on the vine. She wears a gauntlet on her left hand and gazes toward a hooded bird.

KEY MEANINGS

Prosperity, comfort, luxury, rest, reward, restoration, self-appreciation, abundance, beauty, sensuality

UPRIGHT MEANING

This is the card of luxury and abundance when you enjoy life's richness. This is a time not only of financial stability but satisfaction as you get to enjoy what you have created. You may be focused on the material things just now, particularly home improvements, décor and beauty, and also feel comfortable with yourself and within your relationships. The card also shows leisure time and treats, so you attend to your needs and interests, and if you choose, enjoy some spending.

REVERSED MEANING

The reversed card shows financial problems, particularly regarding work, property and land, and neighbors—whatever affects your peace of mind.

THE NINE OF PENTACLES' SYMBOLS

1	**Number IX**	Number of integration and intensity
2	**Standing figure**	Ownership
3	**The nine coins**	Profitability
4	**The robes**	Fertility
5	**The hooded bird**	Pragmatism
6	**The ripened grapes**	Wealth and fertility
7	**The snail**	Slowness and protection
8	**Fertile hills**	Space and shelter

What the Symbols Mean for You

When you are drawn to a particular symbol or feature of a card, it's because it holds a special meaning for you. Here is a guide to interpreting your symbols.

1 NUMBER IX
Nine is the number of integration and intensity. In the minor arcana, nine carries the weight of all the number cards that precede it, holding that energy until the release and expression of the Ten. All the lessons of the previous cards integrate at this stage, so in the material suit of Pentacles, we see material gain—the reward of the suit's journey through work, poverty, recovery, and generosity. Nine in the suit's element of Earth intensifies what is material to us, while the astrological association of Venus in Virgo, for luxury with sensitive awareness, means money is wisely spent, without making a show of wealth.

2 STANDING FIGURE
The female figure stands tall in the grounds of her manor house. Like III The Empress, her garden is her sanctuary. She symbolizes pride in achievement.

3 THE NINE COINS
The six coins on her right under her protective hand represent savings and the three to her left what she might reasonably spend. A tree appears on the ground above each pile as further symbols of growth.

4 THE ROBES
The woman's heavy robe is decorated with flower motifs that are Venus symbols—the orb and cross. Orange is associated with creativity, while the robe's red lining suggests the lining of the womb, for fertility and growth.

See the red lining on the tunic of the just-born Fool, card 0.

5 THE HOODED BIRD
Birds signify spirit communication, and the bird's hood, limitation. The woman gazes at her small bird of prey to show she is aware that material matters take priority; she is happy to limit herself to her home and, for now, does not need to reach beyond her private paradise. This is not materialism, but time to enjoy what she has worked for.

6 THE RIPENED GRAPES
The grapes, tethered to supports, are cultivated rather than wild. This suggests the card's astrological associations tend the vine with care (Virgo) and enjoy great fruitfulness (Venus).

See the ripened grapes on the Ten of Pentacles and King of Pentacles.

7 THE SNAIL
The slow pace of the snail is a reminder to take life slow and easy when we can. Its shell signifies self-protection.

8 FERTILE HILLSIDES
The earthen hills at the horizon shield the manor from adverse weather. They offer space for growth, so your home or place of work supports your activities and future development. This meaning also aligns with the card's Tree of Life sphere of Yesod, which means "foundation." Yesod is also associated with manifestation.

TEN OF PENTACLES

Esoteric Title: Wealth
Number: Ten
Astrological Association: Mercury in Virgo
Element: Earth
Season: Autumn/Fall
Tree of Life Position: Malkuth, the Kingdom, the sphere of experience
Animal Symbol: Dog

DESCRIPTION

Three generations of a family appear by the courtyard arch of their home: an old man, possibly a grandfather, parents, and child. Two dogs sit and stand by the grandfather. Two family crests are displayed on the archway.

KEY MEANINGS

Legacy, inheritance, family, love, wealth, security, connection, community, commitment, marriage, traditions, shared values

UPRIGHT MEANING

This Ten brings wealth and its accumulation but also values and connection—so the focus can be on family and the friends we choose as family. While the card means prosperity, it can specify a legacy, which may be knowledge rather than money. Like the Four of Wands, this Ten can mean weddings and, otherwise, commitment in relationships.

REVERSED MEANING

The reversed Ten means disagreement over money and personal values. There may be conflict around commitment in relationships and issues with tradition and freedom.

THE TEN OF PENTACLES' SYMBOLS

1	**Number X**	The number of completion
2	**Arch**	Protection and transitions
3	**Ripened grapes**	Maturing wealth
4	**The dogs**	Loyalty
5	**The family**	Inheritance
6	**The ten coins**	The world
7	**Tower and house**	Establishment, security
8	**Coats of arms**	Status

What the Symbols Mean for You

When you are drawn to a particular symbol or feature of a card, it's because it holds a special meaning for you. Here is a guide to interpreting your symbols.

1 NUMBER X

Ten, the first double number, marks the ending of one cycle and the beginning of another; the number 10 comprises 1 for beginnings, and the zero, with its circular form, is a symbol of completion. This echoes the card's Tree of Life sphere of Malkuth, the kingdom, for life experience. The meaning of the Tens, whether positive or negative, arises from the nature of the suit: a multitude of generous Pentacles brings abundance.

2 ARCH

The partial arch symbolizes protection and marks the threshold between what may be an inner and outer courtyard. Arches can be portals—here, between public life signified by the coats of arms on the outside of the arch, and the private world of the family within the inner courtyard. As an interpretation, this signifies being on the outside looking in.

See the arch on the Ace of Pentacles and the double arches on the Four of Wands and Five of Cups.

3 RIPENED GRAPES

The grapes symbolize family and prosperity, which links with the card's element of Earth, for the material world. The card's astrological association, Mercury in Virgo, suggests wealth management—the flow of money (Mercury) with careful tending (Virgo); Virgo also suggests care of the body.

4 THE DOGS

The two dogs look up to the old man, who pets them. They symbolize loyalty and friendship.

5 THE FAMILY

The old man stands for the past, the couple for the present and the child, the future. In tarot readings, the left is the past, the center is the present and the right is the future—just as these figures are positioned on the card. Together they symbolize inheritance—passing on money and knowledge from one generation to the next.

6 THE TEN COINS

The ten coins echo the pattern of the ten spheres on the Tree of Life, the central motif of Kabbala (see page 228). The coins are an expression of life, of the world we live in. And yet they float and are not integrated into the image, as if not quite real. In this way, the coins may suggest an idealized rather than real world. We may be idealizing others' lifestyles.

See the coins in the air on the Six of Pentacles.

7 TOWER AND HOUSE

The homestead signifies security and the tower, a lookout to spot potential predators. There's a sense of enclosure here that may be reassuring or suffocating, depending on your position.

8 COATS OF ARMS

The family coats of arms symbolize high status. The lower one, with its image of ships, denotes good fortune; the checkered tiles to its left signify strategy—perhaps in business, bringing in wealth.

See the alchemical emblem on the Two of Wands and the crest on the Six of Cups.

See the checkered sash on the Three of Wands.

PAGE OF PENTACLES

Other Names: Princess, Knave or Jack of Pentacles
Esoteric Titles: The Princess of the Echoing Hills, The Rose of the Palace of Earth
Element: Earth of the suit of Earth

DESCRIPTION

A young person in a sun-drenched meadow holds up a coin. His hold is delicate, almost reverential; this is a precious gift.

KEY MEANINGS

Beginnings, news, money, education, learning, ideas, talent, options, business

UPRIGHT MEANING

As an influence: The card brings beginnings and offers related to money, work, home, education, and travel; this is a great time for new ventures. However, you may need to pay careful attention to financial matters, such as taxes and other payments due, and be sure to examine all aspects of a situation before you act. As an individual, the Page is a younger person, loyal and hardworking, who is beginning to reap the rewards of their efforts.

REVERSED MEANING

Plans are unrealistic or unaffordable. There may also be irresponsible spending or ignored debt that curtails your freedom.

THE PAGE OF PENTACLES' SYMBOLS

1	**The Page**	Young person or situation
2	**Facing right**	The future
3	**The coin**	Talent and reward
4	**Yellow sky**	Awareness
5	**Plowed fields**	Readiness and planning
6	**Meadow and trees**	Discovery and growth
7	**Mountains**	Goals and challenges
8	**Oak-leaf fringe**	Wisdom
9	**Red headgear**	Action and learning

What the Symbols Mean for You

When you are drawn to a particular symbol or feature of a card, it's because it holds a special meaning for you. Here is a guide to interpreting your symbols.

1 THE PAGE

Pages are messengers, bringing news of future events. They also describe young people and young situations. This Page is Earth of Earth—for loyalty, patience, and success through commitment and dedication. However, two Earths can be too pragmatic—and potentially inflexible.

2 FACING RIGHT

The Page looks to our right; the right means the future, so his thoughts are of his next steps.

3 THE COIN

The coin signifies real reward for effort—the coin itself appears as a sporting trophy or award.

4 YELLOW SKY

Clear vision: being fully aware of what your current environment has to offer and appreciating where you are at this moment.

5 PLOWED FIELDS

The Page is deciding where to take his talent, or coin of potential. The world, like the field, is ready to receive what you have to offer.

See the plowed field on the Knight of Pentacles.

6 MEADOW AND TREES

The flower-filled pasture signifies new places and discovery. The four trees to the left, the place of the past, show what the Page has already achieved, and the coin—a new treasure—is the result.

7 MOUNTAINS

Goals and challenges. The Page is only focused on his coin; the journey toward this goal, and the challenges this will bring, is yet to begin.

8 OAK-LEAF FRINGE

The Page's green sleeve has a fringe cut into the shape of oak leaves. Oak is a symbol of wisdom and longevity and foreshadows the oak-leaf plumage on the Knight of Pentacles (see page 158).

See the oak-leaf fringe on the Two of Pentacles and Page of Wands, and the King of Wands' cowl.

9 RED HEADGEAR

Red is the color of action and manifestation. The Page's hat is like that of the rich man on the Six of Pentacles, who epitomizes material success. In this way, the Page is the Six as a young man, full of ambition—so the hat also signifies learning.

KNIGHT OF PENTACLES

Esoteric Title: The Prince of the Chariot of Earth

Element: Fire of the suit of Earth

Major Arcana Link: VII The Chariot

Astrological Associations: Leo and Virgo

Animal Symbol: Black horse

DESCRIPTION

A knight sits astride a black horse, overlooking a plowed field. He holds a single coin, looking beyond the card as if ready to plant it as a seed of future wealth.

KEY MEANINGS

Prosperity, commitment, plans, improvement, stability, patience, investment, loyalty, trust, work, responsibility

UPRIGHT MEANING

As an influence: Work—no matter how tough—is worthwhile, as you will reap the long-term benefits: pay rises, income from investments, and paying off loans. The card reveals how careful planning brings future security. In relationships, the card shows loyalty and signals a long-term love. As an individual, a loyal, reliable person; they may not be spontaneous, but their word is their bond.

REVERSED MEANING

Review your finances and make key decisions about your home and income; stubbornness and lack of vision may lead to loss.

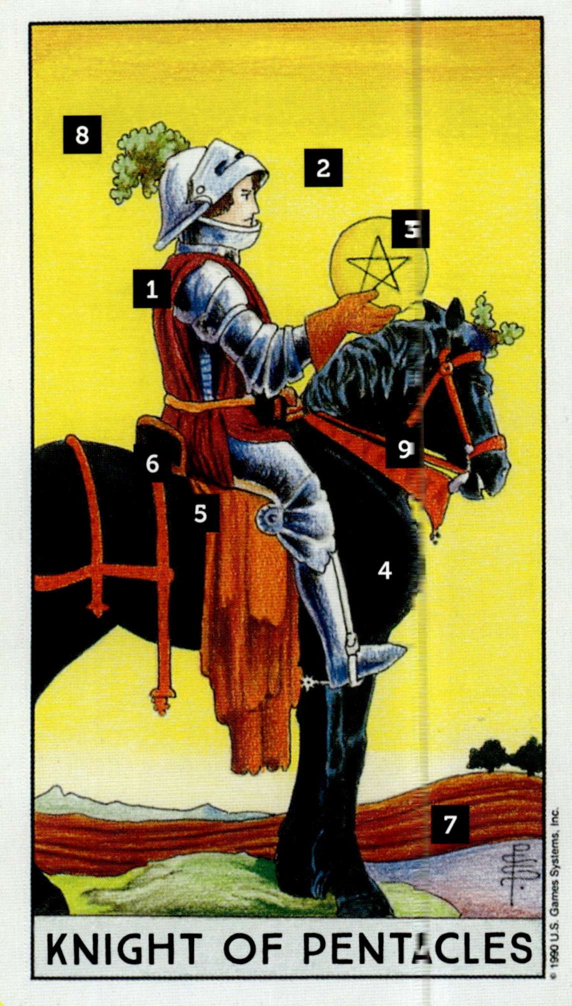

THE KNIGHT OF PENTACLES' SYMBOLS

1	**The Knight**	Change
2	**Facing right**	The future
3	**The coin**	Reward and commitment
4	**Agricultural horse**	Responsibility
5	**Gauntlets and blanket**	Adaptability
6	**Saddle**	Support
7	**Plowed fields**	Seasons and cycles
8	**Oak-leaf plumage**	Wisdom
9	**Red harness**	Action and protection

What the Symbols Mean for You

When you are drawn to a particular symbol or feature of a card, it's because it holds a special meaning for you. Here is a guide to interpreting your symbols.

1 THE KNIGHT

Always on horseback, the Knights are the tarot's agents of change. The Knight of Pentacles is an aspect of card VII The Chariot, and they have the astrological sign of Leo in common (Leo and the other fixed signs are represented by the sphinx on The Chariot). The card's elements are Fire and Earth, giving the meaning of steady progress.

2 FACING RIGHT

The Knight's whole body is turned to us in profile, to the right; the right means the future, so his thoughts are firmly fixed on the years ahead.

3 THE COIN

Whereas the Page of Pentacles explores the right place for his coin or talent, the Knight knows where to invest his time and energy for the greatest return. He holds out his coin with pride, a sign of commitment to work and relationships.

4 AGRICULTURAL HORSE

The horse is a draft, or "heavy" horse so-called due to its ability to haul heavy freight. The horse bears the responsibility of the load, while its color black signifies protection—meaning to manage commitments well.

5 GAUNTLETS AND BLANKET

The gauntlets and blanket show the Knight's readiness for a long journey—but also his adaptability: whatever is ahead, he may need comfort and protection. Both items are also a means of disguise, bringing additional meanings of secrecy and privacy.

See the gauntlet on the Nine of Pentacles.

6 SADDLE

The back of the saddle is high, a symbol of support. The saddle back has also been seen as a book—perhaps a Bible or other book of faith to inspire his journey.

7 PLOWED FIELDS

The Knight might plant his coin in plowed earth to begin a new cycle of growth and harvest. This links with the Knight's Tree of Life sphere of Tiphareth, for beauty and rebirth—guiding you, like the Knight, to work with nature's changing seasons and cycles.

See the plowed filed on the Page of Pentacles.

8 OAK-LEAF PLUMAGE

Both the Knight and the horse have oak-leaf plumage, a reminder of the adage "from acorns, great oaks grow." The oak symbolizes wisdom and asks that you show patience.

9 RED HARNESS

Red symbolizes action, while the agricultural harness signifies structure. Its design protects the horse so the weight of the plow will be balanced and not cause injury. In this way, careful planning and self-care are important now.

QUEEN OF PENTACLES

Esoteric Title: The Queen of the Thrones of Earth
Element: Water of the suit of Earth
Major Arcana Link: III The Empress
Astrological Associations: Sagittarius and Capricorn
Animal Symbols: Goat, rabbit

DESCRIPTION

A Queen in vibrant robes sits on a stone throne in the countryside—her feet are on fertile earth, and flowers bloom around her. She rests a golden coin in her lap.

KEY MEANINGS

Security, prosperity, reward, work, growth, fertility, protection, beauty, nature, resourcefulness

UPRIGHT MEANING

As an influence: This is a card of abundance and well-being: you enjoy more prosperity, tend to your health, and can give practical support to others. It also favors marriage, fertility, children, and spending time in nature; whatever brings you close to the earth and all its sensuality. As an individual, this Queen is grounded and wise, loyal in her friendships and other love relationships. She may offer a gift or a loan.

REVERSED MEANING

Being mean with money or overspending. Overall, neglecting finances, home, and self-care.

THE QUEEN OF PENTACLES' SYMBOLS

1	**The Queen**	Empowerment
2	**Facing left**	The past
3	**The coin**	Achievement and reward
4	**Rich coloration**	Fertility
5	**Uncultivated ground**	Doing groundwork
6	**Throne**	Foundation
7	**Rabbit**	Nature's cycles
8	**Goat's head**	Work and responsibility
9	**Rambling roses**	Sensuality
10	**Closed crown**	Protection

What the Symbols Mean for You

When you are drawn to a particular symbol or feature of a card, it's because it holds a special meaning for you. Here is a guide to interpreting your symbols.

1 THE QUEEN
Queens signify empowerment. As the Queen of Pentacles' suit is Earth, she represents the physical body and pragmatism of card III The Empress (see page 30). The Queen's combined elements are Water and Earth, which is harmonious: Water nurtures the Earth, ensuring growth.

2 FACING LEFT
Seated toward the left side, the Queen appreciates the past. She holds the coin, symbol of her past accomplishments (see below).

3 THE COIN
The coin signifies success and reward. It is her treasure, set on her lap like a cherished child. She holds the coin but gives it space to grow. In this way, the coin represents growing prosperity.

4 RICH COLORATION
The rich colors of the card—red, greens, earth tones, blues, and butter yellow—symbolize fertility, the traditional characteristic of womanhood.

See these colors on III The Empress.

5 UNCULTIVATED GROUND
The ground is part-cultivated but mainly rough, as if nature wants to reclaim it. This signifies that it's important to do the groundwork in new ventures and relationships. Some people—work colleagues, friends, or family—may also need careful tending.

6 THRONE
The Queen's throne is set in soft earth, but it holds her weight. This suggests strong foundations and nurturing roots. The throne is decorated with pears and a nymph—this may be the wood Nymph Pomona, deity of the orchard and fruit trees. The pear is a fertility symbol.

7 RABBIT
The young rabbit is a symbol of the spring and new life. As the earth flourishes, so the Queen lives in tune with nature's cycles.

8 GOAT'S HEAD
The goat's head links with Capricorn, one of the Queen's zodiac signs. This is echoed in the winged goat on the crest of her crown. Capricorn is the sign of work, responsibility, and time.

9 RAMBLING ROSES
The red rose is a symbol of love and passion. Here, the roses appear wild and rambling rather than the cultivated blooms we see on I The Magician, here suggesting sensual relationships.

See the cultivated red roses on I The Magician and VIII Strength.

10 CLOSED CROWN
This is the only closed crown in the tarot—all others are open. The closed crown is a symbol of protection, and being closed to outside possibilities as the focus is purely on the coin: what is on hand.

KING OF PENTACLES

Esoteric Titles: The Lord of the Wide and Fertile Land, King of the Spirits of the Earth	
Element: Air of the suit of Earth	
Major Arcana Link: IV The Emperor	
Astrological Associations: Aries and Taurus	
Animal Symbols: Bull, boar	

DESCRIPTION

A King in a richly decorated robe sits on a black throne by a castle wall. He holds a scepter in his left hand and a golden coin in his right.

KEY MEANINGS

Security, prosperity, reward, work, growth, generosity, protection, status, boundaries, planning, long-term relationships

UPRIGHT MEANING

As an influence: Building wealth for a solid financial future, the card says hard work brings the success you deserve. This is also an auspicious card for work and property. You are ready to accept new responsibility, which gives you status and a sense of pride; it's a call to expand your base and take a step up. As an individual, the King is reliable and future-forward—he creates lasting relationships and security.

REVERSED MEANING

Greed and a lack of trust; there is also the possibility of debt that needs to be managed. A further interpretation is extreme materialism and potential corruption.

THE KING OF PENTACLES' SYMBOLS

1	**The King**	Authority
2	**The coin and scepter**	Achievement and sovereignty
3	**Grapevine design**	Fruits of labor
4	**Boar**	Base instincts
5	**Bull**	Sign of Taurus; sensuality
6	**Flower crown**	Fertility
7	**Armor**	Past battles

What the Symbols Mean for You

When you are drawn to a particular symbol or feature of a card, it's because it holds a special meaning for you. Here is a guide to interpreting your symbols.

1 THE KING

Kings signify authority. As the King of Pentacles' suit is Earth, he represents the physical body and pragmatism of IV The Emperor (see page 34). The King's two elements are Air and Earth. Practical Earth can conflict with idealistic Air, but when balanced, ideas take physical shape.

2 THE COIN AND SCEPTER

On his knee the King balances the coin, symbol of achievement and of his suit element of Earth. He holds it firmly with his left hand—the left hand symbolizes receiving while the right is the hand of giving. The King protects what he has. In his right hand is the scepter, symbol of sovereign authority.

3 GRAPEVINE DESIGN

The grapevine design on the King's robes features ripe purple grapes, the fruits of his labor. Grapes signify wealth and family; the King celebrates and displays his wealth and status, which he has earned through dedicated work.

See the grapevine on the Nine and Ten of Pentacles.

4 BOAR

The King rests his foot on a boar statue to signify victory over primal urges, so the message of this symbol is self-mastery.

See the animal as base instinct in the lion of Strength, card VIII.

5 BULL

Like The Emperor with his ram of Aries throne, the King of Pentacles has the bull for his sensual sign of Taurus. The bull along with the grapes on the card evoke the story of Dionysus, the hedonistic Greek god. Dionysus' lover was killed by a bull and Dionysus turned his corpse into the first grapevine.

6 FLOWER CROWN

The King's crown continues the theme of fertility and the riches of the land with the red flower and fleur-de-lis design of his crown. The fleur-de-lis symbolizes royalty and perfection; the red flower resembles a poppy, which stands for sleep and rebirth. Under the crown is a wreath, symbol of his past victories. Together, these symbols represent the King's fruitful management of his element of Earth.

See the lilies on I The Magician.

See the victory wreath on the Seven of Cups, Six of Wands, and XXI The World.

7 ARMOR

The King shows his armor, a symbol of past battles. It also tells us he is still the warrior underneath the regalia, ready to take up arms.

ACE OF SWORDS

Esoteric Title: Root of the Powers of Air

Number: One

Astrological Associations: The Air signs—Gemini, Libra, and Aquarius

Element: Air

Major Arcana Link: I The Magician

Season: Winter

Tree of Life Position: Kether the crown, sphere of divine light

Compositional Affinity: All minor arcana Aces

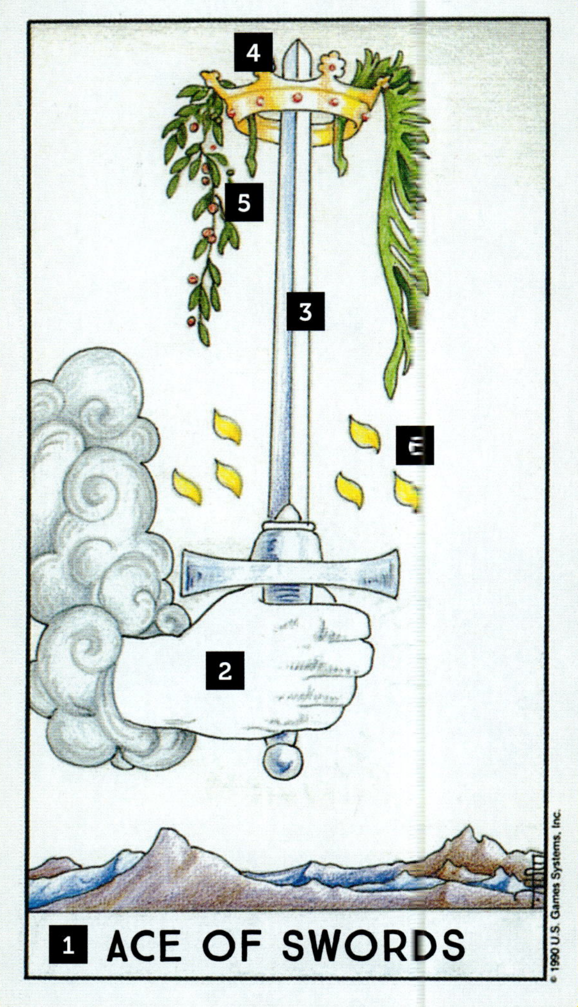

DESCRIPTION

From a cloud, a hand appears brandishing an upright silver sword; it is encircled by a crown hung with olive branch and palm frond. Below are blue and purple mountains.

KEY MEANINGS

Beginnings, success, decisions, clarity, incisiveness, force, truth, ending of conflict, certainty

UPRIGHT MEANING

The Ace brings success across all areas of life, from love to career as obstacles disappear. You find the clarity you need, and in answer to a question, the card gives you a resounding "yes." There's also immediate change in circumstances, as a decision frees you to move forward with confidence. The card also reveals assertiveness and potentially arrogance—so wield that sword with care.

REVERSED MEANING

The reversed Sword reveals conflict and potential criticism—it may be best to withdraw and find the answer elsewhere.

THE ACE OF SWORDS' SYMBOLS

1	**Number I**	Beginnings and oneness
2	**Hand**	Invitation
3	**Upright sword**	Truth and purpose
4	**Crown**	Divine light
5	**Olive branch and palm frond**	Achievement
6	**Golden droplets**	Element of fire

What the Symbols Mean for You

When you are drawn to a particular symbol or feature of a card, it's because it holds a special meaning for you. Here is a guide to interpreting your symbols.

1 NUMBER I

One, or Ace, is the number of beginnings and oneness (feeling "at one" within the self and with the divine). All Aces also relate to card I The Magician in the major arcana, who displays each suit symbol on his altar (see page 22). The first card of its suit, the Ace, holds the essence of its Air element: clarity of thought.

2 HAND

The hand offering the sword represents an invitation and a gift. Traditionally, the right hand is the hand of giving, and the left, the hand of receiving.

See the giving hands on the Ace of Pentacles, Cups, and Wands.

3 UPRIGHT SWORD

With its branch and frond, the sword might resemble a tree, strong and steadfast. Held high above the mountains, the sword rises above challenges and goals: we have the "upper hand." However, the sword is double-edged, so must be handled with care. As with the Queen and King of Swords, the weapon is also a symbol of justice—so the virtue of justice must come to bear, too, if we are the use the gifts of the Ace wisely: in practice, to use integrity rather than rush headfirst.

See the sword on the sphinx on X The Wheel of Fortune and XI Justice.

4 CROWN

The crown is an authority symbol, and a symbol of Kether, also referred to as "the crown"—the card's Tree of Life sphere, meaning divine light. The crown of the head is also the crown chakra, the center of energy that connects the body to the spirit. More literally, the crown is the head or faculty of thinking.

5 OLIVE BRANCH AND PALM FROND

The olive branch means peace, and the palm frond, victory—we can see this as success bringing clarity and peace of mind. The feathery palm frond in the crown resembles a feather and gives us the idiom, "a feather in your cap," in other words, an achievement. The crown, olive, and palm also represent the first three spheres on the Tree of Life (see the Tree of Life illustration on page 228)—Kether, the crown, Chockmah (wisdom), and Binah (understanding).

6 GOLDEN DROPLETS

The six golden droplets are in the form of the Hebrew letter Yod, for fire (a further meaning is "hand of God"—see XVI The Tower, page 82). The number six gives us zain, the sixth letter of the Hebrew alphabet whose symbol is the sword.

TWO OF SWORDS

Esoteric Title: Peace Restored

Number: Two

Astrological Association: Moon in Libra

Element: Air

Season: Winter

Tree of Life Position: Chockmah, the sphere of wisdom

DESCRIPTION

A blindfolded woman sits before us. Crossing her chest, she holds an upright sword in each hand, one tilted to the right, one to the left. Behind her is a rocky seascape at low tide.

KEY MEANINGS

A truce, stalemate, procrastination, uncertainty, mental block, self-protection, avoidance, keeping the peace, low energy, privacy

UPRIGHT MEANING

This Two means a truce, a temporary respite from stress and activity. This card may also show a necessary decision; however, taking too much time to process your thoughts—and staying in your head rather than trusting your intuition—can lead to procrastination and avoidance, perhaps due to fear of conflict. In relationships, the card can reveal someone who crosses you.

REVERSED MEANING

The reversed card intensifies the upright meaning, along with being manipulated and willful deception, so the message is to protect your interests.

THE TWO OF SWORDS' SYMBOLS

1	**Number II**	Duality
2	**Blindfold figure**	Limitation
3	**Two swords**	Two minds
4	**Low tide**	Emerging truths
5	**Waxing moon**	Building energy
6	**Monastic dress**	Privacy

What the Symbols Mean for You

When you are drawn to a particular symbol or feature of a card, it's because it holds a special meaning for you. Here is a guide to interpreting your symbols.

1 NUMBER II

Two, the number of duality and partnership, reveals the need for balance and decisions. The card's astrological association, Moon in Libra, signifies this harmonious balance, which in the conflictual suit of Swords takes considerable effort. The card's Tree of Life sphere of Chockmah, for wisdom, provides guidance—that our inner wisdom, or intuition, will help us come to the right decision.

2 BLINDFOLD FIGURE

The blindfold signifies limitation, as it limits our view. The card may foreshadow The Magician—the woman's hair resembles his and, if she were to wear her blindfold as a headband, symbol of willpower and the mind, she would be able to see the way clearly. If she remains blindfold, she risks the further restriction depicted on the Eight of Swords. One interpretation of the blindfold is that without physical sight, the female figure must rely on her third eye, or intuition.

See the blindfold on the Eight of Swords.

See the headband on I The Magician.

3 TWO SWORDS

Swords, with their element of Air, represent the mind. The two Swords show the female figure is in two minds—she must weigh the options, but is at odds with herself, symbolized by her crossed arms.

4 LOW TIDE

At low tide, we see what has been hidden from view. Underwater or unconscious experience gives way to conscious experience: what lies beneath the surface comes to light. The rocks symbolize emerging issues or truths that may feel dangerous; the moss in the foreground signifies stagnant situations. A further meaning of low tide is waiting, and/or feeling trapped by delay. Until the tide comes in, our ship—the vessel of the self—cannot sail.

See low tide on the Eight of Swords and Eight of Cups.

5 WAXING MOON

The waxing moon represents a phase of thinking. In two weeks' time the moon will become full, which brings a time of expression and release, but for now, energy—and the tension around a decision—continues to build.

See the waxing moon on II The High Priestess and XVIII The Moon.

6 MONASTIC DRESS

The woman's dress is monastic in its simplicity. This signifies she values privacy and has found a safe space away from the water to contemplate her next steps.

THREE OF SWORDS

Esoteric Title: Sorrow
Number: Three
Astrological Associations: Saturn in Libra
Element: Air
Season: Winter
Tree of Life Position: Binah, the sphere of compassion and understanding

DESCRIPTION

Beneath dense clouds in a sky heavy with rainfall, three identical swords pierce a dominant red heart.

KEY MEANINGS

Sorrow, suffering, endings, revelation, heartbreak, betrayal, disloyalty, truth, clarity, painful devotion, healing

UPRIGHT MEANING

The message of this card is intentionally direct: it foretells sorrow and grief. This applies to relationships, from romance to family, but can reveal disloyalty in other life areas, too, as a painful truth comes to light. Through the process of suffering and recovery, you see a situation clearly. Nothing more is hidden, so you make decisions based on fact rather than speculation. In readings the card can show minor procedures and operations, as Swords suggest the action of cutting.

REVERSED MEANING

The reversed card brings more intensity than the upright card, so be prepared for confusion, drama, and necessary disruption—which too will pass.

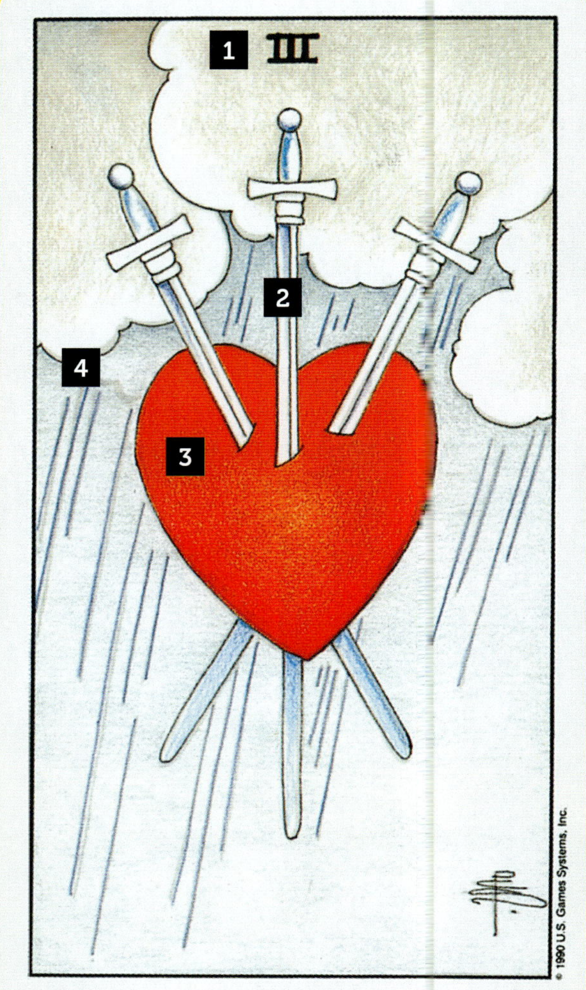

THE THREE OF SWORDS' SYMBOLS

1	**Number III**	Conflict and truth
2	**Three swords**	Sorrows
3	**Heraldic shield**	Reputation
4	**Clouds and rain**	Tears and healing

What the Symbols Mean for You

When you are drawn to a particular symbol or feature of a card, it's because it holds a special meaning for you. Here is a guide to interpreting your symbols.

1 NUMBER III

Three is for creative fulfillment—the beginning, middle, and end or completion. However, in the conflict-driven suit of Swords, dynamic three brings conflict and sacrifice. Three also suggests affairs, with a third person being involved in a relationship, particularly if the card appears with the Seven of Swords (see page 176). The card's astrological association of Saturn in Libra expresses this—severe Saturn bombards peaceful Libra with the harsh truth.

2 THREE SWORDS

Swords represent the mind and, in this card in particular, grief. In Christian art, the Virgin Mary is depicted as Our Lady of Sorrows with seven swords piercing her heart; each sword represents a painful episode relating to her son. In this way, the swords suggest necessary suffering; unavoidable hurt that can only be endured. An additional interpretation is suffering for a good cause—perhaps making a financial or emotional sacrifice, which also links with the card's Tree of Life sphere of Binah, for compassion and understanding.

3 HERALDIC SHIELD

With its symmetrical design, the heart and swords could be a shield. As a simple shield of the heart ruptured by swords, it signifies compromised boundaries and a failure to protect. In heraldry, the top center point of a shield is known as the honor point—on the Three of Swords, the honor point has been pierced by the central sword, suggesting potential damage to our reputation and sense of self.

See the shield on the Six of Cups.

4 CLOUDS AND RAIN

Of the "weather" cards in the deck (see below), this Three is the only one to include rainfall—the others express high drama rather than sadness or grief. Rain naturally symbolizes tears and upset, but culturally rain brings hope and celebration: crops will be watered. Tears also release pent-up emotion and may begin the process of healing after the storm.

See the storm on XVI The Tower.

See the high winds on the Knight of Swords.

FOUR OF SWORDS

Esoteric Title: Rest From Strife

Number: Four

Astrological Association: Jupiter in Libra

Element: Air

Season: Winter

Tree of Life Position: Chesed, the sphere of love and mercy

DESCRIPTION

An effigy of a young knight, his hands in prayer position, is set beneath a window within a church. Three swords are pictured above him, and the fourth appears alongside his tomb.

KEY MEANINGS

Withdrawal, recovery, healing, rest, separation, planning, quietude, safety, sanctuary

UPRIGHT MEANING

The Four means taking time out from projects, work, or relationships. You may need to step away from commitments to rest and rejuvenate—so self-care is key now; the card also favors counseling or other healing therapies. A further meaning is recuperation after illness or an operation and can mean visits to hospital. In love, a relationship goes on hold; you need to press pause to work out how best to proceed.

REVERSED MEANING

When reversed, the card shows enforced time out—so the message is to accept this and use it as an opportunity to think through your options.

THE FOUR OF SWORDS' SYMBOLS

1	**Number IV**	Stability
2	**The four swords**	Stillness
3	**The Knight**	A Templar Knight
4	**Knight's position**	Faith and surrender
5	**Stained-glass window**	The outside world
6	**The church**	Sanctuary

What the Symbols Mean for You

When you are drawn to a particular symbol or feature of a card, it's because it holds a special meaning for you. Here is a guide to interpreting your symbols.

1 NUMBER IV

Four is the number of stability and the element of Earth. The card's element is Air, and Air and Earth weaken, rather than support one another, which brings tension and potential conflict. We see this in the card's astrological association of cerebral Jupiter and sociable Libra. The Knight may have conflicting needs; he cannot abandon society all together but must find time for restorative solitude. The card's Tree of Life sphere of Chesed also embraces the idea of peace. This is the Knight's goal—to find peace through rest.

2 THE FOUR SWORDS

The three swords above the knight are displayed with their hilts downward. These are the swords from the previous card; now they are items for display rather than working weapons. The fourth sword rests alongside the knight's tomb, the sword hilt close to his left hand so he may at any moment take it up and strike.

3 THE KNIGHT

The Knight may be the Templar Knight Baron Robert de Roos (1177–1226/27). At Templar Church, London, there are nine Templar Knight effigies—de Roos is the only knight to have his hands in the prayer position, as on our card. The monk in the stained-glass window (see description at right) may also be de Roos, who briefly became a monk.

4 KNIGHT'S POSITION

The knight is at rest temporarily. Laying on his back, he is vulnerable to attack but trusts in his safety. His hands are in prayer position, symbolizing submission and devotion to a greater power.

5 STAINED-GLASS WINDOW

The colorful stained-glass window shows a monk helping a parishioner—a symbol of the charitable activities of the church beyond its walls. Charity was part of the duty of a medieval knight; the monk depicted may be the Templar Knight Robert de Roos (see The Knight, at left).

See the stained-glass window on the Five of Pentacles.

6 THE CHURCH

The church is a common symbol of sanctuary—a place of refuge during testing times.

See the church on the Three of Pentacles.

FIVE OF SWORDS

Esoteric Title: Defeat
Number: Five
Astrological Association: Venus in Aquarius
Element: Air
Season: Winter
Tree of Life Position: Geburah, the sphere of power and destruction

DESCRIPTION

In the aftermath of battle, three figures remain by an unsettled sea. The victor holds three swords; he is about to take his opponents' remaining two. He takes pleasure in his win.

KEY MEANINGS

Loss, defeat, bullying, cruelty, conflict, stubbornness, endings, upheaval, release, humiliation, obstinacy

UPRIGHT MEANING

What you hoped for does not materialize, so it is wise to accept defeat. In readings the card spells a finite ending and is a message to retreat rather than continue; this is an unwinnable conflict. The clarity this ending brings, however, is a release; it is time to regather and heal with no guilt or regret. Specific meanings include the end of a friendship, bullying in educational establishments or the workplace, and more generally, strife and arguments.

REVERSED MEANING

When reversed, the card's meaning brings more criticism and extremity so you may find a situation ends more dramatically and, thankfully, quickly.

THE FIVE OF SWORDS' SYMBOLS

1	**Number V**	Tests
2	**Abandoned swords**	Lost faith
3	**Body language**	Abuse of power
4	**Ripped clouds**	Violence
5	**Green and red disguise**	Subterfuge

What the Symbols Mean for You

When you are drawn to a particular symbol or feature of a card, it's because it holds a special meaning for you. Here is a guide to interpreting your symbols.

1 NUMBER V

Five is the number of imbalance and disruption; as an odd number, nothing is settled. Number five in the suit of Swords for Air, or the mind, means mental disruption. As the number of fingers on the hand, five is also associated with human experience—and all of life's attendant tests and challenges. In the Five of Swords astrology, we have loving Venus in unconventional Aquarius—which may explain the context for the battle (symbolized by Geburah, Tree of Life sphere of power and destruction). One might be too idealistic and even fanatical about a certain outcome that proves impossible to achieve.

2 ABANDONED SWORDS

In medieval times, a knight's sword was a symbol of his faith. To relinquish your sword in battle was to lose your faith and purpose.

3 BODY LANGUAGE

Two figures have their backs turned to away; one man has his head in his hands, a gesture of despair. The bigger figure dominates the image, just as he has dominated the fight. The expression on his face is snide—cruel, even, as if he has taken pleasure in his opponent's loss. This is not matter of fact; it's personal, and more hurtful for those involved. We do not see the opponent's faces, a sign that through battle they are humiliated and lose their sense of identity.

4 CLOUDS

Slashed clouds are a symbol of violence. In this suit of Air, we see the destruction of battle in the sky rather than on the ground—the slashed clouds are the only evidence for the war that has taken place.

See the slashed clouds on the Knight of Swords.

5 GREEN AND RED DISGUISE

The merchant has red and green attire. Red is for action and desire, green for growth and abundance. The victor has achieved what he desired and now has an abundance of swords as his reward. However, his lack of armor and colors may have intentionally deceived his victims, tricking them into seeing him as benign rather than violent. In this way, the red and green may have disguised his true intentions.

SIX OF SWORDS

Esoteric Title: Earned Success

Number: Six

Astrological Association: Mercury in Aquarius

Element: Air

Season: Winter

Tree of Life Position: Tiphareth, the sphere of beauty and rebirth

DESCRIPTION

A man, woman, and child sail toward a peaceful shore. They carry six swords with them but no luggage; we do not see their faces and they are fixed on their destination.

KEY MEANINGS

Moving on, travel, escape, hope, peace, relief, protection, healing retreat, new focus

UPRIGHT MEANING

The Six shows healing and moving on after a period of stress. Past pressure dissipates, and you feel a sense of resolution and completion; troubles are over and brighter times beckon. In relationships, the card can show recovery after arguments or potential separation—whatever brings you the most peace. Further interpretations include travel, short breaks away, and moving home.

REVERSED MEANING

The reversed card expresses feelings of powerlessness as you cannot find the solution you need just now—but it will come in time.

THE SIX OF SWORDS' SYMBOLS

1	**Number VI**	Peace of mind
2	**Six swords**	Self-protection
3	**Three figures**	A new story
4	**Far shore**	Reward
5	**Waves and stillness**	Change and navigation

What the Symbols Mean for You

When you are drawn to a particular symbol or feature of a card, it's because it holds a special meaning for you. Here is a guide to interpreting your symbols.

1 NUMBER VI

Six is the number of harmony and peace. It also represents a stage of completion—in that a battle or period of stress is finally over. As the element of the suit of Swords is Air, for the mind, together the number and element signify peace of mind. The card's astrological association, Mercury in Aquarius, means a new focus. Aquarius, sign of idealism meets fast-moving Mercury, so the boat journeys toward a new shore.

2 SIX SWORDS

The six swords appear with their hilts down so the boat's occupants are safe from the blades. The weapons also create a protective shield at the front of the boat, again keeping them safe from attack. As swords are the symbol of the mind, this expresses the idea of blocking out intrusive thoughts of the past and focusing on the present moment.

3 THREE FIGURES

The number three is for the beginning, middle, and end of a story. The trio of travelers—who appear to be a father, mother, and child—have completed a chapter. With no luggage, they are free of the past, ready to begin again. This new start resonates with the card's Tree of Life sphere of Tiphareth, for rebirth.

4 FAR SHORE

The shore ahead looks idyllic—the gentle hills and trees are symbols of a fruitful future. This suggests the idea of the promised land, an ideal. Here, the shore is the goal, the reward for troubles overcome.

5 WAVES AND STILLNESS

The water to the left of the boat is still, for peace, while the water on the right is agitated, for past ups and downs. In this way, the two forms of water symbolize parallel states of mind; the boatman must steer his course with grace. Just as he pulls his oar through the waves, his past experiences will help him sail ahead and reach the far shore.

SEVEN OF SWORDS

Other Names: The Thief
Esoteric Title: Unstable Effort
Number: Seven
Astrological Association: Moon in Aquarius
Element: Air
Season: Winter
Tree of Life Position: Netzach, the sphere of endurance, instinct, and desire

DESCRIPTION

A youth clad in a fur-trimmed hat and boots steals five swords from a camp site in broad daylight. Two swords remain, set upright in the earth.

KEY MEANINGS

Dishonesty, lies, theft, deceit, an impostor, betrayal, insecurity, transgression, disguise

UPRIGHT MEANING

This Seven often appears in readings to show fear of loss, or as a warning to protect yourself from deception. This applies to the stealing of ideas as well as possessions. The Seven also shows legal issues and sharp practice in business; it is time to think laterally to protect your interests. However, more positively, the card also encourages you to seek unique solutions to problems that will help you succeed. On a practical note, the card is a reminder to secure your car, home, and other valuable property.

REVERSED MEANING

The meaning is like that of the upright card but advises you not to fall victim to others' dishonesty or greed; it is still possible to outwit them.

THE SEVEN OF SWORDS' SYMBOLS

1	**Number VII**	Number of potential
2	**The stolen swords**	Injustice
3	**Thief's attire**	Trickery
4	**The sunlit camp**	Daylight robbery
5	**On tip toe**	Parody of stealth

What the Symbols Mean for You

When you are drawn to a particular symbol or feature of a card, it's because it holds a special meaning for you. Here is a guide to interpreting your symbols.

1 NUMBER VII

Seven is the number of potential. Sevens are traditionally associated with mysteries—including the mysteries of the unseen future—along with luck, divinity, and magic. The combination of mystery and the Air element means everything being in our head, yet to be realized. The Moon in Aquarius gives us the intuition of the magical moon with idealistic, detached Aquarius—which suggests that the thief instinctively knows when to strike and can detach himself from the consequences of crime. The card's Tree of Life sphere of Netzach also brings in the meanings of instinct and desire—in this case, a desire for other's property.

2 THE STOLEN SWORDS

Swords are a symbol of faith and justice; so stolen swords denote injustice and lost faith. The swords are arranged in two groups of five and two. Five are in the hands of the thief—five is the number of mankind and human experience. The thief appears to grin as he runs off, as if pleased with himself for leaving the two swords behind as a show of mercy.

See the male figure's cruel grin on the Five of Swords.

3 THIEF'S ATTIRE

The youth wears a fancy fur-trimmed hat and boots which contrasts with his workaday trousers and tunic. He might have stolen his red accessories or worn them deliberately to fit in with a crowd before cheating them of their swords. Red is the color of action, creativity, and passion, seen in XI Justice and I The Magician. In this Seven, the thief manifests his desire for other's power by stealing their possessions.

4 THE SUNLIT CAMP

The thief steals when least expected—in daylight, not at night when guards would be on duty. The tent doors are all open, so this may be an opportunistic rather than calculated crime. No one has noticed the thief's intrusion, and he commits his crime openly without any respect for authority.

5 ON TIP TOE

The thief runs on tip toe to steal away from the camp, but there is no need: it is daylight, and no one is around to prevent him (we see a group of soldiers in silhouette, far from camp). The tiptoeing is a parody of stealth, an ego-boost as he takes his prize.

EIGHT OF SWORDS

Esoteric Title: Shortened Force
Number: Eight
Astrological Association: Jupiter in Gemini
Element: Air
Season: Winter
Tree of Life Position: Hod, the sphere of majesty and the mind

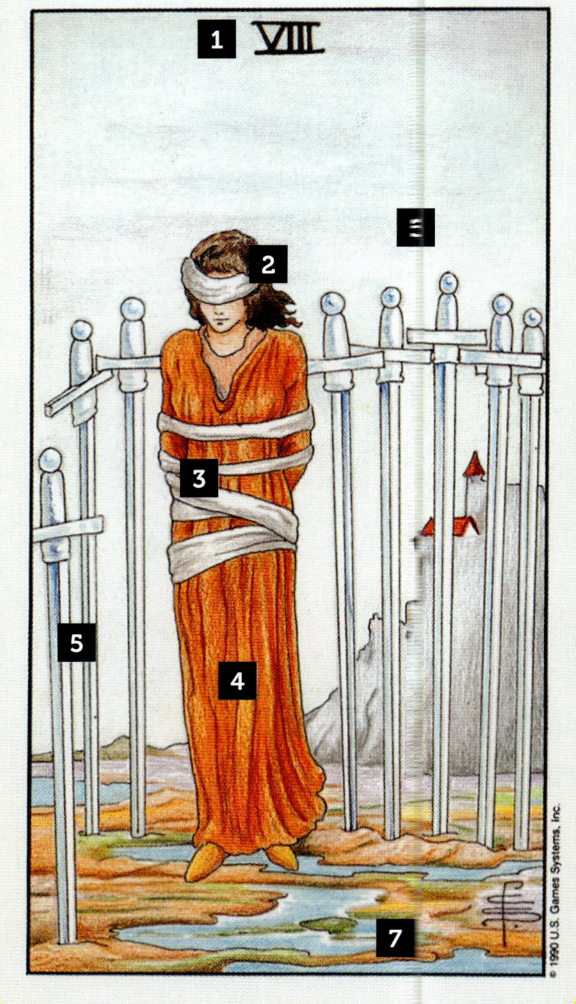

DESCRIPTION

A lone woman in a red dress is tied and blindfold. Eight upright swords are placed around her on a rocky shoreline; behind her is a fairy-tale castle.

KEY MEANINGS

Restriction, limitation, unwanted thoughts, negativity, options, perception, abandonment, othering

UPRIGHT MEANING

The Eight means restriction and overthinking. This manifests as frustration, blocks, and unreasonable demands; a sense of duty may keep you from breaking free, but it is time to untangle your commitments. In your social circle you may feel distanced from friends, but support is there should you ask. In romance, a partner may be emotionally unavailable. A further meaning is debt or other agreements that limit your freedom.

REVERSED MEANING

The reversed meaning of the card is similar to the upright meaning but with a sharper focus and deeper frustration. However, there is room to negotiate.

THE EIGHT OF SWORDS' SYMBOLS

1	**Number VIII**	Cycles and renewal
2	**Blindfold**	Limitation
3	**Binds**	Victimhood
4	**Woman in orange**	The Other; the witch
5	**Eight swords**	Unwanted thoughts
6	**Uneven division**	Fears
7	**Low tide**	Truths

What the Symbols Mean for You

When you are drawn to a particular symbol or feature of a card, it's because it holds a special meaning for you. Here is a guide to interpreting your symbols.

1 NUMBER VIII

Eight, number of fulfillment, change, and renewal, is also the lemniscate (infinity symbol) for the infinite flow of energy. Eight in the card's element of Air means a change in the way of thinking. The astrological association for the Eight is Jupiter in Gemini, which places expansive Jupiter with sociable Gemini; if we can expand our thinking, we gain perspective—and, in the case of the maiden, break free to re-enter society. The card's Tree of Life sphere of Hod, for the mind, suggests that logic is the answer: we can think our way out.

See the lemniscate on I The Magician, VIII Strength, and the folded arms in the Nine of Cups.

2 BLINDFOLD

The blindfold signifies limitation, as it restricts our view of the world. However, the woman's hair is unbound, free to the wind—signifying that she has free will; she needs to see things another way.

See the blindfold on the Two of Swords.

3 BINDS

The woman is bound from her arms to her hips, but the binds are loose. She could release herself, but if she becomes accustomed to this feeling of helplessness, she remains trapped by negative thoughts. However, like the demons on the Devil card with their loose chains, she too can set herself free.

See the loose chains on XV The Devil.

4 WOMAN IN ORANGE

The bound woman conjures the specter of the witch about to be burned at the stake. In this context, she is the "other," the victim that society blames and rejects. Her dress is orange, color of fire and flames.

5 EIGHT SWORDS

The swords are traditional symbols of justice and faith and, in this suit, thoughts. The eight swords—or our thoughts—are an advantage or disadvantage, depending on how we manage them. At first glance the swords appear to imprison her, but she is not surrounded. And if she shook free of her loose binds and blindfold, the swords could be her allies: she could wield one and, protected, make her way back to the castle, symbol of civilization.

6 UNEVEN DIVISION

The swords fall into two groups of three and five—or the Three and Five of Swords. These cards may represent anxieties that keep us stuck: fear of heartbreak (the Three) or defeat (the Five).

7 LOW TIDE

As low tide can reveal rocks and other elements of our subconscious mind, it can signify truths and the danger of these truths surfacing. Equally, low tide also brings the idea of being left behind or stranded.

NINE OF SWORDS

Esoteric Title: Despair and Cruelty
Number: Nine
Astrological Association: Mars in Gemini
Element: Air
Season: Winter
Tree of Life Position: Yesod, the sphere of foundation and the unconscious

DESCRIPTION

In the dead of night, a figure in white sits up in bed, hands to their face in a gesture of anguish. Nine horizontal swords appear above and behind them.

KEY MEANINGS

Disturbance, anxiety, stress, worries, nightmares, sleep patterns, depression, entrapment

UPRIGHT MEANING

This is the card of anxiety and, more broadly, disturbance. Pay close attention to your thoughts; you may be feeling anxious in response to a recent event, such as relationship issues or pressure of work, or suffer random anxiety. This Nine can occasionally reveal depression and panic disorder and, if so, consider professional guidance. More literally, the card expresses whatever disrupts your sleep, such as physical discomfort, nightmares, or insomnia.

REVERSED MEANING

When reversed, there may be guilt or despair—which will dissipate as you move through this cycle. It is important to ask for support if needed.

THE NINE OF SWORDS' SYMBOLS

1	**Number IX**	Number of integration and intensity
2	**The figure in bed**	Anxiety made conscious
3	**The nine swords**	Mental anguish
4	**The bedspread**	Daytime perspective
5	**Bed motif**	Victimhood

What the Symbols Mean for You

When you are drawn to a particular symbol or feature of a card, it's because it holds a special meaning for you. Here is a guide to interpreting your symbols.

1 NUMBER IX

Nine is the number of integration and intensity. In the minor arcana, nine carries the weight of all the number cards that precede it, until the release that comes with the Ten. All the lessons of the previous cards integrate at this stage, so this Nine bears the culmination of the journey through the suit from the Ace of victory through to a truce, heartbreak to defeat, peace, theft, and restriction. Nine in the suit's element of Air, for the mind, symbolizes mounting thoughts, resulting in anxiety. Mars in Gemini signifies the stress of forceful Mars in agreeable Gemini; Gemini, sign of the twins, also expresses the angst of being in two minds.

2 THE FIGURE IN BED

The figure in bed is too anxious to sleep or has just awoken from a nightmare; this relates to the card's Tree of Life sphere of Yesod, for the unconscious mind. He sits upright in bed but is not present in spirit. This sense of otherworldliness is also suggested by the sleeper's ghostly white nightdress.

3 THE NINE SWORDS

The swords are horizontal, with interlocking hilts. One anxious thought leads to the next. The formation of swords gives the impression of prison bars, and a feeling of being trapped by our thinking. The three lower swords appear to pass through the figure—through the crown of the head, the third eye and the heart. The swords disable the upper chakras, or energy points of the body: the crown for spiritual connection, the third eye for intuition, and the heart for love. Repetitive, negative thoughts can disconnect us from our innate wisdom.

4 THE BEDSPREAD

The figure covers his eyes so cannot see the bright quilt with its zodiac-themed patches and red roses. The red rose symbolizes love and the zodiac glyphs, balance and perspective; every patch is identical, creating a balanced design, while the twelve signs signify the expansiveness of the cosmos. However, the troubled figure cannot see the bigger picture on the quilt; only daylight will bring clarity.

See roses on III The Empress and VIII Strength; see the roses and lilies on I The Magician and on the gowns of the supplicants in V The Hierophant.

5 BED MOTIF

The carved scene on the bed base shows one person lunging at another in an attacking stance, illustrating the internal world of the man in bed who feels attacked by his own mind.

TEN OF SWORDS

Esoteric Title: Ruin

Number: Ten

Astrological Association: Sun in Gemini

Element: Air

Season: Winter

Tree of Life Position: Malkuth, the Kingdom, the sphere of experience

DESCRIPTION

A man lies facedown on a beach at night with ten swords are embedded in his back. The light over the distant mountains may be the beginning of sunset or sunrise.

KEY MEANINGS

Endings, outcomes, release, shock, change, betrayal, completion, acceptance, renewal

UPRIGHT MEANING

This Ten means a sudden ending. It may apply to a group of people rather than an individual, so can reveal the end of a relationship or project or losing a job or status due to restructure of a business. Though direct, the card gives you the clarity you need; there is no doubt that the situation you are enquiring about is over. However, this card, like XIII Death, does not mean physical death. Instead, it says this ending must come so that new opportunities and ideas may flourish.

REVERSED MEANING

When reversed, the upright meaning is accompanied by stress and clinging on to what is past. The message is to trust what comes, and release what you cannot hold.

THE TEN OF SWORDS' SYMBOLS

1	**Number X**	Number of completion
2	**The ten swords**	Endings
3	**Night and day**	Coming light
4	**The figure's hand gesture**	Earth and heaven
5	**The red robe**	Blood

What the Symbols Mean for You

When you are drawn to a particular symbol or feature of a card, it's because it holds a special meaning for you. Here is a guide to interpreting your symbols.

1 NUMBER X

Ten, the first double number, marks the ending of one cycle and the beginning of another; the number 10 comprises 1 for beginnings, and the zero, with its circular form, is a symbol of completion, which also aligns with the card's Tree of Life sphere of Malkuth, for experience. The meaning of the Tens, whether positive or negative, arises from the nature of the suit: a multitude of Swords brings conflict and endings. The card's astrological association is Sun in Gemini, a happy, light-hearted combination that suggests the brighter future that comes after our recovery from the Ten.

2 THE TEN SWORDS

The ten swords pin down the figure from neck to hip. A group of three swords stands perfectly upright, while others appear individually placed—but regardless of their source, all accumulate to immobilize the man. The ten swords, therefore, symbolize the end of the situation in question.

3 NIGHT AND DAY

The yellow hue of the sky may be sunrise or sunset; it tells us that there is light beyond the blackness of this ending. The black and yellow sky above the horizon may also express the happy times before the ending and the blackness after.

See the sunrise/sunset on XIII Death and XIV Temperance.

4 THE FIGURE'S HAND GESTURE

The figure, although facedown, makes the sign of blessing in his right hand. Two fingers are extended, and the others folded into the palm, a symbol of the known and unknown worlds—or earth and heaven; maybe the prone figure will return in another carnation. This gesture also communicates the idea of other forms of consciousness, and how shock news throws us into an altered reality.

See this symbol on V The Hierophant and the Six of Pentacles.

5 THE RED ROBE

The prone figure's red robe symbolizes blood, the life force, but there is no sign of blood where the swords tips pierce the body. This may relate to the card creator A. E. Waite's comment that this Ten "is not especially a card of violent death."

PAGE OF SWORDS

Other Names: Princess, Knave, or Jack of Swords
Esoteric Titles: The Princess of the Rushing Winds, The Lotus of the Palace of Air
Element: Earth of the suit of Air

DESCRIPTION

A young person takes a defensive position on a windswept hilltop. He holds a large sword in both hands as if prepared to wield it, but wears no battle armor.

KEY MEANINGS

Beginnings, news, intelligence, detail, legal issues, contracts, vigilance, defense, strategy, ambition

UPRIGHT MEANING

As an influence: The card brings necessary action—from legal agreements such as contracts to applications for work, this is the time to pay attention to detail and follow procedure. There's a feeling of pending trouble, or at the least, some disturbance, so consider the best ways to protect your interests. As a person, the Page is an ambitious young person, quick-witted, and eager to take on a new challenge.

REVERSED MEANING

When reversed, the card traditionally means gossip and misinformation. There may be setbacks or delays with official paperwork.

THE PAGE OF SWORDS' SYMBOLS

1	**The Page**	A young person or situation
2	**Facing left, sword right**	The future and the past
3	**The sword beyond**	Perceived threat
4	**Hilltop**	Vision and risk
5	**Clouds and tree**	Doubt; invisible troubles
6	**Ten birds**	Messages and worries

What the Symbols Mean for You

When you are drawn to a particular symbol or feature of a card, it's because it holds a special meaning for you. Here is a guide to interpreting your symbols.

1 THE PAGE

Pages are messengers, bringing news, and also describe young people and young situations. This Page is Earth of the suit of Air. Air denotes intellect and strategy, so there may be some self-conflict due to pragmatic Earth clashing with idealistic Air.

2 FACING LEFT, SWORD RIGHT

The future and the past. The Page faces left but holds his sword to the right, as if ready to protect himself from troubles arising on all fronts—from past issues and those to come. The Page's stance is uneven, as if trying to find the right position for defense.

3 THE SWORD BEYOND

The tip extends beyond the frame of the card, as if we can only imagine the extent of the Page's blade. He needs to appear powerful to compensate for his lack of experience in battle—he is not dressed for fighting. In this card, the incomplete sword, therefore, signifies worry over compromised or broken boundaries: the threat of invasion by the enemy, or invasive thoughts.

See the sword hidden beyond the card frame in the Knight of Swords, Two, Five, and Nine of Swords.

4 HILLTOP

The hilltop signifies vision and risk. To gain a vantage point, the Page must be visible to others and open to the elements—the threat of rain and the forceful wind. This is rough terrain that says this is a place of discomfort.

5 CLOUDS AND TREE

The clouds symbolize doubt, and the windswept tree, invisible troubles.

See the clouds on VI The Lovers.

6 TEN BIRDS

Birds are believed to be a sign from the spirit world. As earthly messengers, or couriers, they bring news. Collectively, they can also represent worries and, here, trouble on the horizon.

KNIGHT OF SWORDS

Esoteric Titles: The Prince of the Chariot of the Wind

Element: Fire of the suit of Air

Major Arcana Link: VII The Chariot

Astrological Associations: Taurus and Gemini

Animal Symbols: White horse, bird, butterfly

DESCRIPTION

A knight charges ahead, about to attack his enemy. He gives his horse full reign to gallop at speed and, with raised weapon, gives a battle cry.

KEY MEANINGS

Conflict, courage, drama, aggression, truth, sudden decisions, arguments

UPRIGHT MEANING

As an influence: The card signifies disputes and arguments; there's sudden drama as whatever has been kept below the surface erupts. This applies particularly in love relationships and work, but at the least, you see where the trouble lies. As a person, the Knight of Swords is a driven and astute individual, willing to endure conflict to get the results he desires.

REVERSED MEANING

When reversed, the card means stress and suffering due to unfair opposition. It's also the card of potential scandal—but this too will pass.

THE KNIGHT OF SWORDS' SYMBOLS

1	**The Knight**	Change
2	**Riding in from the right**	Future trouble
3	**Red cape and plume**	Passion and energy
4	**The sword beyond**	Perceived threat
5	**Ragged clouds**	Ruthlessness
6	**Birds and butterflies**	Thought

What the Symbols Mean for You

When you are drawn to a particular symbol or feature of a card, it's because it holds a special meaning for you. Here is a guide to interpreting your symbols.

1 THE KNIGHT

Always on horseback, the Knights are the tarot's agents of change. The Knight of Swords is an aspect of card VII The Chariot, and they have the astrological sign of Taurus in common (Taurus and the other fixed signs are represented by the sphinx on The Chariot). The card's elements are Fire and Air, which relate to storms and hurricanes. With his raised sword, the Knight strikes in a lightning flash.

2 RIDING IN FROM THE RIGHT

The Knight rides in from the right of the card, the place of the future. He warns of troubles and conflict, and rides against the wind: what he brings will be unexpected.

3 RED CAPE AND PLUME

Red is the color of passion and energy. The Knight's red cape comes to life in the wind—a reminder of the card's elements of Fire and Air. His plume takes the shape of wings, another symbol of the card's element of Air and the mind. Plans take flight.

4 THE SWORD BEYOND

The sword extends beyond the card, so we see less than half of the weapon. The rest is deliberately left to the imagination—in conflict, perceived threat is half the battle. The incomplete sword can also reveal anxiety and worry about problems that may or may not materialize.

See the sword beyond the card frame in the Page of Swords, and Two, Five, and Nine of Swords.

5 RAGGED CLOUDS

The ragged clouds show us that this knight is tearing up the sky and forcing nature to his will. As he will cut through whatever is in his way, these torn clouds symbol ruthlessness.

See the clouds on the Page of Swords and VI The Lovers.

6 BIRDS AND BUTTERFLIES

The motifs decorating the horse collar look out of place on the horse's collar; their innocence conflicts with the Knight's predetermined aggression. The butterflies and birds symbolize the Air element and represent thought.

See the butterflies engraved in the Queen of Swords' throne.

QUEEN OF SWORDS

Esoteric Title: The Queen of the Thrones of the Air	
Element: Water of the suit of Air	
Major Arcana Link: III The Empress	
Astrological Associations: Virgo and Libra	
Animal Symbols: Bird, butterfly	

DESCRIPTION

We see a Queen on her throne on a hilltop wearing a distinctive cloud cloak. She holds an upright sword and makes a gesture with her left hand.

KEY MEANINGS

Intelligence, judgement, ambition, clarity, freedom, decisions, instinct, intuition, strength, autonomy, singlemindedness

UPRIGHT MEANING

As an influence: The card brings the gifts of perception and perspective. It's a time for quick thinking and putting together clear strategies. Call upon your inner strength and wisdom, and be prepared to stand alone; in relationships, too, you may need to prioritize your own interests. As an individual, the Queen traditionally represents a single person. As a personality, she is ambitious, wise, and direct.

REVERSED MEANING

Stress and lack of understanding lead to fractious relationships, feeling attacked, and receiving little compassion.

THE QUEEN OF SWORDS' SYMBOLS

1	**The Queen**	Empowerment
2	**Facing right**	The future
3	**White robes**	Purity of intention
4	**Red bracelet**	Venus: Mercy and redemption
5	**The sword**	Authority and judgement
6	**Winged creatures**	Thinking
7	**Hand gesture**	Openness
8	**Two sickles**	Divine judgement
9	**Cloud cloak**	Freedom
10	**Blue sky**	Truth and clarity

What the Symbols Mean for You

When you are drawn to a particular symbol or feature of a card, it's because it holds a special meaning for you. Here is a guide to interpreting your symbols.

1 THE QUEEN

Queens signify empowerment. As the Queen of Swords' suit is Air, she represents the mind of card III The Empress (see page 30). The Queen's combined elements are Water for emotion and Air for the mind, which sit comfortably together—provided they stay in tune.

2 FACING RIGHT

The Queen sits in profile, facing right, which means her focus is on the future.

3 WHITE ROBES

White is a color of the element of Air. The queen's white tunic almost merges with the clouds, as if she could be part of the sky and the element itself. White symbolizes purity, so here, purity of intention.

4 RED BRACELET

The red bracelet on the Queen's right wrist suggests the Venus symbol seen on III The Empress, and it is also a symbol of mercy and redemption.

See the Venus symbol on III The Empress.

5 THE SWORD

The sword in the hands of a Queen is a symbol of judgement. As it dominates the image, the weapon shows a potential imbalance between harsh judgement and mercy or empathy. Held vertically, the sword also symbolizes boundaries.

See the sword of retribution on XI Justice.

6 HAND GESTURE

The queen's raised hand evokes her suit element, as her palm is open to the air. Her hand could also hold the scales of mercy (see The Sword, at left), linking with her sign of Libra, the scales. A further meaning is a gesture of readiness before giving a knighthood.

7 WINGED CREATURES

The throne features a winged cherub and butterflies to signify the Queen's suit of Air and the mind (butterflies also adorn her crown). However, these butterflies, symbols of thought, are carved in stone and made to last. Whatever is dreamed of must be created in solid form.

See butterflies on the Knight and King of Swords.

8 TWO SICKLES

Toward the base of the throne is a pair of sickles, which symbolize divine judgement (see The Sword, at left). An alternate reading is two crescent moons, for intuition.

See the moon on II The High Priestess and XVIII The Moon.

9 CLOUD CLOAK

The Queen's cloak has a butterfly clasp (see Winged Creatures, above) and is decorated with clouds. This design connects her directly to her hilltop skyscape, so she becomes part of nature, free to go where she chooses.

10 BLUE SKY

Blue is the color of truth. All words and actions, for the Queen, are for the sake of truth and clarity.

KING OF SWORDS

Esoteric Titles: The Lord of the Wind and the Breezes, the Lord of the Spirits of the Air
Element: Air of the suit of Air
Major Arcana Link: IV The Emperor
Astrological Associations: Capricorn and Aquarius
Animal Symbols: Bird, butterfly

DESCRIPTION

The King sits in the same landscape as his consort, the Queen—a blowy hilltop up in the clouds. He wears billowy white-blue robes and holds a sword upright in his right hand.

KEY MEANINGS

Clarity, decisions, wisdom, judgements, contracts, conflict, strategies, ambition, ultimatums, instinct, communication

UPRIGHT MEANING

As an influence: It is time for a strategy as the head, rather than the heart, takes charge: your mind may be in overdrive, particularly if you are working or studying hard. Also, the card often brings contracts, agreements, disputes, and decisions. There's also an element of judgement here, so there may be legal or official proceedings. As a person, the King is incisive, wise, and courageous but may lack empathy and patience.

REVERSED MEANING

Mental overload or feeling manipulated by others' unreasonable demands. Ruthlessness and potential cruelty; feeling embattled.

THE KING OF SWORDS' SYMBOLS

1	**The King**	Authority
2	**The sword**	Judgement and wisdom
3	**Blue robes**	Truth
4	**Purple cloak**	Intuition, status
5	**Winged creatures**	Thinking
6	**Two moons**	Cycles and phases

What the Symbols Mean for You

When you are drawn to a particular symbol or feature of a card, it's because it holds a special meaning for you. Here is a guide to interpreting your symbols.

1 THE KING

Kings signify authority. As the King's suit is Swords, which takes the Air element, he represents the mind of IV The Emperor (see page 34). The King's other element is also Air. Double-Air means great intellect and ambition, so the King is full of ideals; the downside is that he may appear elusive, living in his own world.

2 THE SWORD

The sword in the hands of a King is a symbol of judgement, but he holds it at an angle, unlike the perfectly straight card of the Queen of Swords and XI Justice; while his sword could be ceremonial, it could be used in battle at a moment's notice. This is part of this King's power—he can wield his weapon both ways, so the sword signifies his experience and wisdom.

See the sword of retribution on XI Justice.

3 BLUE ROBES

The King's blue robes are a symbol of truth—as in "true blue." With his sword, he cuts to the heart of a matter. In this way, blue says that the truth will soon be made clear.

4 PURPLE CLOAK

In early printings of the Rider Waite Smith deck, the King's cloak is a brown, earthy color—given the card is double-Air, this would reveal how the King's decisions (the mind) are grounded in reality (Earth). Here, the cloak is purple, a symbol of intuition, royalty, and status.

5 WINGED CREATURES

The throne features butterflies and a fairy (see Two Moons, below) to signify the King's suit of Air and the mind. Butterflies, symbols of thought, are carved in stone and made to last, to signify realized intention. A winged cherub appears on the King's golden crown, a symbol of his connection with God or the divine.

See butterflies on the Knight and Queen of Swords.

6 TWO MOONS

The two moons may be the waxing and waning crescents of Titania, the largest moon of Uranus, which rules Aquarius, one of the King's zodiac signs. Titania is named after Shakespeare's Titania, the Fairy Queen. The moons and butterfly make a crest on the throne, symbolizing cycles and phases. An alternative reading is two sickles, for divine judgement (see Queen of Swords, page 188).

ACE OF WANDS

Esoteric Title: Root of the Powers of Fire
Number: One
Astrological Associations: The Fire signs—Aries, Leo, and Sagittarius
Element: Fire
Major Arcana Link: I The Magician
Season: Spring
Tree of Life Position: Kether the crown, sphere of divine light
Compositional Affinity: All minor arcana Aces

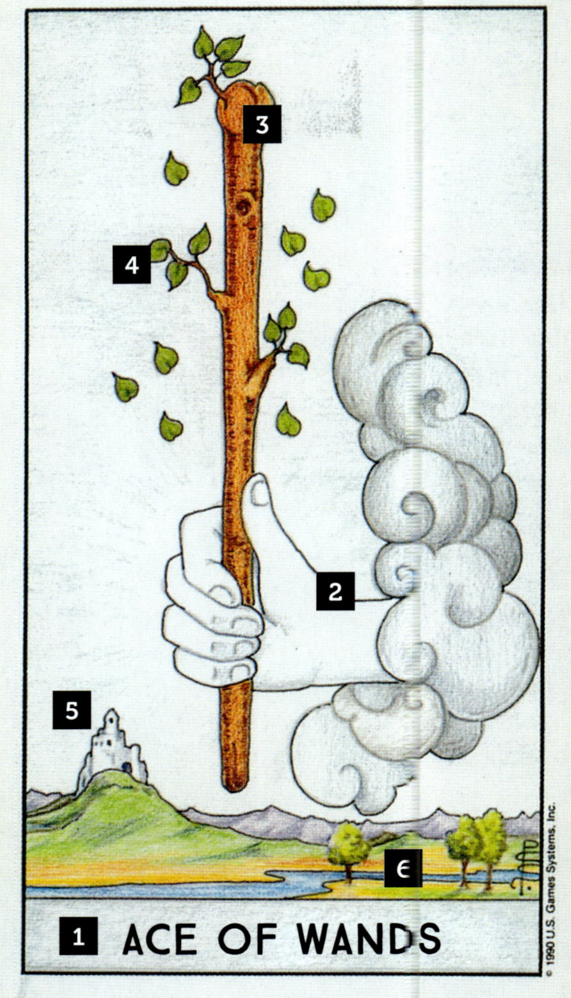

DESCRIPTION

A hand appears from a cloud, holding an upright wand with buds and falling leaves. Below is a castle on a hilltop above a fertile valley.

KEY MEANINGS

Beginnings, passion, new ventures, opportunity, travel, enterprise, career, solutions, creativity, growth, virility, courage

UPRIGHT MEANING

A new passion begins. This Ace brings fiery, dynamic energy—so you experience sudden flashes of motivation and inspiration; whatever has been stuck shifts dramatically. Travel, new contacts, and passion bring excitement and soulful adventures. This is also an auspicious card for creativity and inventiveness; problems can be solved in a flash.

REVERSED MEANING

The reversed card can show fertility issues, creative blocks, and overall, delay. You may need to see a situation in a new light.

THE ACE OF WANDS' SYMBOLS

1	**Number I**	Beginnings and oneness
2	**Hand**	Invitation
3	**Wand**	Purpose
4	**Leaves**	Growth and hope
5	**Castle**	Ambition and desire
6	**Valley**	Opportunity

What the Symbols Mean for You

When you are drawn to a particular symbol or feature of a card, it's because it holds a special meaning for you. Here is a guide to interpreting your symbols.

1 NUMBER I

One, or Ace, is the number of beginnings and oneness (feeling "at one" within the self and with the divine). All Aces also relate to card I The Magician in the major arcana, who displays each suit symbol on his altar (see page 22). The first card of its suit, the Ace, holds the essence of its Water element: pure emotion and spiritual connection, shown by the card's Tree of Life sphere, Kether, for divine light.

2 HAND

The hand offering the chalice represents an invitation and a gift. Traditionally, the right hand is the hand of giving, and the left, the hand of receiving.

See the giving hands on the Ace of Pentacles, Cups, and Swords.

3 WAND

The wand is a symbol of power and purpose and, in this card in particular, its phallic shape is a symbol of male fertility. The wand sprouts three buds—three is the number of Fire, the card's element. The ten attached leaves lead us to card X The Wheel of Fortune, which expresses the nature of Fire: the upside is that the spirit of adventure can bring great reward, but on the downside, we risk getting burned. Number ten also relates to yod, the tenth letter of the Hebrew alphabet, which also means "fire."

See Yod droplets on XVI The Tower, XVIII The Moon, and the Ace of Swords.

4 LEAVES

There are eight floating leaves—symbols of growth—around the wand. Eight relates to VIII Strength: in the fourteenth-century Visconti Sforza card, Strength is a man wielding a wand-like club to subdue a lion. The total number of leaves is eighteen, which may refer to the eighteenth letter of the Hebrew alphabet, Tzaddi, meaning "hope."

5 CASTLE

The white hilltop castle is a symbol of potential, ambition, and desire. If this is our dream, we may use our magic wand to manifest it.

See the fairytale castle on the Seven of Cups and the Eight of Swords.

6 VALLEY

The valley, with its flowing blue water and trees, gives not only the obvious meaning of fertility but also opportunity. There is rich, level ground in which to plant our wands—our fresh ideas—and see them grow.

TWO OF WANDS

Esoteric Title: Dominion

Number: Two

Astrological Associations: Mars in Aries

Element: Fire, for the soul

Season: Spring

Tree of Life Position: Chockmah, the sphere of wisdom

DESCRIPTION

A well-dressed man holds a globe in his right hand and a tall wand in his left. To his right is a second wand, held in a ring. From battlements, he looks out over a fertile landscape.

KEY MEANINGS

Partnerships, planning, support, vision, energy, willpower, talent, adventure, friendship, progress, work, confidence, nature, spiritual pathways

UPRIGHT MEANING

This Two holds a vision for the future, so this is a time of planning—to look ahead, inspired by what is possible in work, projects, and relationships. From a strong position you see the way ahead clearly and have the energy to create what you desire. Whether this applies to a new venture, travel plans, or partnership, give this early stage of development your full attention. A further meaning of the card is personal development as you discover a new spiritual path or inspiring practice.

REVERSED MEANING

When reversed, the card shows frustration as plans do not materialize due to a personality clash or because it simply isn't the right time.

THE TWO OF WANDS' SYMBOLS

1	**Number II**	Partnership and duality
2	**Two Wands**	A doorway
3	**Man and globe**	Vision
4	**Battlements and beyond**	Status and ambition
5	**Rose, cross, and lily**	Alchemy

What the Symbols Mean for You

When you are drawn to a particular symbol or feature of a card, it's because it holds a special meaning for you. Here is a guide to interpreting your symbols.

1 NUMBER II

Two as the number of duality suggests partnership and expansion: when we make a connection with something or someone other than ourselves, a new energy comes into play. The card's astrological association is Mars in Aries, for willpower and determination—which must be well directed, just like the two carefully positioned wands.

2 TWO WANDS

The single wand held by a ring at its base symbolizes the pure Fire of the Ace, which is now contained; it represents work already done. The second wand is a symbol of the man's intentions and completes the form of a doorway to the future: spiritually, this may be a portal to other realms of experience and consciousness. This meaning of expanded experience resonates, too, with the card's Tree of Life alignment with Chockmah, sphere of wisdom.

See the temple pillars as portal on II The High Priestess.

3 MAN AND GLOBE

The male figure wears a red hat, which denotes action and the Fire element of this suit. This is literally a "fire in the head," so he is ablaze with inspired ideas. The globe is a symbol of the earth and ecology, which signifies seeing the bigger picture. With his wand in his left hand and the globe in his right, he is ready to wave his magic wand to push forward his agenda. With his global vision, he wants to take over the world—hence the card's esoteric title of dominion.

4 BATTLEMENTS AND BEYOND

Standing behind castle battlements, the male figure has a clear view from on high. This is a position of command from which he surveys his domain—so he may be the landowner, looking beyond his known territory, or a traveler, taking in the view on his journey. Either way, he is ready to conquer the heights of the distant mountains, a symbol of his goals.

5 ROSE, CROSS AND LILY

The red rose, black cross, and white lily are the colors of alchemy. As an emblem, it represents Rosicrucianism, an old order devoted to the study of alchemy and occult practices. Displayed here as a crest, it associates the male figure with the fictional hero Christian Rosenkreutz, whose story inspired Rosicrucianism. In the story, Rosenkreutz's family crest is like that shown on our card—so in this way, our male figure is also the hero about to begin his adventure.

See the cross and rose motif inset below the three coins on the Three of Pentacles.

See the roses on III The Empress and VIII Strength, and the roses and lilies on I The Magician.

THREE OF WANDS

Esoteric Title: Established Strength
Number: Three
Astrological Associations: Sun in Aries
Element: Fire, for the soul
Season: Spring
Tree of Life Position: Binah, the sphere of compassion and understanding

DESCRIPTION

From a clifftop, a merchant with his back to us looks out over a bay. He holds one budding wand; two others stand upright close by. His three ships sail the waters below.

KEY MEANINGS

Results, success, prosperity, determination, good luck, progress, travel, enterprise, creativity, collaboration, support, relationships

UPRIGHT MEANING

The card signifies great results. Plans—maybe those you made in the Two—have evolved, and you now see progress and reward. A key element of this success is trusting your past decisions or having the confidence to follow through a project and getting the right support. In relationships, you may meet someone new and, in projects, you are drawn to the unusual rather than the mundane. Now is the time for further adventure.

REVERSED MEANING

When reversed the card shows miscommunication and delay—however, this is such a positive card when upright that any issues are minor and quickly resolved.

THE THREE OF WANDS' SYMBOLS

1	**Number III**	Creative power
2	**Three Wands**	Intention and protection
3	**Figure, fully turned**	Vision and trust
4	**Attire**	Action and growth
5	**Checkered sash**	Strategy
6	**Boats at sunrise**	Hope and fortune
7	**Distant shores**	Future goals

What the Symbols Mean for You

When you are drawn to a particular symbol or feature of a card, it's because it holds a special meaning for you. Here is a guide to interpreting your symbols.

1 NUMBER III

On the card, the Three is expressed as three boats, three wands, and the three buds on each wand. Three is the number of creative fulfillment—the beginning, middle, and end or completion. It relates to the element of Fire—Sun in Aries, the cards' astrological association, characterizes this fire as determination and forthright communication. The card's Tree of Life sphere of Binah brings understanding and gentleness to brazen fire so, like the successful merchant, it burns brightly without burning out.

2 THREE WANDS

The wands form the shape of a triangle, symbol of the card's Fire element. The wands have nine buds in total—nine is the number of cumulation, for the merchant's experience and the ships' cargo as an accumulation of goods. He holds one wand, symbol of his intention to create wealth. The two other wands represent his success to date and are positioned behind him as protective markers.

3 FIGURE, FULLY TURNED

Uniquely in the deck, the central figure is completely turned away from us. This represents his single focus: that his ships fare well, and he attains his goals. The man, a merchant, has used his fire to create opportunity but must now wait for the results; he must have faith in his decisions.

4 ATTIRE

The merchant has red and green attire. Red is for action and desire, green for growth and abundance. He wears a headband, symbol of determination. The arm holding the wand is armored, which tells us that he has battled to get this far—and will continue to protect his interests.

See the partial armor on IV The Emperor.
See the headband on I the Magician.

5 CHECKERED SASH

The checkered sash may symbolize the light and shade of our life experience. The sash also resembles a chess board; no doubt the merchant has made the right moves to ensure his success.

See the check motif on the Ten of Pentacles.

6 BOATS AT SUNRISE

The lemon sky tells us this is early dawn, when boats set sail. According to A. E. Waite, the co-creator of the cards, "these are his [the merchant's] ships, bearing his merchandise." Boats and tides signify potential good fortune. Here, they also represent hope.

7 DISTANT SHORES

The distant shores and purple mountain are symbols of the merchant's ambition and goals.

FOUR OF WANDS

Esoteric Title: Perfected Work

Number: Four

Astrological Association: Venus in Aries

Element: Fire

Season: Spring

Tree of Life Position: Chesed, the sphere of love and mercy

DESCRIPTION

Two young people hold up flower garlands. They stand by a city wall and before them is a bower of fruit and flowers held by four wands in bud.

KEY MEANINGS

Freedom, reward, joy, childhood places, holidays, celebration, honeymoon, creativity, energy, domestic happiness

UPRIGHT MEANING

This card brings happiness, celebration, and appreciation. You may have time away for travel, social occasions, and holidays—in readings this Four often comes up to show honeymoons, too, and returning to favorite places. New love comes in and established relationships feel content and close; full of motivation and inspired ideas, you may work on improving a property or finding a dream house. This is a creative time, too, so your projects flourish, and collaborations are also favored.

REVERSED MEANING

When reversed, the card can reveal some minor delays to plans but otherwise the positive upright meaning holds true.

THE FOUR OF WANDS' SYMBOLS

1	**Number IV**	Stability
2	**Arbor**	Fruitfulness
3	**Wands**	Growth and purpose
4	**The couple**	Celebration
5	**City wall**	Boundaries
6	**Two arches**	Protection
7	**Sunshine skies**	Energy and well-being

What the Symbols Mean for You

When you are drawn to a particular symbol or feature of a card, it's because it holds a special meaning for you. Here is a guide to interpreting your symbols.

1 NUMBER IV

Four, the number of stability, is the perfect fit for the card's element of Fire, which energizes plans and burns through problems. The card's astrological association is sensitive Venus in headstrong Aries: a deeply creative pairing—provided the balance is right. Chesed, the sphere of love and mercy, supports the gentleness of love planet Venus, too.

2 ARBOR

The wedding arbor is hung with fruits and flowers, symbols of abundance and fertility. Two wands have red ribbon bows; red is for passion and the life force. The ribbon signifies birth, too, as it is like an umbilical cord, while the crescent shape made by the arbor fruits and flowers on a frame resembles a cradle for a baby to come. This is a time of fruitfulness.

See the red ribbons as infinity symbols on XXI The World.

3 WANDS

Wands signify manifestation—the result of powerful intention. Here, they evoke the Celtic festival of Beltane with the wands as maypoles, fertility symbols that were also decorated with flowers. The four wands also suggest growth; they make the framework for the arbor, but this could also be the start of a permanent building, a structure that the celebrating couple can grow into.

4 THE COUPLE

The couple appear as young people or older children, raising garlands in a gesture of celebration; this is also illustrated by the dancing couple at the bottom-left of the card. Each figure wears wreaths, a symbol of success, and Roman togas, echoing the Floralia, the Roman flower festival. Equally, the couple might be the May Queen and King, part of the Beltane festival (see Wands, at left). They express joyful energy—one of the card's principal meanings.

5 CITY WALL

The city castle wall marks a boundary. The building is well maintained, with no crumbling brickwork. As an interpretation for your situation, this symbol says that your personal boundaries are protected and strong, too.

6 TWO ARCHES

Arches signify protection. The two arches appear as part of a larger arch; this stands for the two people—the couple—being protected by family and society.

See the two arches as the bridge in the Five of Cups.

7 SUNSHINE SKIES

The bright yellow sky is a symbol of awareness, energy, and clarity. The yellow is the color of ripened corn, so the scene (along with Beltane; see Wands, at left) might also reference the Celtic festival of Lammas, celebrated on the first day of harvest. Yellow tells us all is well and acts as a symbol of well-being.

See the yellow sky as a symbol of energy on I The Magician and IXX The Sun and as a symbol of health on VIII Strength.

FIVE OF WANDS

Esoteric Title: Strife
Number: Five
Astrological Association: Saturn in Leo
Element: Fire
Season: Spring
Tree of Life Position: Geburah, the sphere of power and destruction

DESCRIPTION

On open ground, five young men hold up a wand as if to fight or show their might. There is no one focus or clear goal; the wands point in various directions and are not aligned.

KEY MEANINGS

Tests, competitions, play, practice and rehearsal, challenges, frustration, ego, strength, debate, pride, determination, confidence

UPRIGHT MEANING

This Five is a card of tests. You can win and overcome the challenges they present—from competitions and examinations to miscommunication, particularly in work and relationships. These tests also present an opportunity to develop resilience, particularly concerning self-interested individuals who try to dominate; rather than withdraw, be sure you are heard. Further meanings include rehearsals and practice, and potential disruption to plans and travel; check arrangements carefully.

REVERSED MEANING

The reversed meaning is misinformation as what you hear may be confusing or untrue. A further interpretation is temporary restriction.

THE FIVE OF WANDS' SYMBOLS

1	**Number V**	Tests
2	**Five wands**	Purpose
3	**Buds**	Stages of development
4	**Lush ground**	Potential
5	**Attire**	Individuality

What the Symbols Mean for You

When you are drawn to a particular symbol or feature of a card, it's because it holds a special meaning for you. Here is a guide to interpreting your symbols.

1 NUMBER V

Five is the number of imbalance and disruption; as an odd number, nothing is settled. Five is also the number of mankind and all of life's attendant tests and challenges. Number five in the suit of Wands for Fire, or the soul, brings restlessness. The card's astrological association is harsh Saturn in extrovert Leo—a contrary pairing of gloom and optimism. As a card meaning, this suggests the frustration of being tested and held back. The cards' Tree of Life sphere of Geburah, for power and destruction, gives us insight into the card's negative potential—but this association with power may also guide you to take your power back.

2 FIVE WANDS

Wands symbolize intention and power, but here, the power is dissipated as each wand points in a different direction. Some of the wands make triangle shapes—the triangle is the symbol of Fire, the card's element. The way the wands all make different angles also tells us that each person in the group has their own angle, or take, on the situation. As youths, they are necessarily self-interested, working out how best to wield their wand, or power.

3 BUDS

The buds signify stages and phases of growth. One wand is without buds. Two wands have three, and one wand has four. They young men may look a similar age, but the buds—along with their differently colored clothing—show that they are at different stages of development. The men with wands with zero and two buds appear to be struggling with the weight of their wand more than the others.

4 LUSH GROUND

The big swathe of greenery represents growth and potential. The earth has the feel of springtime, the wands' season; the tussle we see with the youths is the beginning of their journey to maturity.

See the lush ground on VIII Strength.

5 ATTIRE

The youths wear different colors to show their individuality. Some sport boots, others shoes; one has a headband, symbol of willpower, and one has a cap waiting for its feather, emblem of honor—from the idiom "a feather in your cap."

See the headband on the Three of Wands and I The Magician.

SIX OF WANDS

Esoteric Title: Victory
Number: Six
Astrological Association: Jupiter in Leo
Element: Fire
Season: Spring
Tree of Life Position: Tiphareth, the sphere of beauty and rebirth
Animal Symbol: White horse

DESCRIPTION

A man on a white horse is celebrated in a parade. He holds a single wand circled with a laurel wreath; five other wands are raised in his honor.

KEY MEANINGS

Success, triumph, acknowledgment, respect, appreciation, happiness, visibility, promotion, reward for work

UPRIGHT MEANING

This joyful Six brings great good news. It reveals weddings, parties, and other group celebrations and signifies well-deserved achievement—such as a promotion in your career, or success in examinations, contests, and creative projects. You win respect for your work and others acknowledge and appreciate your talent. In romantic relationships, the card shows that feelings are articulated (and reciprocated) or going public as a couple. As an answer to a yes-or-no question, this Six is a resounding yes. A further interpretation is winning a court case.

REVERSED MEANING

The reversed card shows delayed news—so you may need to wait for a decision. A further meaning is dealings with an arrogant individual.

THE SIX OF WANDS' SYMBOLS

1	**Number VI**	Peace
2	**Six wands**	Earned success
3	**The horseman**	Victory and power
4	**Riding to the right**	Transformation
5	**White horse**	The future
6	**Green caparison**	New territory; possibilities
7	**The crowd**	Society

What the Symbols Mean for You

When you are drawn to a particular symbol or feature of a card, it's because it holds a special meaning for you. Here is a guide to interpreting your symbols.

1 NUMBER VI

Six is the number of harmony and peace. As with all the minor arcana Sixes, it represents a stage of completion—which here is crowned with success. As the element of the suit of Wands is Fire, for the soul, the peaceful Six keeps the ego under control; the horseman is victorious and proud but not arrogant. The card's astrological association, resilient Jupiter in optimistic Leo, signifies working through obstacles and keeping perspective.

2 SIX WANDS

The horseman holds up one wand in triumph, a symbol of his singular victory; this individuality is also denoted by the wand's single bud. The wand and wreath are also a symbol of fertility and fruitful endeavors. The five wands held by the crowd relate to the number five, the number of experience—so the horseman's expertise accounts for his success.

3 THE HORSEMAN

The horseman with his laurel wreath, symbol of victory and leadership, appears in profile like a Roman emperor on a coin. His wreath crowns him with power.

4 RIDING TO THE RIGHT

In tarot, the right side means the future; the horseman is firmly fixed on the path ahead.

5 WHITE HORSE

The white horse is a symbol of success. The horse gives us a knowing look in acknowledgment, though, that this is a parade—the real success has come from hard work. A further meaning of the horse is transformation as it carries the rider forward. The animal can also be seen as the vehicle of the soul, which aligns with the card's element of Wands, associated with the soul.

See the white horse on XIX The Sun.

6 GREEN CAPARISON

The horse is largely covered by a caparison, a protective covering. The green folds suggest a landscape—the new, fresh territory that comes with success, which evokes the card's Tree of Life sphere of Tiphareth, for beauty and rebirth.

7 THE CROWD

The card shows two people, and we see the headgear of a possible third and the blue robe of a fourth. One man looks toward our horseman and the other into what we assume is a crowd, symbol of society. The horseman is seen by society, and publicly acknowledged with their victory wands.

SEVEN OF WANDS

Esoteric Title: Valor

Number: Seven

Astrological Association: Mars in Leo

Element: Fire

Season: Spring

Tree of Life Position: Netzach, the sphere of endurance, instinct and desire

DESCRIPTION

Towering over a clifftop landscape, a young man stands in a defensive pose. He brandishes his tall wand as six wands rise from unseen hands as if to invade his territory.

KEY MEANINGS

Effort, defense, challenges, courage, advantage, competition, negotiation, determination, boundaries

UPRIGHT MEANING

This Seven is the card of effort and of overcoming all obstacles. It acknowledges the energy you have invested to date and the work that remains to be done; with determination, you can succeed. In business and projects, this Seven reveals tough negotiations and, in relationships, having the difficult conversations to break through blocks to understanding. There's a passionate dynamic to this card, too, as you stand strong, willing to protect your boundaries and fend off challenges to your position. A further meaning is advocacy work, and fighting for a cause you believe in.

REVERSED MEANING

When reversed, the card shows an array of problems that feel too demanding to deal with. The message is to prioritize what to tackle first rather than hesitate.

THE SEVEN OF WANDS' SYMBOLS

1	**Number VII**	Number of potential
2	**The young man**	Willingness
3	**The wands**	Power and intention
4	**The clifftop world**	Displacement
5	**Green tunic**	Growth and protection

What the Symbols Mean for You

When you are drawn to a particular symbol or feature of a card, it's because it holds a special meaning for you. Here is a guide to interpreting your symbols.

1 NUMBER VII

Seven, number of potential, stands for mystery, luck, divinity, and magic. The combination of mystery and the Fire element can be interpreted as burning desire, while Mars in Leo brings intensity and extroversion: this translates as strength in action—which describes the youth steadfastly defending his land. The card's Tree of Life sphere of Netzach is associated with instinct and desire—in this card, expressed as courage.

2 THE YOUNG MAN

The young man stands astride a river, a foot on each bank. He calls to mind the *Colossus of Rhodes*, the huge statue of sun god Helios depicted astride the harbor of Rhodes; Helios also stood strong to defeat would-be invaders.

3 THE WANDS

Wands are symbols of intention, power, and magic. As far as we know, the brandished wand is bigger than those we see partially, showing the man's dominance. Also, the brandished wand has five buds, as opposed to the two and three buds on the other six wands, suggesting he is further developed in his ideas and thoughts than his potential opponents.

4 THE CLIFFTOP WORLD

This is the world in miniature—cliffs, high hills, or mountains with a river running through a valley. The buds on the wands offer up a clue to the meaning of this reduction. In total there are twenty, which gives us XX Judgement. On Judgement, figures rise from the dead; here in the Seven, six wands rise from an unknown source. Both cards suggest strange territory—imaginal, surreal spaces that exist outside reality. It is rare to see these odd proportions; here it may be a reminder that dedication to a cause can be transformational.

5 GREEN TUNIC

Green is the color of nature and growth. The green expanse of the man's tunic is greater than the green land below, meaning that this land represents him—he is part of it, and it must be protected.

EIGHT OF WANDS

Esoteric Title: Swiftness

Number: Eight

Astrological Association: Mercury in Sagittarius

Element: Fire

Season: Spring

Tree of Life Position: Hod, the sphere of majesty and the mind

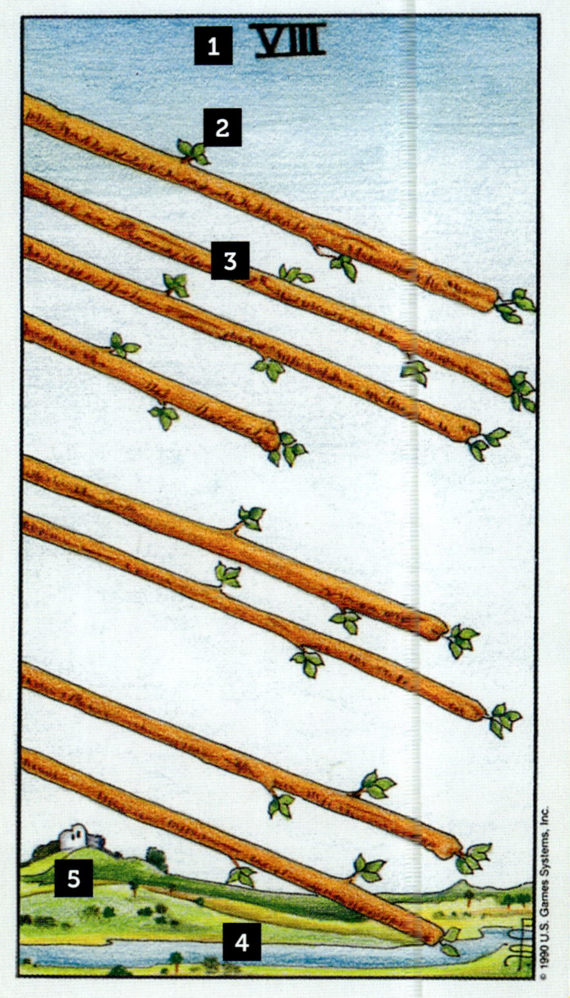

DESCRIPTION

From the left of the card, eight wands fly in formation in a downward motion. Below is a hill, white dwelling, and flowing river.

KEY MEANINGS

News, communication, travel, high energy, motivation, strong relationships, opportunities, spiritual guidance

UPRIGHT MEANING

This card's meaning is communication—so this is a sociable and even frenetic time as you receive more messages, emails, and offers than usual as events speed up. At home, the card shows visitors and potential arrangements; however, it is up to you to discern which to act upon so you can prioritize your time rather than jump at every opportunity. There is also great news concerning travel, love relationships, and spiritually; you feel deeply connected with your guidance.

REVERSED MEANING

The reversed card shows communication issues and a need for patience. A further interpretation is jealousy.

THE EIGHT OF WANDS' SYMBOLS

1	**Number VIII**	Cycles and renewal
2	**Buds**	Beginnings and growth
3	**Eight wands flying**	High energy
4	**Land and river**	Nurturing and security
5	**White house**	Dream come true

What the Symbols Mean for You

When you are drawn to a particular symbol or feature of a card, it's because it holds a special meaning for you. Here is a guide to interpreting your symbols.

1 NUMBER VIII

Eight sideways is the lemniscate (infinity symbol) for the infinite flow of energy. The number of fulfillment, change, and renewal, Eight in the card's element of Fire signifies passion and high energy, depicted as the eight flying wands. The astrological association is Mercury in Sagittarius, for movement and travel—a powerful, fast-moving combination. The card's Tree of Life sphere of Hod, for majesty and the mind, also expresses this dynamic energy.

See the lemniscate in I The Magician, VIII Strength, and in the folded arms on the Nine of Cups.

2 BUDS

Each of the eight wands has three buds, symbols of beginnings and growth. Number three is for Fire, the card's element; three is also emphasized in the wand's groupings (see Eight Wands Flying, at right).

3 EIGHT WANDS FLYING

Wands are a symbol of purpose and magic. Eight identical wands have already made their ascent and are flying downward toward land. They appear as rungs on a ladder, symbol of divine connection (the biblical Jacob's Ladder reached from earth to heaven). The ladder also represents ambition, as it takes us to new heights. The wands are arranged in three distinct groups—one group of four and two groups of two. Three is the number of the Fire element, as for the sets of three buds (see Buds, at left); and the two and four take us back to the Two of Wands, card of planning, and Four of Wands, card of reward, which together add up to the celebratory Six. The positivity of these previous cards culminates in the Eight, sending our mood—and energy—sky-high.

4 LAND AND RIVER

The verdant landscape with its blue, flowing river symbolizes fertility, peace, and security.

5 HOME

The eight wands are homeward-bound. When they land, they will form the framework of the white house; their energy is directed and creative. The house symbolizes a dream come true.

See the dream house on the Ten of Cups.

NINE OF WANDS

Esoteric Title: Great Strength
Number: Nine
Astrological Association: Moon in Sagittarius
Element: Fire
Season: Spring
Tree of Life Position: Yesod, the sphere of foundation and the unconscious

DESCRIPTION

A male figure with a head bandage stands before a row of upright wands; in the background is a green hilly landscape. Holding a tall wand, he looks warily to the left.

KEY MEANINGS

Stability, strength, defense, past wounds, protection, responsibility, resources, experience, resilience

UPRIGHT MEANING

The card reveals strength, resourcefulness, and overall, emotional resilience during a time of stress. You may experience this as a phase of intense work, overdue projects, tough negotiations, and legal issues or in general feeling challenged and battle-weary. On a positive note, you are clear about your boundaries and will defend them to the hilt; also, others see your struggle and offer you the support and encouragement to continue. A further meaning of the card is keeping your ideas and knowledge to yourself.

REVERSED MEANING

When reversed, you may be dealing with obstinacy and defensiveness, which applies to romantic relationships, too. Hold your ground.

THE NINE OF WANDS' SYMBOLS

1	**Number IX**	Number of integration and intensity
2	**The man's pose**	Defense
3	**The row of wands**	Experience
4	**The bandage**	Psychic wound
5	**Green landscape**	Boundaries

What the Symbols Mean for You

When you are drawn to a particular symbol or feature of a card, it's because it holds a special meaning for you. Here is a guide to interpreting your symbols.

1 NUMBER IX

Nine is the number of integration and intensity. In the minor arcana, nine carries the weight of all the number cards that precede it, until the release that comes with the Ten. All the lessons of the previous cards integrate at this stage, so this Nine bears the culmination of the journey through the suit from the Ace of inspiration to manifestation, tests, victory, effort, opportunity, and here, defense. Nine in the suit's element of Fire, for the soul, symbolizes strong passions. The Moon in Sagittarius signifies wisdom in practice—the ability to draw upon your experience to safeguard your position.

2 THE MAN'S POSE

The man stands close to his wand as if for comfort as well as protection as his battles may not be over—he could attack or defend himself in an instant. He looks to his left, the place of the past, with a wary expression; experience tells him to expect further demands on his energy, but he is ready for whatever arises.

3 THE ROW OF WANDS

Eight wands form a row behind the figure. They appear to rise from the earth behind him, while he stands before them like a guard, holding up his wand in warning to potential invaders. As symbol, the wands signify the man's wisdom gained from experience; he protects his reputation.

4 THE BANDAGE

The bandage covers a wound, symbol of survival. This is also a psychic wound, sign of past emotional distress which resonates with the card's Tree of Life sphere of Yesod, for the unconscious self. The male figure has endured much to reach this point and, because of his wound, he may be defensive rather than defended. He could be I The Magician, exhausted by the work of magic—his headband repurposed as a temporary bandage.

See the headband on I The Magician.

5 GREEN LANDSCAPE

Unusually, the land has no particular features—no river, trees nor house, so simply represents the principle of territory. The double line under the landscape marks its boundary, which the male figure stands to protect.

TEN OF WANDS

Esoteric Title: Oppression

Number: Ten

Astrological Association: Saturn in Sagittarius

Element: Fire

Season: Spring

Tree of Life Position: Malkuth, the Kingdom, the sphere of experience

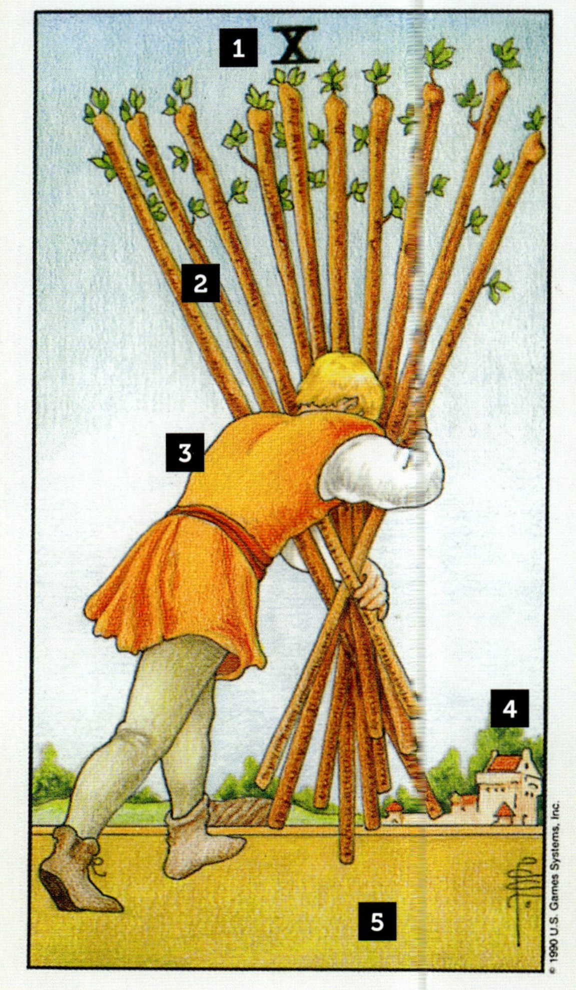

DESCRIPTION

A laborer strides under the weight of ten wands, which partially block his vision. Before him lie a plowed field and manor house.

KEY MEANINGS

Responsibility, burdens, duty, workload, oppression, pressure, resourcefulness, perspective

UPRIGHT MEANING

This Ten tells of potential overwhelm, when we are working—or otherwise giving—to the maximum. The card's traditional meaning is heavy responsibilities; there is constant pressure to be productive, although the tasks feel increasingly challenging. The card often means temporary pressure, but if you continue to work at this pace, you lose perspective—so it is time to prioritize and review how best to use your energy and resources. A further meaning is emotional burdens and carrying issues from the past. Overall, relationships may suffer as all your energy is focused elsewhere.

REVERSED MEANING

When reversed, the card shows an inability to see beyond immediate demands—so you may neglect you own needs.

THE TEN OF WANDS' SYMBOLS

1	**Number X**	Number of completion
2	**The ten wands**	A burden
3	**The laborer's pose**	Oppression
4	**Manor house and farm**	Distant reward
5	**Foreground**	Isolation

What the Symbols Mean for You

When you are drawn to a particular symbol or feature of a card, it's because it holds a special meaning for you. Here is a guide to interpreting your symbols.

1 NUMBER X

Ten, the first double number, marks the ending of one cycle and the beginning of another; the number 10 comprises 1 for beginnings and the zero, symbol of completion. The meaning of the Tens, whether positive or negative, arises from the nature of the suit; too many fiery wands become demanding and oppressive. The card's astrological association of Saturn in Sagittarius means hard work and discipline in the freedom-loving sign of Sagittarius—resulting in a struggle to keep sight of the bigger dream.

2 THE TEN WANDS

The wands are taller than the laborer and take up more space than his body; they are too heavy for him to carry. The make the shape of X, the card's number, emphasizing completion and that this is the last phase of a process. The card's Tree of Life sphere of Malkuth, sphere of experience, guides us to use our experience to manage this responsibility.

3 THE LABORER'S POSE

With his head down and gripping all ten wands, the laborer strives forward despite his oppression. His view is obscured not just by his wands but by his right hand, which symbolizes limitation. He carries the weight with his upper arms and shoulders—as in the idiom "a weight on your shoulders" to describe a mental or emotional burden.

See the blindfold, symbol of limited view on the Two and Eight of Swords.

4 MANOR HOUSE AND FARM

The manor house and farm signify status and, for the laborer, distant reward. He makes his way toward the manor to bring its occupants his wands, the fruits of his labor. As he cannot see clearly and his load is heavy, it may be some time before he reaches his destination and claims his reward. A further reading of the manor is unequal relationships: the labor is the servant, the family of the manor his masters.

5 FOREGROUND

The laborer walks toward the manor, but his foot is positioned next to the double line that divides the foreground from the background. This symbolizes his separation from the fertility and reward symbolized by the distant manor; his realm is flat and empty.

PAGE OF WANDS

Other Names: Princess, Knave, or Jack of Wands

Esoteric Titles: The Princess of the Shining Flame, The Rose of the Palace of Fire

Element: Earth of the suit of Fire

Animal Symbol: Salamander

DESCRIPTION

A young person in a desert landscape stands before three pyramids. He holds a staff, or wand, and gazes at the two buds at the top.

KEY MEANINGS

Beginnings, news, ideas, inspiration, imagination, travel, communication

UPRIGHT MEANING

As an influence: The card brings beginnings and creative pursuits, along with opportunities for travel and communication. This is a time for new discovery—to explore, be inspired, reach out, make new contacts, forge plans, and expand your vision. As a person, the Page is young and bursting with ideas to set the world alight.

REVERSED MEANING

When reversed, the card means miscommunication and delay. There's a struggle for true meaning in conversations, leading to frustration.

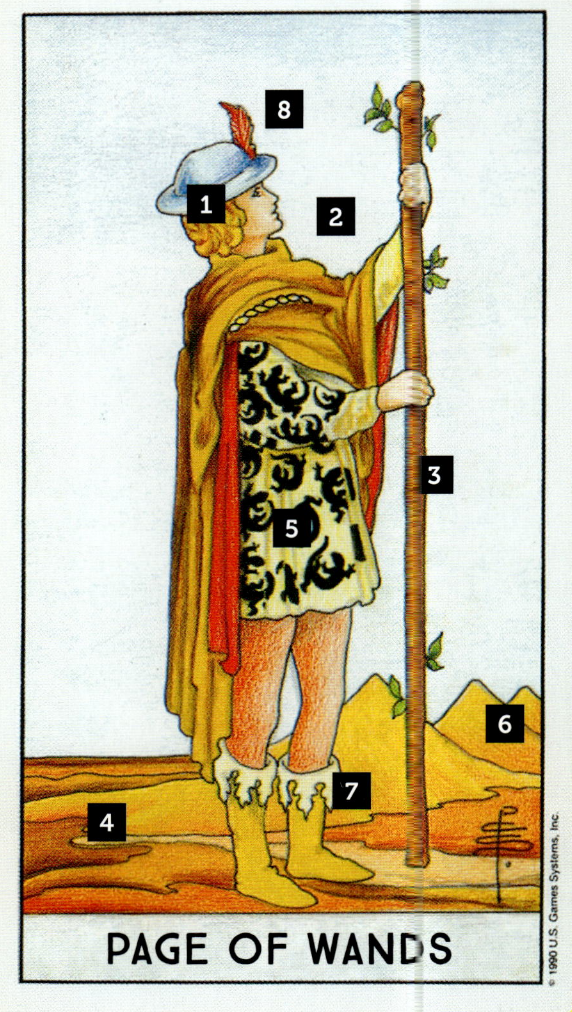

THE PAGE OF WANDS' SYMBOLS

1	**The Page**	Young person or situation
2	**Facing right**	The future
3	**The wand**	Purpose, energy
4	**Desert**	Potential
5	**Salamander tunic**	Rebirth and passion
6	**Pyramids**	Wisdom and foundation
7	**Oak-leaf fringe**	Wisdom and longevity
8	**Red feather**	The life force

What the Symbols Mean for You

When you are drawn to a particular symbol or feature of a card, it's because it holds a special meaning for you. Here is a guide to interpreting your symbols.

1 THE PAGE

Pages are messengers, bringing news of future events. They also describe young people and young situations. This Page is Earth of the suit of Fire—for passion, travel, creativity, and communication. Earth and Fire create the positive combination of passive (Earth) and active (Fire) elemental energies.

2 FACING RIGHT

The Page looks to our right; the right means the future, so his thoughts are of his next steps.

3 THE WAND

The wand is a symbol of creativity and growth. Taller than the Page, this says that his ideas are greater than he is. His ideas are yet to manifest fully, but he is carefully tending them, symbolized by the wand's five buds. Five is the number of human experience—the Page is yet to experience the world. The wand also resembles a torch, symbolizing the spirit of adventure and discovery and, of course the magic wand, for manifesting heaven on earth—or making thoughts reality.

See the magic wand on I The Magician.

4 DESERT

The desert colors of hot oranges and red underscores the card's element of Fire. This may be arid land, but much growth is possible—and the Page with his budding wand tells us that anything is possible when we imagine it.

See the desert on the Knight of Wands and IV The Emperor.

5 SALAMANDER TUNIC

The salamander, with its mythically fireproof skin, appears on the Page's tunic to denote passion and rebirth. It is a soul symbol, signifying deep dedication.

See the salamander tunic on the Knight and King of Wands.

6 PYRAMIDS

The pyramid represents the elements of Earth and Fire. The Pyramid with its square base stands for the Earth element while its triangular body signifies the element of Fire—so the pyramid is Fire grounded by Earth. Inspiration and creative fires burn, but do not burn us out. In this way, the pyramid also symbolizes strong foundations, and here, the wisdom of respecting our energy.

See the three pyramids on the Knight of Wands.

7 OAK-LEAF FRINGE

The Page's boot fringes are cut into the shape of oak leaves. Oak is a symbol of wisdom and longevity. However, this symbol also resembles a flame, echoing the Fire element of the suit.

See the oak-leaf fringe on the Page and Two of Pentacles and the King of Wands' cowl; see the flame motif on the King of Wand's crown.

8 RED FEATHER

The flame-like feather is red, for action and manifestation. This signifies life and vitality.

See the red feather in 0 The Fool, XIX The Sun, and XIII Death.

KNIGHT OF WANDS

Esoteric Title: The Prince of the Chariot of Fire
Element: Fire of the suit of Fire
Major Arcana Link: VII The Chariot
Astrological Associations: Scorpio and Sagittarius
Animal Symbols: Chestnut horse, salamander

DESCRIPTION

With its front legs rearing up as if to dance over the sand, a chestnut horse charges across the desert. The armored knight holds a staff in his right hand.

KEY MEANINGS

Action, adventure, speed and control, news, change, travels, creativity, invention, volatility, spontaneity

UPRIGHT MEANING

As an influence: This is a card of speed and inspiration—communication, new ideas and projects, travel, and new relationships and romance abound. The Knight shifts energy, unlocking problems and hurtling through obstacles, and often shows house moves and new work. As an individual, an unpredictable, spontaneous person who is wonderful company but needs lots of attention.

REVERSED MEANING

Creative blocks, delays to travel and other plans; also, lack of motivation. An additional meaning is burnout.

THE KNIGHT OF WANDS' SYMBOLS

1	**The Knight**	Change
2	**Riding in from the right**	News
3	**Reins and wand**	Controlled impulses
4	**Five buds**	Creativity and growth
5	**Salamander motif**	Dedication
6	**Red feathers**	Vitality
7	**Three pyramids**	Creative fire

What the Symbols Mean for You

When you are drawn to a particular symbol or feature of a card, it's because it holds a special meaning for you. Here is a guide to interpreting your symbols.

1 THE KNIGHT

Always on horseback, the Knights are the tarot's agents of change. The Knight of Wands is an aspect of card VII The Chariot, and they have the astrological sign of Scorpio in common (Scorpio and the other fixed signs are represented by the sphinx on The Chariot). The card's element is double Fire, which makes for a volatile energy that, without control, can run amok.

2 RIDING IN FROM THE RIGHT

The Knight's gaze is to the left for the past, but he appears to come from the right, the future. He brings you up to speed with news.

3 REINS AND WAND

The wand on this card is a symbol of power, echoed in the horse's wildness; it's as if the wand is part of the horse. The Knight has him on a tight rein, so he doesn't throw the Knight from his saddle. This joint symbol reminds us to temper our impulses rather than be ruled by them.

See power in balance in the sword and scales of Justice, card XI.

See the wand as power in I The Magician.

4 FIVE BUDS

The wand's five buds signify news and ideas. The Knight sees all five clearly. As with the Page, the number five means "mankind," which relates to tests and experience.

See the five buds on the Page of Wands.

5 SALAMANDER

The salamander motif acts as a totem flame retardant: in myth, salamanders—symbols of passion and rebirth—had fireproof skin and could pass through fire unharmed. In this way, we see the Knight's dedication to the fire of his own nature; the flames licking at his armor are a part of him.

See the salamander tunic on the Page and King of Wands.

6 RED FEATHERS

Red stands for action and manifestation, and signifies life and vitality. This plumage is much more prominent than the Page of Wand's small feather, showing us the greater power of the card.

See the red feather on the Page of Wands, 0 The Fool, XIX The Sun, and XIII Death.

7 THREE PYRAMIDS

The pyramids symbolize wisdom and foundation, and their triangular form represents the card's element of Fire. Three pyramids—three as the number of Fire—gives even more intensity.

See the three pyramids on the Page of Wands.

QUEEN OF WANDS

Esoteric Title: The Queen of the Thrones of Flames
Element: Water of the suit of Fire
Major Arcana Link: III The Empress
Astrological Associations: Pisces and Aries
Animal Symbols: Black cat, lion

DESCRIPTION

In a desert landscape, a queen sits on a throne decorated with lions and sunflowers. A black cat at her feet, she holds a tall wand and a single sunflower.

KEY MEANINGS

Empowerment, communication, self-expression, soulfulness, sensuality, creativity, leadership, focus, growth, identity, meaningful connections

UPRIGHT MEANING

As an influence: Intuition, soul purpose, and identity are the prime messages here. This is your time for self-expression and speaking your truth, so communication is key. It's a dynamic card, so it's time to manifest desires—from travel to writing a book or tackling a new role at work. In love, relationships bloom. As an individual, this Queen is full of creative energy and is highly attuned to those she holds close.

REVERSED MEANING

There may be poor communication and disconnection, so the focus is keeping projects and relationships on track. An additional meaning is professional jealousy.

THE QUEEN OF WANDS' SYMBOLS

1	**The Queen**	Empowerment
2	**The sunflower**	Growth and optimism
3	**The wand**	Purpose
4	**Lion throne**	Courage and protection
5	**Two and three dimensions**	Manifestation
6	**Cat amulet**	Sensuality
7	**Black cat**	Deep relationships
8	**Pyramids**	Wisdom and foundation
9	**Golden robes**	Self-value

What the Symbols Mean for You

When you are drawn to a particular symbol or feature of a card, it's because it holds a special meaning for you. Here is a guide to interpreting your symbols.

1 THE QUEEN
Queens signify empowerment. As the Queen of Pentacles' suit is Fire, she is the soul aspect of card III The Empress (see page 30); her fiery, assertive nature is represented by Aries, one of her zodiac signs. The Queen's combined elements are Water and Fire. As water puts out fire, there may be inner conflict between determined Fire and sensitive Water—so energy must be managed carefully.

2 THE SUNFLOWER
As a singular bloom and throne decoration, the card's sunflowers represent the sun. The living flowerhead is virtually the same size as the queen's face; by identifying with the flower, she says she, too, holds its powerful light. Overall, a symbol of growth and success.

See the sunflower on card XIX The Sun.

3 THE WAND
The Queen holds the wand in her right hand, the hand of giving; it is a symbol of the Queen's power and purpose. It sprouts three buds, the number of the Fire element. The wand is also a torch, which carries fire; as it is unlit, it signifies our potential to burn brightly.

4 LION THRONE
The lions represent Sekhmet, an ancient Egyptian lion goddess who breathed fire. As guardians of the throne, they denote strength, protection, and power—Sekhmet means, "She who is powerful."

See the lion on card VIII Strength.

5 TWO AND THREE DIMENSIONS
We see the sunflowers and lions as surface pattern on the throne and as manifest three-dimensional objects—a symbol of thoughts becoming reality.

6 CAT AMULET
The clasp holding the Queen's cloak depicts Bastet, the Egyptian cat goddess, which signifies protection and sensual pleasure.

7 BLACK CAT
The black cat is Bastet (see Cat Amulet, above). The cat is also the witch's familiar, so symbolizes deep relationships.

8 PYRAMIDS
Rather than vast aridity, here are three pale pyramids denoting the idea of desert. Maybe the Queen has arrived at her destination at the edge or plates of the desert: to the right is gray stone, suggesting civilization. The pyramids symbolize wisdom and foundation, and their triangular form represents the Queen's suit of Fire.

See the pyramids on the Page and Knights of Wands.

9 GOLDEN ROBES
Gold symbolizes wealth and success and echoes the sunshine energy of the sunflowers. The Queen shows her energy and is clear about what she can achieve; she does not hide her talent.

KING OF WANDS

Esoteric Titles: Lord of the Flame and Lightning, The King of the Spirits of Fire

Element: Air of the suit of Fire

Major Arcana Link: IV The Emperor

Astrological Associations: Cancer and Leo

Animal Symbols: Salamander, lion

DESCRIPTION

In flamboyant orange robes, this King sits on a matching throne decorated with salamander and lion motifs. He holds a tall budding wand in his right hand.

KEY MEANINGS

Passion, soulfulness, communication, travel, energy, inspiration, wisdom, culture

UPRIGHT MEANING

As an influence: It's time to create and be inspired—you will get the support and interest you need. This card is also about following your soul path and honoring your skills and wisdom. Overall, there can be greater communication, sharing of culture, and travel opportunities now. As an individual, this King is a free spirit eager to learn rather than judge. He loves to talk and listen, making him a great friend or travel companion.

REVERSED MEANING

Restriction and thwarted plans; feeling you are not following your truth. A person who is egotistical and potentially obsessive.

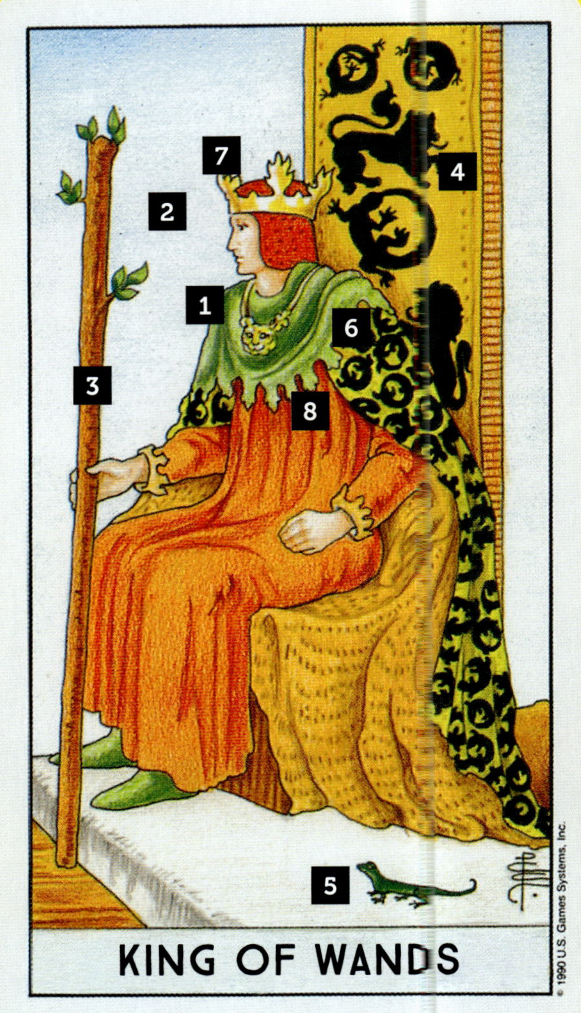

THE KING OF WANDS' SYMBOLS

1	**The King**	Authority
2	**Facing left**	The past
3	**The wand**	Power and intention
4	**Lions**	Courage and protection
5	**Salamander**	Passion and rebirth
6	**Robes and cloak**	Fire under control
7	**Crown and cap of maintenance**	Secure identity
8	**Oak-leaf fringe**	Wisdom and longevity

What the Symbols Mean for You

When you are drawn to a particular symbol or feature of a card, it's because it holds a special meaning for you. Here is a guide to interpreting your symbols.

1 THE KING

Kings signify authority. As the King of Wands' suit is Fire, he represents the soul of IV The Emperor (see page 34). The King's two elements are Air and Fire for the mind and the soul. Fire needs air to burn, so the elements are supportive provided neither seeks to dominate; otherwise, too much fire burns us out, or ideas cannot fly.

2 FACING LEFT

In tarot, the left means the past. The King is surveying the territory he has traveled so far.

3 THE WAND

The King holds the wand in the right hand, the hand of giving; it signifies his powerful intentions and ability to manifest what he desires. It has four green buds—four is the number of the element of Earth, which stabilizes volatile Fire. If we see the wand as a torch, it also stands for our potential to illuminate and inspire.

4 LIONS

The throne is decorated with heraldic lions, for Leo, one of the card's signs. The lion head also appears on the King's necklace to signify courage and strength—a protective amulet.

See the heraldic lions on the Queen of Wands.

5 SALAMANDER

A salamander motif decorates the King's cloak and throne—and appears live, on the right of the card. The creature stands for the Fire element, passion, and also rebirth because it was fabled to have fireproof skin (see Knight of Wands, Salamander, page 214).

See the salamander on the Knight and Page of Wands.

6 ROBES AND CLOAK

The salamander is a symbol of protection on the King's cloak—worn to control the fire symbolized by the color orange of his robes. The combined meaning is passion under control.

7 CROWN AND CAP OF MAINTENANCE

The crown features a flame design, for the Fire element, complemented by a red cap of maintenance that is worn to secure the crown in place. The flame crown and red cap affirm the King's identity as Fire—a dedicated and driven individual.

8 OAK-LEAF FRINGE

The King's cowl has an oak-leaf fringe, to symbolize the qualities of the oak tree: wisdom and longevity.

See the oak-leaf design on the Page of Wands and the Page and Two of Pentacles.

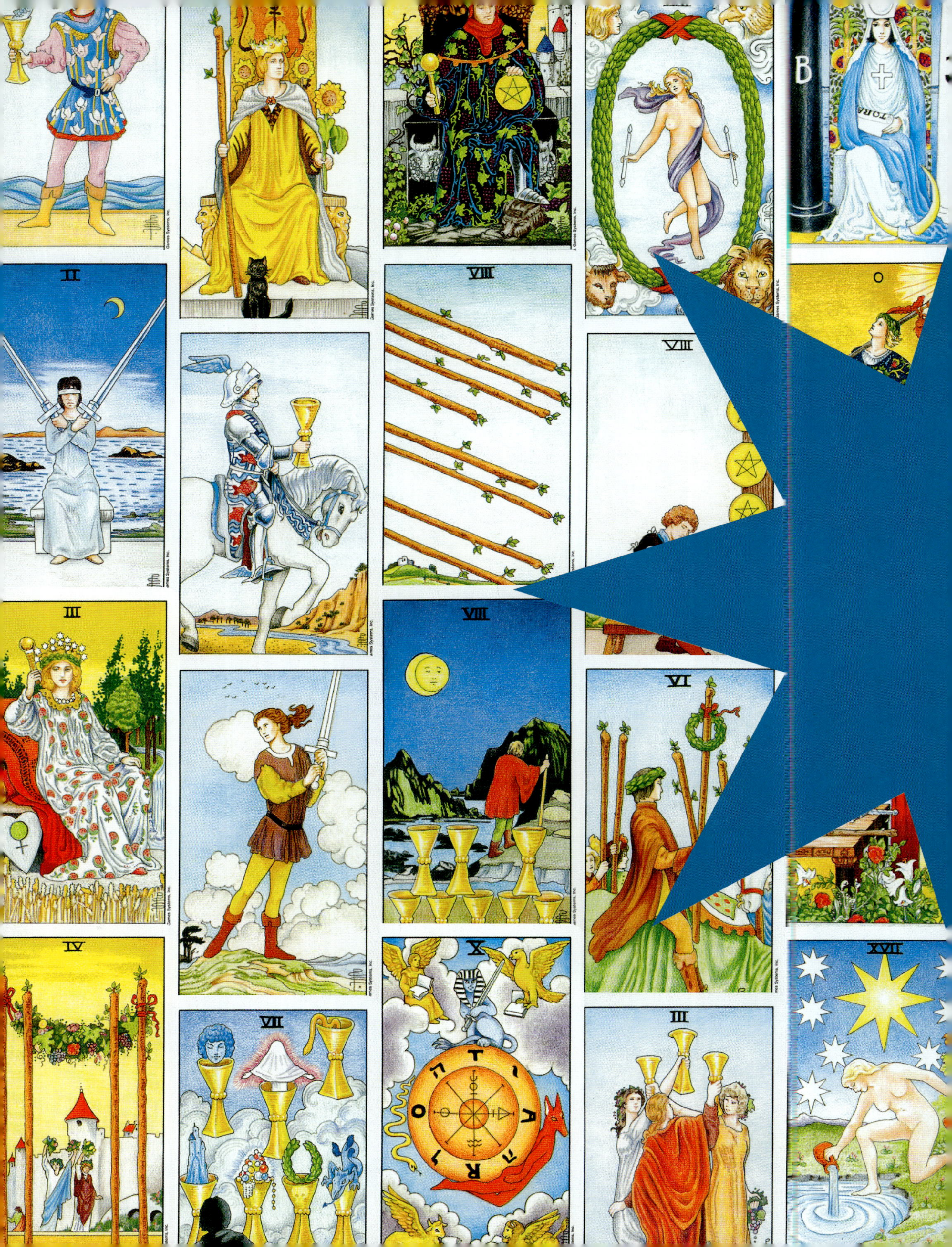

B
TORA

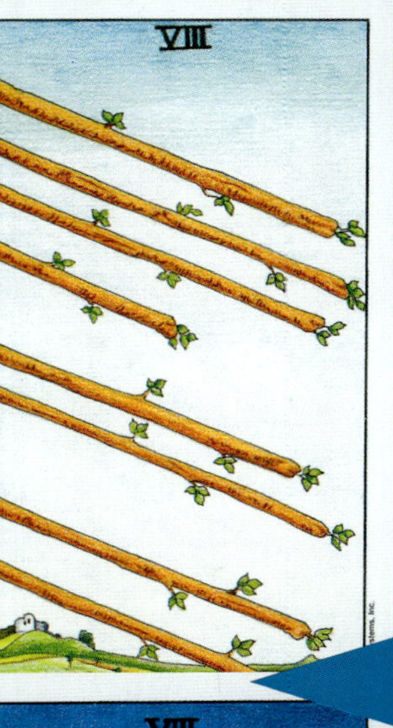
VIII

VIII

VIII

VI

VII

X

III

XVII

CHAPTER 4

READING TECHNIQUES AND FURTHER SPREADS

In this chapter, we take symbol-reading further with Instant Intuitive Focus (see Exercise sidebar, at right), a technique that helps you move more deeply into the symbols and messages your cards hold. Further, it releases you from card interpretations: you are free to intuitively choose the symbol you need in this moment, then write about it or draw it in your tarot journal (see Journaling sidebar, opposite).

The following spreads are inspired by three symbols in the cards—the Wheel, X, and star. And there is guidance, too, on designing your own spreads using the card diagrams in chapters 2 and 3 as a starting point.

EXERCISE: INSTANT INTUITIVE FOCUS

This is one of those exercises you can enjoy alone as a daily ritual, share in a group as a warm-up before reading together, or, if you have more time, practice as an extended meditation.

First, find a card. Go through all the cards face up and choose one you are instantly drawn to; alternatively, shuffle and dip into the deck, choosing one card at random. However you select your card, do it quickly; let your hands do the choosing, not your mind. This way, you avoid overthinking and connect with your intuition.

- Place your card before you, face down.
- Next, center yourself (see chapter 1). When you feel calm and balanced, make this request: "Show me what I need to see now."
- Open your eyes and turn your tarot card face up. Now half-close your eyes. Imagine you're following a small bird that alights on part of the card to draw your attention to it. Let your gaze be curious, just noticing where you or your bird goes on the card. You might find you're holding the card more closely as one element calls to you (your body often tells you what is needed as it expresses our unconscious desires). You may be drawn to a number, color, or tiny detail: this is your symbol for today, and it holds meaning for you.
- Feel that you can reach into the card and touch your symbol as if it were real. Does it have a texture, a sound, a color? Sense its qualities and how you feel.
- Quickly, write down or draw your symbol in your tarot journal (see sidebar, opposite). What does it tell you about you or your situation now? Your unconscious mind has chosen this symbol for a reason.
- Write or draw your impressions or speak them aloud.

If you feel ready, you can now go deeper with your symbol.

COMMUNING WITH YOUR SYMBOL

When you find you are naturally connected with a card symbol, you can begin a conversation. Think about a question. What would you like to ask?

- Close your eyes and visualize your symbol—imagine you are taking it from the card into your third eye (the chakra, or energy point between your brows).
- Ask your question in your mind and settle yourself to listen. Rather than ask a direct question, you can simply make a request for guidance.
- See what arises then, using your nondominant hand, draw or write the response.

We use the nondominant hand to prevent complication; we can only be simple and direct when using unfamiliar muscles to write.

Make a note of your findings in your tarot journal (see sidebar at right)—you will find, over time, that you begin to build your personal lexicon of symbols. You can also look up your symbol in the Appendix (pages 228 to 234). Your interpretation may be different from the meaning given there, and that is fine; always go with what is intuitively right for you.

Tip: *Display your card where you can see it during the day and, if you work with crystals, place the crystal associated with that card next to it to bring in energy. If you don't have the crystals mentioned in the card profiles, you can use any others with which you feel an affinity.*

RECURRING SYMBOLS

If you regularly journal your readings, you can flip back over the last few months (or years, if you're a journal devotee) and highlight the cards and symbols that recur for you. A symbol or card recurs because we are still in the energy of that card or symbol. Positively, this could be a sign for you that you are on your path, and the recurrence reassures you of this. A further reason is because there is something we need to learn and, until that is done, the card or symbol stays with us. So if a certain card haunts you from one reading to the next, take note. Anna told me how she got XV The Devil card in virtually every reading about work for three years. When she left her job, the Devil—her former manager—disappeared. As soon as we change the situation that the card relates to, the card often disappears from our readings.

JOURNALING: FINDING YOUR POWER SYMBOL

Whenever possible, journal your readings. Always add the date, and sketch out your cards, writing down your interpretations and how you feel. A great way to do this is to use tarot-card stickers (which can be perfect if you find it hard to decipher your own handwriting)! Review your reading notes regularly and update with your comments: Which cards were prescient for you? Which related to an event that later happened? Look for symbols that connect cards. For example, in a reading you may see XVII The Star and IX The Hermit, who has a star in his lamp, so the star will be a key symbol for you; self-guidance and cosmic guidance, for example, may well be the theme of your week or month. You might be drawn to the sunflower on the Queen of Wands and the sunflowers in the Sun's garden (which appear in the same reading) and if so, the sunflower is your symbol. Make a note in your journal—write or sketch the symbol with the date. You can see these symbols as guides, and you can meditate with them (see Communing with Your Symbol, above).

Further Spreads

STAR OF GUIDANCE

This spread takes the eight-pointed star from XVII The Star to reveal your talents, challenges, and potential. As the seven smaller stars on the card symbolize the seven classical planets, this reading uses the values associated with each planet for the card positions.

Shuffle your cards and focus on a question or request. You might say, "Show me what I need to see about this [x] situation," or simply, "What do I need to see today?" First, lay down the Significator card, face down, which gives you the theme of the reading. Turn over this card last. Then continue laying cards from the top of the deck in the order shown, face down. When you are ready, turn over cards 1 through 8 and begin your reading.

S Significator card: the theme of the reading
1 You and your situation
2 Mercury: Immediate influences; what's flowing in your life
3 Mars: Challenges; conflict and power struggles
4 Venus: Relationships; love and partnerships
5 Saturn: Lessons; what you're learning, or what lesson is repeating
6 Jupiter: Skills and experience; how you shine in the world
7 Moon: What is hidden from you; unconscious beliefs
8 The Sun: The outcome; your greatest potential at this time

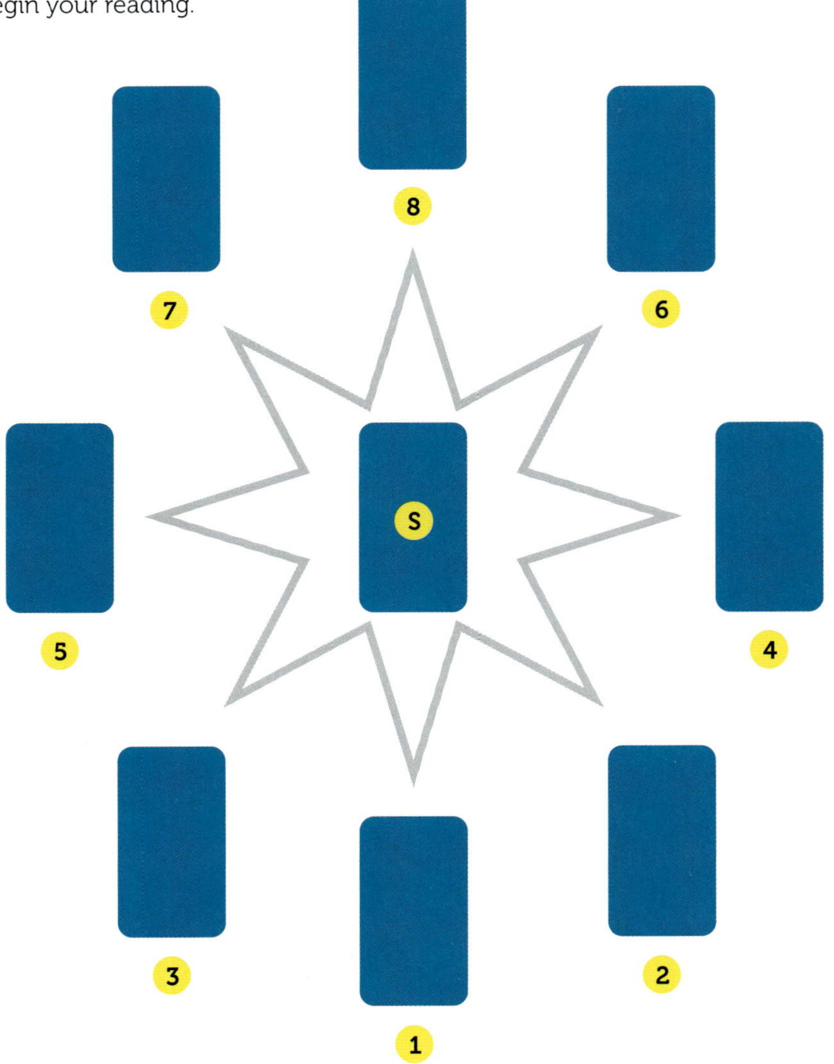

THE TEN: ENDINGS AND BEGINNINGS

The Ten is based upon the Roman numeral X, which appears on sixteen major arcana cards and eight minor arcana cards. The ten is the number of endings that make way for beginnings; this layout is designed to reveal what will be released and what is to come.

Shuffle your cards and ask your question (see Star of Guidance, opposite), then lay down six cards as shown below, face down. When you are ready, turn them face up and begin your reading.

1 What's coming to an end
2 What's before you: What to do now
3 What supports you financially
4 What supports you emotionally
5 A secret about this situation
6 What's coming next

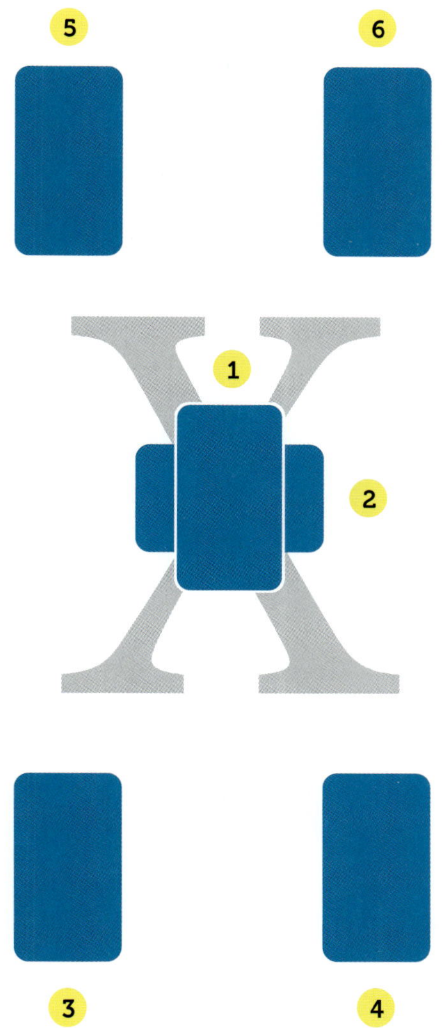

FORTUNE'S WHEEL: CYCLES OF CHANGE

Based around card X The Wheel of Fortune, this spread explores cycles of growth, fulfillment, release, and gratitude. You can interpret the cards as they stand or lay a second wheel of cards on top of the first, so you have two cards for each position. The second card offers another aspect of the situation and often validates your interpretation of the first card. Have a pendulum on hand, too, to ask the wheel a question (see Working with a Pendulum, at right).

Shuffle your cards and ask your question (see Star of Guidance, page 224), then lay down eight cards as shown below, face down. When you are ready, turn them face up and begin your reading.

1 What to appreciate
2 What to reflect on
3 What to release
4 What's over
5 Underlying support
6 What I need to share
7 What's getting stronger
8 Blessings

Working with a pendulum: Hold a pendulum in the center of the wheel. Say, "Show me where am I now in this cycle." Let the pendulum move, tuning in to its subtle vibration, and see which card it takes you to. This gives you a position on the wheel. Do bear in mind that your position represents current influences, which shift as the Wheel and our lives turn.

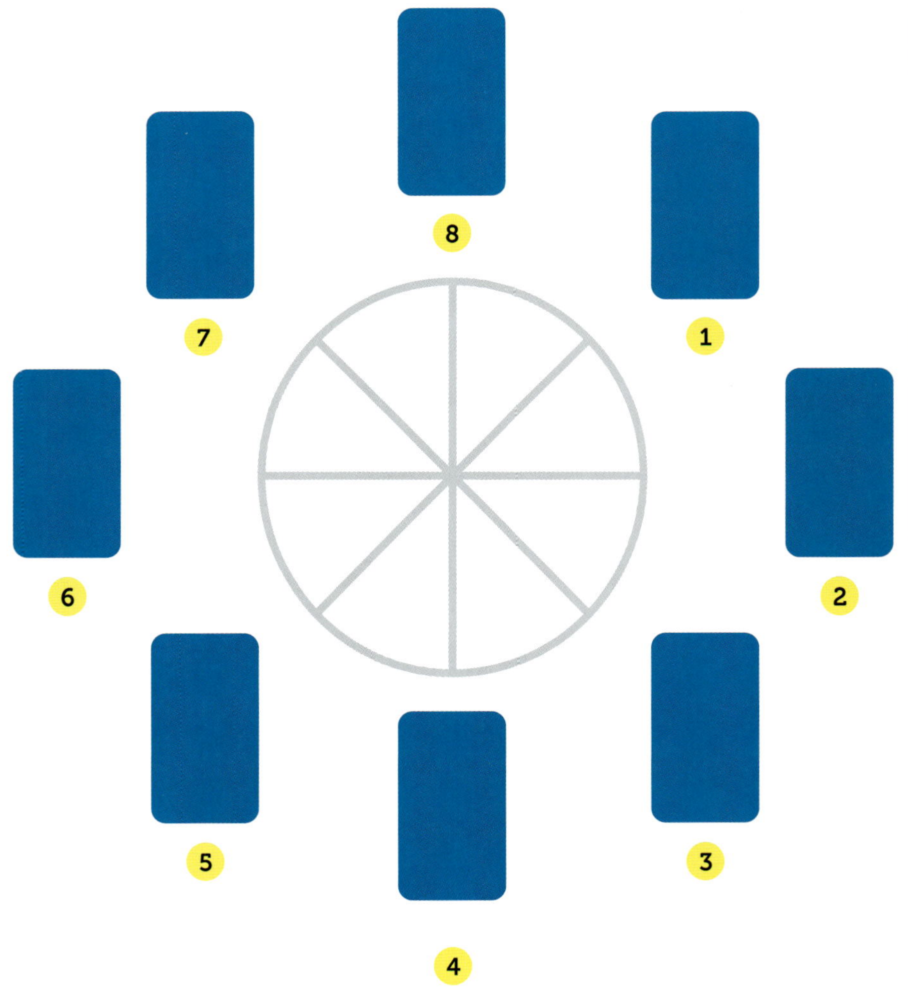

Creating Your Own Spreads

Designing your own tarot spreads gives you an opportunity for play, which activates intuition. Creativity and intuition are interconnected. Whenever you feel out of touch with yourself, creativity, which involves using your hands, brings you back into alignment; you sense your knowing again. Drawing—sketching cards and card positions—coloring, writing by hand, or any other craft you enjoy feeds your tarot development and practice.

To craft your own spread, flip through this book until you land on a card that speaks to you today. Look at the annotated card with the symbol meanings. As a starting point, take a symbol meaning and turn it into a statement or question that will become a card position. For example, on XI Justice we have "pillars," meaning "boundaries"; "cloak and clasp" meaning "illumination," and "the mural crown," for authority. To translate these into a three-card spread, see below.

Naturally, you can interpret Justice's symbol meanings or those given for any of the other cards in a way that feels right to you.

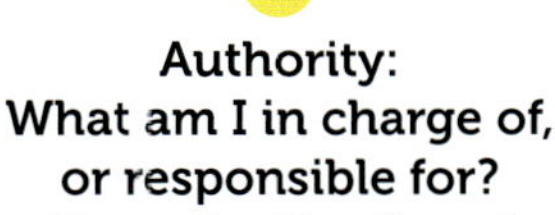

1

Authority: What am I in charge of, or responsible for?
Example: The Ten of Wands. Feeling you are responsible for everything; there is too much to do.

2

Boundaries: What do I need to protect?
Example: Three of Cups. Your social life; making time for friendship and love.

3

Illumination: What do I need to see now?
Example: XX Judgement. It is time to review where you are; what can you revise or improve—or it may be time to release the responsibilities revealed by card 1.

APPENDIX

The Tree of Life Pathways and the Major Arcana

Each major arcana card is linked with a pathway on the Tree of Life, the central motif of the mystical Judaic system of teachings called Kabbala. The numbered pathways show the flow of the creative force.

1. **Kether**, the sphere of divine light
2. **Chockmah**, the sphere of wisdom
3. **Binah**, the sphere of understanding
4. **Chesed**, the sphere of love
5. **Geburah**, the sphere of power and destruction
6. **Tiphareth**, the sphere of beauty and rebirth
7. **Netzach**, the sphere of endurance, instinct, and desire
8. **Hod**, the sphere of majesty and the mind
9. **Yesod**, the sphere of foundation and the unconscious mind
10. **Malkuth**, the Kingdom, the sphere of experience

The Tree comprises ten sephirots, or spheres, that describe the story of creation and are aspects of our spiritual experience on earth. The pathways between each sephira show approaches to divinity, or ways of understanding God. Understanding a cards' Tree of Life pathway gives more depth to its meaning.

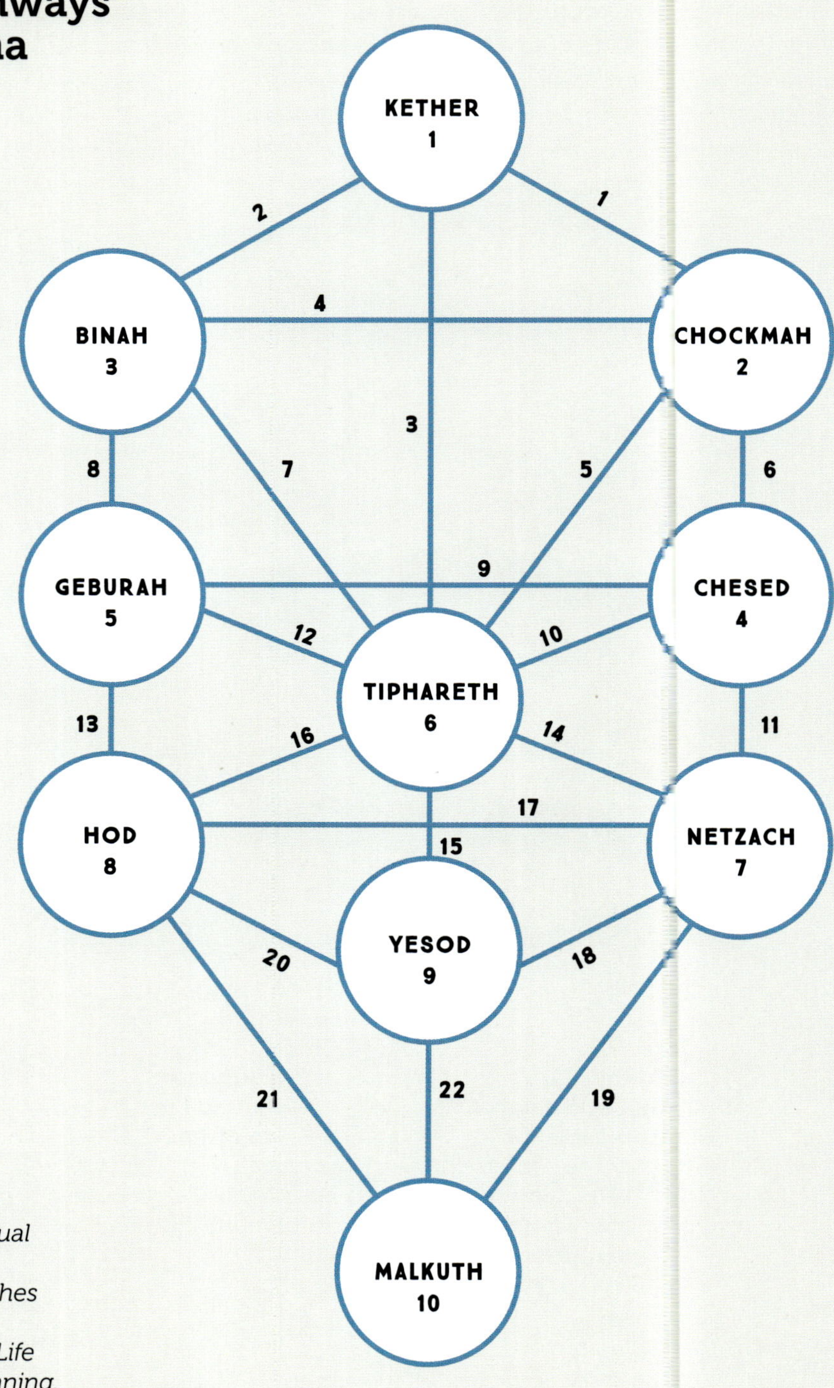

Planetary Days: When to Read

Each major arcana card has an associated day of the week. This day derives from the planet associated with the card, or its zodiac sign (and the planet associated with that sign). For example, I The Magician takes the planet Mercury, while VI The Lovers has the astrological sign of Gemini—also ruled by Mercury. Mercury's day of the week is Wednesday, so you can lay a Magician or Lovers spread on a Wednesday to bring in the cards' planetary energy to support your reading. Below are the day associations for the major arcana cards and their spreads.

Day of the week	Ruling planet	Spread
Monday	Moon	II The High Priestess
		VII The Chariot
		XVIII The Moon
Tuesday	Mars	IV The Emperor
		XIII Death
		XVI The Tower
		XX Judgement
Wednesday	Mercury	I The Magician
		VI The Lovers
		IX The Hermit
		XVII The Star
Thursday	Jupiter	X The Wheel of Fortune
		XIV Temperance
Friday	Venus	III The Empress
		V The Hierophant
		XI Justice
		XII The Hanged Man
Saturday	Saturn	XXI The World
		XV The Devil
Sunday	Sun	VIII Strength
		XIX The Sun

Quick-Reference Major Arcana Meanings

0 The Fool:
Beginnings, innocence, risk

I The Magician:
Action, ambition, manifesting

II The High Priestess:
Intuition, wisdom, secrets

III The Empress:
Abundance, resources, nurture

IV The Emperor:
Order, authority, boundaries

V The Hierophant:
Unity, marriage, education

VI The Lovers:
Love, decisions, maturity

VII The Chariot:
Drive, progress, victory

VIII Strength:
Resilience, patience, courage

IX The Hermit:
Reflection, solitude, quest

X The Wheel of Fortune:
Fate, luck, cycles

XI Justice:
Fairness, decisions, balance

XII The Hanged Man:
Waiting, sacrifice, spirituality

XIII Death:
Release, transformation, beginnings

XIV Temperance:
Negotiation, diplomacy, precision

XV The Devil:
Limitation, binds, habits

XVI The Tower:
Breakdown, breakthrough, revelation

XVII The Star:
Hope, guidance, healing

XVIII The Moon:
Illusion, doubt, mysteries

XIX The Sun:
Joy, optimism, growth

XX Judgement:
Review, second chances, the past

XXI The World:
Success, completion, expansion

Quick-Reference Minor Arcana Meanings

	CUPS	PENTACLES	SWORDS	WANDS
Ace	Love	Money	Success	Inspiration
Two	Partnership	Choices	Inaction	Planning
Three	Celebration	Talent	Sorrow	Travel
Four	Boredom	Stability	Retreat	Enjoyment
Five	Loss	Exclusion	Defeat	Tests
Six	Reunion	Generosity	Peace	Victory
Seven	Confusion	Potential	Theft	Effort
Eight	Departure	Reward	Limitation	Movement
Nine	Wishes	Comfort	Anxiety	Strength
Ten	Happines	Inheritance	Finality	Burdens

Court Cards: As Influences

	CUPS	PENTACLES	SWORDS	WANDS
Page	Socializing	Learning	Detail and documents	Good news
Knight	A proposal	Growing prosperity	Opposition	Speed
Queen	Love, relationships	Support, sensuality	Independence	Creative power
King	Emotional balance	Achievement	Mental focus	Innovation

Court Cards: As People

	CUPS	PENTACLES	SWORDS	WANDS
Page	Sensitive	Reliable	Vigilant	Expressive
Knight	Idealistic	Steady	Forthright	Dynamic
Queen	Intuitive	Wise	Incisive	Inspiring
King	Conciliatory	Pragmatic	Strategic	Free-spirited

A–Z of Card Symbols

SYMBOL	MEANING	PAGE NUMBER
Angel	The zodiac sign of Aquarius; guidance	59, 61, 120–121
Ankh	Male virility	35–36
Apple	Female fertility	35–36
Apron	Protection (Eight of Pentacles)	150–151
Archangels		
Michael	Courage and protection (XIV Temperance)	74–76
Gabriel	Bringer of divine messages (XX Judgement)	98–100
Raphael	Love and healing (VI The Lovers)	42–44
Uriel	Wisdom, truth, and light (XV The Devil)	78
Archway	Transitions and protection	154–155
Armor	Defense, battles	35–36, 47–48, 162–163
Background or sky		
Neutral	Openness, potential	67–68, 136–137, 148–149
Blue	Truth and clarity	112–113, 188–189
Yellow	Energy, well-being, awareness	51–52, 63–64, 156–157, 198–199
Bandage	Psychic wound	208–209
Bell(s)	(Ace of Cups) News, (Five of Pentacles) the outcast	108–109, 144–145
Beggars	Poverty, frustration	144–145
Bench	Support	140–141, 150–151
Birds	Thoughts, worries	184–185, 186–187
Bird, ibis	Soulful expression	87–88
Bird, hooded	Pragmatism	152–153
Blanket	Adaptability and secrecy (Knight of Pentacles)	158–159
Blindfold	Limitation	166–167, 178–179
Blood	Life, death, and sacrifice	116–117
Blue fabric, flowing	Element of water; flowing feelings	124–125
Boar	Base instincts	162–163
Bracelet, red (Queen of Swords)	Symbol of Venus, associated with love; also, mercy and redemption	188–189
Buds	Beginnings, growth; also stages of development	200–201, 206–207, 214–215
Bull	The zodiac sign of Taurus; sensuality	59, 61, 162–163
Butterflies	Thoughts	186–187
Caduceus	Balance and peace	110–111
Canopy of stars	Divine navigation	47–48
Caparison (Six of Wands)	New territory; possibilities	202–203
Castle	Imagination, ambition, desire	120–121, 192–193
Cat	Sensuality; deep connection	216–217
Chains	Habit	79, 81
Chalices (Cups), two (XIV Temperance)	Miracles	75–76, 108–135
Chariot	Self-containment	47–48
Church	Sanctuary, rest	170–171
Child	Innocence	95–96
City	Society, civilization	150–151
Cloak	Protection; can also denote high or low status	63–64, 116–117, 142–143

Clouds	Doubt	43–44, 184–185
Clouds, ripped	Violence	172–173
Coin	Symbol of the suit of Pentacles and the element of Earth: The material world; achievement, reward	136–163
Coins, falling	Gifts	146–147
Coat of arms (Ten of Pentacles)	Status	154–155
Colors		
Black	Protection	116–117, 150–151, 158–159
Blue	Truth, communication	39, 41, 128–129, 134–135, 150–151, 190–191
Gold	Wealth and success	135
Green	Growth, potential, protection, magic	202–203, 204–205
Orange	Creativity	148–149, 152–153
Purple	Intuition	148–149, 190–191
Red	Action, passion	39, 41, 122–123, 134–135, 146–147, 150–151, 156–157, 158–159, 186–187
Yellow	Awareness, intelligence	63–64, 134–135
White	Purity	188–189
Corn	Well-being	31–32
Corn ears (Death's flag)	Harvest	71–72
Cottage in the countryside	A dream life	110–111
Crayfish	Instinct, vulnerability	91, 93
Cross, Fylfot	The cosmos	67–68
Crosses, three	The trinity (Father, Son, Holy Spirit)	39, 41
Crowd	Society	202–203
Crown	Authority	35–36, 142–143
Crown, closed	Protection	160–161
Crown, flower	Fertility	162–163
Crown, jellyfish (King of Cups)	Trust	134–135
Crown, moon	Stages and cycles	27–28
Crown, papal	Spiritual authority	39, 41
Crown, solar	The future	75–76
Crown, star	Authority and guidance	31–32, 47–48
Crutches	Support	144–145
Cup	Element of Water, for the heart; emotions, love, relationships. The womb, fertility; as chalice, faith; an invitation	108–135
Darkness	Limitation	79, 81, 83–84
Date palm	Fertility	27–28
Demon	Enslavement	79–80
Desert	Potential	212–213
Dog	Instinct and loyalty	19–20, 154–155
Dove and Eucharist	Divine spirit	108–109
Droplets (Ace of Cups)	Divine grace	108–109
Droplets, golden (XVI The Tower)	Hebrew letter Yod, meaning "fire"	83–84
Eagle	The zodiac sign of Scorpio	59, 61
Feather	Success	124–125
Fish, leaping	Optimism	134–135
Fish, red	Passion	130–131
Fish, talking	Psychic communication	128–129
Flag	Unity	99–100

Nine	Accumulation, integration, intensity	124–125, 152–153, 180–181, 208–209
Ten	Endings and completion	126–127, 154–155, 182–183, 210–211
Oak-leaf fringe	Wisdom	138–139, 156–157, 158–159, 212–213, 218–219
Path	The unknown	91, 93
Pebbles	Intuition	132–133
Pearls	Wisdom	31–32, 132–133
Pentacle	Element of Earth, for the body and material concerns. Money, abundance, achievement	136–163
Pentagram	Perfection and protection: The five elements of Earth, Air, Fire, Water, and Spirit	136–137
Pentagram, inverted	Materialism and evil	79–80
Pillars (High Priestess)	Severity and mercy	27–28
Pitchers	Resources	87–88
Pomegranate	Fertility	27–28
Pool	The unconscious mind	75–76, 87–88, 91, 93
Pyramid	The element of Fire: Foundation	214–215, 216–217
Quartered circle	Grounded ideas	140–141
Rabbit	Nature's cycles	160–161
Rain	Sadness, tears, release, healing	168–169
Rainbow	Miracles and reward	126–127
Ram's head	Sign of Aries	35–36
Red feather	Life force	19–20, 71, 73, 95–96, 212–213, 214–215
Reins	Controlled impulses	214–215
Rising dead (XX Judgement)	Rebirth	99–100
River	Continuing life	71, 73
Riverbank	Safety	130–131, 206–207
Rivulets	Healing	87–88, 108–109
Robe or cloak, blue	Truth	27–28, 150–151, 190–191
Robe or cloak, red	Action	35–36, 39, 41, 122–123, 146–147, 186–187, 196–197
Robe, monastic	Protection	55–56
Rose, rambling	Sensuality	160–161
Rose, red	Love and passion	31–32, 136–137
Rose, white	Idealism	19–20, 27–28
Salamander	Passion, rebirth	212–213, 214–215, 218–219
Sash, checkered (Three of Wands)	Strategy	196–197
Scales	Mercy; precision, weighing up	63–64, 146–147
Scallop	Fertility	132–133
Scepter	Sovereign authority	134–135, 162–163
Scroll	Wisdom	27–28, 134–135
Serpent-girdle	Infinity	23–24
Shadow figure	Limited access; being in the dark	120–121
Shield	Unifying forces	47, 49
Ship	Changing fortunes	134–135, 138–139
Shroud	What is awakening within us	120–121
Sickles (Queen of Swords)	Divine judgement	188–189
Sleeve lining	The womb and birth	19–20
Slippers, green	Stepping in to magic	134–135
Snail	Slowness and protection	152–153

Snake	Risk, wisdom, flattery	43–44, 120–121
Sphinxes	Mysteries and wisdom	47–49, 59–60
Staff	Support	47, 49, 55–56
Star maiden	Eternal youth	87–88
Stone, uncarved (Three of Pentacles)	Future potential	140–141
Stone plinth	Solidity	142–143
Stonemason	Mastery	140–141
Suit symbols (Wand, Sword, Cup, Pentacle)	Elemental power	23–24
Sun, full	Clarity, consciousness, energy	23–24
Sun, symbol (dotted circle)	Spiritual illumination	75–76
Sun, white	Pure consciousness	19–20
Sun-moon	Heart's path; awakening intuition	122–123
Sunflower	Growth and optimism	95–96, 216–217
Sunset	Cycles and endings	71, 73
Sword	Element of Air, for the mind: Retribution, decisions, truth, purpose, faith	63–64, 164–191
Sword, abandoned	Lost faith	172–173
Tails (demon, XV The Devil)	Transgression	79–80
Tether	Trust	67–68
Tetragrammaton	Divine connection	75, 77
Throne	Foundation	160–161
Tower	Old structures, ego	83–84
Tree	Growth	67–68, 150–151
Tree, young	Youth	114–115
Tree of Knowledge of Good and Evil	Temptation and sexual experience	43–44
Tree of Life	Healing and eternal life	43–44
Tree, World Tree (Yggdrasil)	Salvation	67–68
Trumpet	Awakening	99–100
Twilight	The liminal world; the in-between	91–92
Tunic, striped (Nine of Cups)	Humility	124–125
Valley	Opportunity	192–193
Veil	Hidden futures	63–64
Venus glyph	Love	31–32
Yellow sky	Clarity	51–52
Yod (Hebrew letter)	Fire	84, 92, 109, 165
Wall	Protection	95–96
Wand	Element of Fire, for the soul. Travel, communication; directed energy, purpose, intention, magic	23–24, 192–219
Wands, double-ended	The Collective	103–104
Watchtowers	Gateways	91–92
Water	Emotion	75–76, 91, 93, 108–109, 130–131
Water babies	Motherhood	132–133
Water lilies	True feelings	108–109, 128–129
Waves	Change	174–175
Wheel	Rebirth	59–60
World dancer	Oneness	103–104

ABOUT THE AUTHOR

Liz Dean is a writer, tarot-reader, and divination teacher. She is the author of 24 books and tarot decks, including international bestsellers *The Ultimate Guide to Tarot*, *The Ultimate Guide to Tarot Spreads*, *Tarot by Numbers*, HBO's *Game of Thrones Tarot*, and *The Magic of Tarot*. She has taught at Reader's Studio, New York; the Omega Institute, New York State; in Perth, Melbourne and Sydney for the Tarot Guild of Australia; and the London Tarot Conferences and for the World Divination Association, among many others.

Liz began reading professionally at Psychic Sisters within the famous Selfridges department store, London, and now reads and teaches privately for a global client list. A former editorial director in illustrated book publishing, commissioning mind-body-spirit titles, Liz also held the position of coeditor of the UK's leading spiritual magazine, *Kindred Spirit*. She lives by the sea in Sunderland, in northeast England.

www.lizdean.info
@lizdeantarot

ACKNOWLEDGMENTS

With thanks to my agent, Chelsey Fox of Fox and Howard Literary Agency; my editors, Jill Alexander, Meredith Quinn, and Jenna Nelson; and my husband, Michael Young. Thanks to my UK Tarot Conference friends, including Robbie Pearson for his wonderful take on the Eight of Swords' sword positions.

In memory of Elizabeth Cunningham, the best friend a girl could have, and mentor extraordinaire, Jonathan Dee.

Further Reading

The Ultimate Guide to Tarot: A Beginner's Guide to the Cards, Spreads, and Revealing the Mystery of the Tarot by Liz Dean (Fair Winds Press, 2015)

Tarot Mysteries: Rediscovering the Real Meaning of the Cards by Jonathan Dee (Zambezi, 2003)

The Tarot: A Key to the Wisdom of the Ages by Paul Foster Case (Macoy Publishing Company, 1975)

The Pictorial Key to the Tarot by A. E. Waite (Dover Publications, 2005)

The Golden Dawn: An Account of the Teachings, Rites and Ceremonies of the Order of the Golden Dawn by Israel Regardie (Llewellyn Publications, 1982)

INDEX